A CHILD IN COMMUNITY

Veronika van Duin

Dear Andy,
lots of love
Veronika

UPFRONT PUBLISHING
LEICESTERSHIRE

A CHILD IN COMMUNITY

ISBN 1 84426 055 0

First Published 2002 by
UPFRONT PUBLISHING
Leicestershire

A CHILD IN COMMUNITY

To my children – Helen Barbara, Rachel, Martin
who grew up in community and
enjoyed it as much as I did
and to my other daughter – Ruthie
who has become such a dear friend.

ACKNOWLEDGEMENTS

My grateful thanks go to Siobhán Porter; my sisters, Agnes and Elizabeth; Ruth Horan and Sheila Pružina for reading, and smiling, and correcting my work. And to my husband, Rob, who says he will read it some day!

Special thanks go to the Camphill Foundation for financial assistance, and without whom this book might not have been written.

OTHER WORKS BY THE AUTHOR

- *Homemaking as a Social Art*, London, Sophia Books (imprint of the Rudolf Steiner Press), 2000
- *The Art of Living*, Kate Roth Publications, 1999

AUTHOR'S NOTE

There are many ways of writing a biography. Because of the unusually vibrant and pictorial nature of my childhood, I have chosen to approach it as my memory dictates. The images, colour, sounds and smells of the events have always been more striking than the actual facts, and the love that surrounded me still fills me with wonder and delight. My sisters remarked, when they read *A Child in Community*, that I had told it well but that they did not remember it in quite the same way, and started to recount *their* memories. I could only laugh and enjoy, because for each of them, other events and different people featured in their tales. And yet we grew up together, had the same parents and the same friends and went to the same schools. How personal is the unconscious!

A Child in Community describes *my* memories, as a fairy tale tells of truths in images. What facts there are, speak for themselves. But all of it is true, a child's perspective being always subjective and full of imagery. I have tried to let the reader grow up *with* me, feeling, hearing, tasting and seeing the magic that was the community in which I was born and raised.

I would like to conclude this note with a slightly altered version of the words of the Announcing Angel from the Austrian Christmas Play that I saw, year after year, throughout my childhood. She proclaims somewhat in this vein:

> I come but to say, now all is ended,
> I trust there are none that I have offended.
> If ought of import I did omit,
> My ignorance the cause of it.
> Say I have pleased, so all's made right,
> And I wish you a right good read!

Veronika
Ireland, 2001

Contents

Chapter I
THE BACKGROUND YEARS

Growing up in a community does not necessarily mean that one doesn't know one's parents. I knew mine very well. There were some children with whom I grew up who could truthfully have said that their parents seemed a bit remote, too busy, or too troubled to bring them up properly. They would say that community life negated family life. I cannot say this. My family was strong, identifiable and warm. We loved each other and knew our parents well. My home was secure, warm and bright. Certainly, it was strange according to the books that I read. We didn't see our father go out to work, and our mother was not at home in the kitchen. Someone else cooked the meals in the vast basement kitchen. But my mother ordered them and set the menus, not unlike a grand home might have seen. My father, however, was the gardener, and my mother was the great lady and this, too, did not fit the picture of a normal lifestyle. We did not belong to the landed gentry. My parents were Jewish refugees, always to retain a rather strong German accent. We learnt to speak English somehow, by drawing on what we heard around us, but definitely not from parental example. I knew we were a Christian family, but my parents had been declared Jewish by Hitler, and so I learnt very early the difference between the Jewish nation and the Jewish religion.

My father's hands were rough and callused, and in the winter the wet earth made large and surely painful cracks in his skin. The fingertips were always raw. My mother's hands were soft, her squarish nails clean, though the surfaces were ribbed. I used to love rubbing my fingers over them. Too little calcium when she was a child growing up in the Viennese Jewish quarter? My father smelled of warm sweat, Three Nuns tobacco, soap and earth. My mother smelled of 4711 eau de cologne and Imperial Leather soap. My father smoked a pipe. My mother carried a bunch of keys, rolled her light blond hair in a bun at the nape of her neck and wore a white apron, though she was not the housekeeper of our home. She was the matron of Heathcot House, a home for children in need of special care.

Originally, Heathcot had been a small manor house, and we rented it from its owner, we being the Camphill Community. The community owned another country house across the River Dee, called Camphill, and a larger manor called Murtle, also on the other side of the river. Later, the Newtondee estate, and then Cairnlee House were acquired, so now we had a farm too. Heathcot was rented by the family of Peter Roth, who was one of the founder members of Camphill. By the time I lived there, however, the house had been given over to the care of severely physically handicapped children, and Peter's parents were gone.

My parents found their way to Camphill in very differing ways. As children we loved to hear their life stories and would ask endless questions in order to get them started. My father fell into the trap much more easily than did my mother, but one could get her going, particularly when on holiday. She was always so very busy. My father, digging straight rows of good earth, would stop, light his pipe and talk, stories flowing effortlessly from his lips. There were so many, and so varied yet similar ones to drink in as a small child, that I no longer know which story was true, which imagined, which accurate and in what order the events happened. Thus, when I dig into my childhood memories, my father's history unravels in its own particular fashion and probably only some of the following tales are actually fact. But they are true within my soul and so must stand the test of real historians.

He always seemed to have time. Sometimes, when walking to the garden, my hand safely tucked inside his roughened palm, he would skip a little to the tune of an old German student song. Later I learned that these songs were not always the most pleasing to the ears of some of the co-workers because they had been adopted by the Nazis and raised such painful memories. My father, though he had for a short time been in a concentration camp (one of his stories that in fact did not add up, or perhaps I confused him and his stepfather, who died in Oranienburg), bore no animosity towards the songs themselves. He recognised their innocence, bearing them not a grudge. Long before Hitler, there had been the German student's days of his youth, and these he cherished, singing the songs as though to cleanse them. He used to say that Hitler was a madman and madness was an illness. I never once caught any whiff of hatred or condemnation; only sadness, acceptance and sometimes, fear.

The fear surfaced when he met anyone in uniform, most of all the local constable. With the greatest of respect, bordering on the servile, my father would greet him and chat with him. Going down to the police station in the village made him change his clothes and put on a clean tie. He said that you never knew with the police, and still he believed the British bobby was fair and agreeable. He told us how the Nazis carried guns and shouted a lot. How impressed he was with the manners and quiet speech of the constable who stamped his passport! Or papers. It was a great day when he became naturalised; my father declaring that only the British could imagine that to be un-British was to be unnatural, hence the term 'naturalisation'. He always said, with a twinkle in his voice, that he quite agreed with this sentiment. He admired the Queen and all that the monarchy stood for: honour, truth, justice and protection of the weak. He remained grateful till his death to the country that gave him asylum from Hitler's madness.

My father, Bernhard Lipsker, was born breech, on 6 March 1913 in Hamburg, Germany. His mother had only just become a widow. His father shot himself after realising that he had lost his considerable fortune in a financial scam, of which there were many at the time. So my grandmother bore him alone, gave birth to him and began to raise him, working as a servant to earn money. She married again, but it is doubtful from the stories that my father told if she did this for love. But a woman alone, trying to raise a son in the Jewish circles of that day, had no voice. She needed a husband. The family moved to Berlin, though when is unclear because my father never told us dates, and as these are my memories I can't fill them with facts that were irrelevant at the time.

My father's stepfather was not a nice man. After a sister was born, he became abusive towards his stepson. My father used to say that it was worth taking the punishment because he loved his sister and he did it for her. He also loved his mother very much and took the beatings for her too. On one occasion, his sister, who apparently also treated him with contempt when she was very little, broke something, and my father said that he had done it. From that time on, she loved him too, and their affection for each other lasted forever. However, the mistreatment became more than my father could bear, and being a large child, he hit back. He must have been perhaps twelve years old, though this fact is not in my memory, but rather in my imagination as I listened to his stories of a childhood so sad. Strangely, he always made the bad bits sound interesting and he never blamed anyone. He used to say it must have been hard to take on someone else's child.

The Jewish social workers intervened and my father went to what he called 'the orphanage'. This was, according to him, a wonderful place. The houseparents must have been special people because they took him to their hearts. My father spoke very highly of them and of their encouragement, because he proved to be a very clever boy. He thought he might become a rabbi. He loved school, always being second to the top. (At the top was a German boy, of course.) His scholarliness endeared him to his houseparents. He told us little about friends or a social life (though I am sure he had both from the few photographs that we still have), but seemed always to be studying.

Of his mother he spoke with the greatest of affection. He loved her so very much. Reading between the lines, and hearing the longing in his voice as he talked about her, even as a child I knew that he must have missed her terribly. From photographs, of which his sister had saved a few, prior to being sent away from his mother, his appearance was neat, tidy and slim. Afterwards he looked fat and anxious behind his glasses. He ate as compensation. I remember how he loved food and loved a glass of beer (which my mother only allowed him to drink on holidays). His sister told us that he used to meet up with his mother in the park and she would feed him cakes and sweets. He never went home again, but had to be content with park visits from his mother and sister.

As a young man, he went to university in Berlin. He had decided to study physics, mathematics and philosophy. I remember him telling us that one of his early professors was Einstein. In fact, I think his professor was called Närnst, an equally prominent and famous physicist of his day. My father's connection to Einstein came about when on a journey with his stepfather, who introduced him to that great man of learning. He loved to tell us about how Einstein said that a real scientist, if following his knowledge through, would have to arrive at God. My father said that science and philosophy were close brothers, if studied properly.

University was wonderful. He met other bright young people and became politically involved. With the rise of Hitler, his political choices were limited, so he joined the communist party and became the leader of the youth section. His political equivalent in the Nazi party was a very close friend. On the day that all Jews were beaten out of the university, he was sent a note not to attend that morning. He could not continue his studies after that, nor his friendship with the young man who saved him. There were not many places open to intellectual Jews, so he enrolled at a seminary for training teachers. Once again, Hitler spoiled it all by declaring there to be no need for Jewish teachers, just before he took his final exam. So he began to seek a profession that would get him out of Germany. His political acumen led him to the belief that there would be a war, and that Britain would be the place to be, should this happen. He sought a place of training as an orchardist, or fruit gardener, as they were called. Until he found a suitable apprenticeship, he worked as a teacher (though without his diploma), in one of the few remaining Jewish schools, in Danzig. Though it was a German town, it was just inside Poland, and this meant travelling across the Polish Corridor by train everyday, as he still lived in Berlin. In order to do this, my father bribed the train guards with liquor.

Finally, he found a market garden that would take him on. His story now goes like this: someone came and locked them all in a nasty, dark shed and they could not get out for a long time. They were hungry, thirsty and dirty and then one day someone left the door unlocked by mistake and so he escaped. This is how he told us of his short imprisonment in Oranienburg concentration camp. Or is it all a figment of my imagination? Probably what happened was that the gardener, who had taken on Jews to train those who wanted to leave Germany, was aware of their vulnerability and did indeed lock them in a garden shed on an occasion in which the Nazis were inspecting his work. He owned land in Neuendorf, a lovely part of Berlin. He took great risks to help the Jews and would have known how to protect them.

This was a particularly exciting story that he told us, and as so many of them were about so many people as well as about the concentration camps, they flood my mind. It was only a few years ago that my sister told me that what he had meant may have been merely a tale. In spite of all the war stories that he told us, in my innocence I did not realise that he might have had personal experience of Hitler's camps. How did he get out? Did incarcerated Jews ever get out? Had he merely seen one in passing?

My father had an unusual friend whom he very dearly loved. Her name was, at that time, Hertha Sielmann. She was the most beautiful woman he had ever met and she allowed him to live in her house. But on Tuesdays and Thursdays, he had to sleep somewhere else because she had visitors. I used to wonder why he couldn't meet her friends. Again, it was years later when I realised that they lived together and that her 'friend' was the man who kept her. She was what we might have called a high-class call girl, free to take her lovers as long as she kept first place for the man who paid for her keep. This remarkable woman, twenty years his senior, loved my father, and cherished his bright personality and extraordinary powers of thinking. She introduced him to the Jewish Welfare Centre and he became a functioning social worker. She also introduced him to the works of Rudolf Steiner.

This was the greatest revelation of his life. Through Steiner's books, he found his way to Christianity, but, needless to say, under the Nazis, his beliefs were not valid when set against his parentage, so he remained a registered Jew. He would have been ashamed to deny it, in any case.

Was it this influential woman who paid huge sums to get him out of the camp? Was it her 'owner', a good German Aryan, who paid? We don't know, especially as we do not know if he ever *was* in a camp; but one day he found himself with a suitcase on his way to Gerrard's Cross in Buckinghamshire, sponsored to work there as a gardener. A friend of his called Maude Jellinek, who lived in England, helped my father, his sister and Hertha Sielmann to get out of Nazi Germany. His hunch about learning agriculture had paid off. Hertha Sielmann followed him to London soon after.

His sister, who was a trained nurse, refused to leave Germany at first; but when a group of patients were admitted to her hospital, obviously suffering from malnutrition and torture, and all were Jewish (is this too one of his stories?), she let herself be sponsored out and arrived in Margate. Here she worked as a nurse, later moving up to Edinburgh as a theatre sister. It was by the good graces of many outstandingly generous people such as 'Auntie Maude', as my father liked to call her, that so many Jewish lives were saved.

My father's mother died of cancer before the war, and his stepfather died in a concentration camp. This was the only time I ever experienced my father not to be full of love. He spoke about his stepfather's death with a certain undercurrent of satisfaction.

Wanting to work with biodynamics, which Rudolf Steiner taught as a new method of agriculture, my father moved to Sunfield Homes, in Clent, to work in Broome Farm. Here he entered the world of children in need of special care, for the first time. Though employed as a gardener, he could hardly avoid the children and he was very happy to be in the environment of a place that was working with the ideas of Rudolf Steiner. Steiner's untold wealth of insight had led to him founding educational establishments for the so-called uneducable, and Sunfield was a pioneer centre of curative education in England.

However, now that he had really found a place that he loved, the fates stepped in again. He did not get on very well with the farmer there, and war had broken out, causing the disaster at Dunkirk. The British Government decided it to be prudent to intern all enemy aliens. As my father had moved to a farm in Essex that was within a three-mile radius of the coastline, he was invited to step down to the police station, just for registration. My father, being nervous owing to his previous experiences with uniformed men, asked permission to bring his toothbrush. This was deemed quite unnecessary, which worried him even more. When leaving Germany, he had been allowed only one suitcase and had sensibly filled it with books by Goethe and of course, his toothbrush. He really wanted his toothbrush, but he went along without it, and so without it also to Liverpool and a boat bound for Ontario, Canada.

The ship boasted a 'mad captain', my father said. He locked the enemy aliens, all of them good German Jews, into the dining room. It must have been stifling, and as they crossed the Irish Sea and sailed into the Atlantic Ocean, it must have been putrid with the stench of vomit. However, my father was always a good sailor. He said being born in Hamburg gave him sea legs, it being one of the biggest ports in Europe. Then he told us such an exciting thing. He said the crew mutinied and locked up the captain and let all the prisoners out. So my father volunteered for submarine spotting, and had a great voyage over the Atlantic looking for U-boats and icebergs.

They landed in Canada and boarded a train that chuffed slowly over the prairie and there, in the middle of it, dumped them all. These intellectual Jews, who had probably never touched hammer and nails, were now given tools and wooden boards, and told to build their huts in the middle of the flat, empty prairie in deepest Ontario. Did they suffer from the little black, biting flies? Probably. They certainly suffered quite a bit, but nothing could have been as bad as the lack of books to read! My father instantly spotted the one man with a book. This was Alex Baum (or Carlo Pietzner, I can't remember which, but he met both of them again once he had arrived in Camphill). Whoever it was, he was reading a book by Steiner. Needless to say, my father borrowed it.

He said the time in Canada wasn't bad, but he had a tooth pulled without anaesthetic. Then he would open his mouth and show two rows of strong, unblemished yellow (from tobacco) teeth, with a gap at the back. He never had a filling in his life.

Being a gardener had its perks, and he set to work growing food for the camp. He also applied without let up to be repatriated to England. Gradually they were all sent back; the stupidity of interning frightened Jewish refugees who were fleeing from

Hitler's megalomania finally got through to the British Government, against whom my father would not hear a bad word. One could, he used to say, have one's political idealism, but to be British and a Member of Parliament was a good thing to be. Although he also always said, 'A good man makes a bad politician.'

Anyway, there he was, back in Liverpool, and straight back into internment, this time on the Isle of Man. There were two camps, one for women, and the other for married men. Here he met up with his sister, and attended a lecture given by Dr König. This is the story that I remember, but my sister tells me that it was even more remarkable that he met this great man at all. It actually happened outside Liverpool before his trip to Canada, in a holding camp of thousands of 'enemy aliens', waiting to be shipped out to the colonies. To pass the time, they entertained each other with lectures and it was here that my father actually met Dr König for the first time. Apparently the camp was very civilised indeed and people could even study and share their knowledge.

My father was determined that he wanted to go to the community that Alex Baum (or was it Carlo Pietzner?) had told him about, and that Dr König was now mentioning in his lecture. He wanted to practise anthroposophy as he had read about it in Rudolf Steiner's books. He applied for release, and being a gardener, he was offered a place near Aberdeen in Scotland and arrived one morning very early outside the door of Heathcot House. Only then did he discover that he had indeed arrived in the Camphill Community, the place where biodynamics and curative education as well as community living were happily combined and practised.

Here, too, he met my mother. I always imagined him sitting on the steps of the half-moon porch decorated with phoney Grecian pillars in the Georgian style of the previous century, in a striped convict's suit with a black target on the back, and my mother opening the door to this criminal and falling instantly in love! Actually, I don't really think it was like that, but the picture pleases me, and when I remember without really thinking, their meeting always appears in my mind's eye in this guise. This was because my father had a way of telling his life story in very few words, but the vivid images he called up in my mind filled all the gaps. I lived his story with him, seeing the Nazis in their black leather, hearing them march, seeing the shed in which he was locked up, hearing the noise of the vomiting refugees as they puked up their insides confined in the dining room of the prison ship. I felt his tooth being pulled. I saw the man lying on his tummy, reading the only book in the camp! I could never quite picture his life with Hertha. He was very reticent about this time. But I could see the classroom with rows of little Jewish boys and girls and I envied them their lessons. To have had my father for a teacher must have been wonderful. He knew such a great deal and never spoke down to anyone.

My father spoke exactly the same way to me, my mother or to Dr König, which I thought privately was very brave of him. Most people held their breath when Herr Doctor came to lunch and they called him *Vater*, which I found very strange and a bit contrived, coming from grown-ups. But maybe this was because they were Germans. My parents were *not* German; my father came from Berlin, and my mother from Vienna, in Austria. My father always said that Berliners were not really German, because they had a sense of humour.

My father, always portly as far back as I can remember, wore wire-rimmed spectacles, round as the fashion then dictated. Later on, in my adolescence, his concession to modern times was to change to square wire-rimmed spectacles. My father, as you can see, was a conservative, and I never saw him without a tie, even when at work in the garden. I think he probably voted for the party, though he never really told us what he favoured. Some time in the Sixties, my mother was invited to visit the United States for a conference in the American Camphill Community, but my father was refused a visitor's permit because he had been a member of the Communist Party! He found this highly amusing. He said there was nothing so strange as the political mind, you never knew which way it would turn, especially if it was American. But he did take care not to enter Berlin. Although it was not part of East Germany, it lay right in the middle of that country, and he did not think that it was sensible or safe to go there.

My father did, however, return to Germany after the war, to

visit his sister, who had gone back just as soon as she thought it prudent; but he always felt a little nervous and really only went to see her. He said that German people were too serious not to be tempted to repeat their folly. By this action it was clear that he *had* suffered. His tone of voice when speaking about his mother, was filled with echoes of unimaginable pain. Sometimes I used to dream of not having my mother and of making bargains with strange creatures to keep her with me. The pain of this nightmare made me scream. For my father, this was no nightmare but actual reality on a daily basis.

Being shipped to Canada was much less fun than he made it sound and trying to grow vegetables on virgin ground cannot have been all pleasure. Also, the pain of the tooth pulling clearly stuck in his mind. Most of my father's life seemed to be one disappointment or deprivation after the other. How could he stay so sane, so kind and reasonable?

One might think from my father's cheerful description of his life that he felt no pain about the disasters that came upon him. This would not be true. He simply told us what he remembered and told it like a story, or like a history lesson. He would describe the rise and fall of Hitler in just such a conversational tone, and when he came to the punchline, he would say, 'And now comes the important part!' And gesticulate with his index finger held upwards to command attention. We would certainly stop and listen because you could be sure it *was* the important bit.

This short and physically unremarkable man had an intelligence that shone, and a personality that crackled. They said of him that when he entered a room everyone gave him their full attention. He was witty and bright and did not have a great deal of time for fools. He loved to teach; he was a born professor turned gardener. He came to Camphill because he wanted to learn more about Rudolf Steiner's spiritual science, or anthroposophy, as my father called it, and because he wanted to apply this marvellous new philosophy to daily life. He was a man who wanted to put his money where his mouth was. Being a communist was only because he had not yet discovered *community* as practised by Camphill, he always said.

Concerning the coming about of the Camphill Community,

my mother's story says it all. She was born in 1912 in a small town in Poland called Brzozow. Because Jews do not really celebrate birthdays, she was never too sure of the exact date but it was definitely in the summertime, so it was fixed for 8 August. Poland was at that time a part of the Austro-Hungarian Empire, so my mother was an Austrian by birth. She told us that she lived in a ghetto and I used to imagine it to be a sort of circle of small huts with a pole fence around it that served to protect the Jews from the pogrom. I knew better than to ask my mother what a pogrom was. She would not have explained it to us as colourfully as my father did. He told us about the Cossacks on their magnificent white chargers, with hoofs like soup plates and plumes on their helmets, and their very fierce dances. He explained how they hated the Jews, but I never really understood why. It seemed that so many people hated Jews – not just the Germans, but the Russians too. I saw these large, rich and smart fair-haired men, heard the thunder of their horses as they swooped down in the dead of night to see if Jews really ate babies. I saw the flaming torches that they clutched in mailed fists, setting fire to the circle of huts. Somehow pictures that I had seen of medieval knights in armour and warlike Vikings got mixed up in my imagination and I covered these hybrids in Russian embroidered shirts and set them on white horses. They were grand but monstrous, and they brought destruction to the small, dark folk who were my ancestors.

I was very proud to be Jewish and certainly did not want to be German. The Jews had prophets amongst them, teachers, doctors, professors and other learned people. Only later did I hear about the bankers and moneylenders. I also knew that most of them were modest tailors, or otherwise engaged in merchants' business. Farmers and gardeners were scarce in the history that my father gave me. The rabbi was the most important person in the ghetto, as my father tried to explain to me. He set the rules of the group. I was proud to know that my Uncle Joseph, my mother's youngest brother, was destined to become a rabbi.

Although my mother said that they left Poland because of the First World War, I always imagined it was to escape another pogrom. My mother, under the age of two and wearing all her clothes at the one time, fled from Poland to Vienna, a civilised town with churches and schools.

My mother describes the flight from Poland rather like the film of *Fiddler on the Roof*. She said they went with all their possessions piled high in a *Leiterwagen*, a sort of wooden cart with railed sides. The children sat on the back, swinging their legs, or walked behind when going up a steep hill, pushing the loaded cart to help the yoked oxen along. My mother was so padded with clothes, her best coat on the outside of the layers, that her arms stuck out at either side. She cannot remember how long it took them. She said they spent a night in a house, where she was put to bed with an eiderdown so high that she couldn't see over the top and she wondered if she would ever be rescued from it. Did they get a train for part of the way? How did their belongings arrive? Did they walk all the way behind the wagon pulled by the two oxen? My mother, at eighteen months or thereabouts, was too young to remember clearly.

They travelled with six children, my mother being the youngest at the time and my grandmother pregnant. Two more children, both boys, were born in Vienna. The child who made the journey from Poland to Austria in his mother's womb was born with an epileptic condition as well as having special needs. In Vienna they lived in cheap accommodation, at one time above a cinema. There never seemed to be any peace. My mother tells of the loud and repetitive piano music that accompanied the silent movies of her day. She would be unable to sleep, either from hunger or from the noise. They were very, very poor, sometimes relying on charity.

My grandparents belonged to the Hassidic Jews, a seriously devout sect wearing prayer shawls and side locks of hair and doing a lot of praying and reading the Talmud. My grandfather considered this the right way to spend his days, rather than working to earn their living. He probably hoped that God would provide, though he did take odd jobs as they came his way. And so they were exceedingly poor as well as having to raise eight children. My mother was one of five girls, the other three being sons. Aba, her older brother, was not always a good boy, my mother used to say, but she loved him possibly the best. My grandfather was apparently very hard on him, chastising him and giving him very little freedom. He was to become a rabbi but the boy disliked learning. He was active and full of humour, even when I first knew him, which was well after the war.

As children, my mother always said, they played and sang and went for long walks, even though they were hungry and they hardly ever had new shoes. They invented a language all of their own called 'bulafun', which she taught to us and we taught to special privileged friends. What a way to keep secrets! In spite of her attempt to tell us that her childhood was fun, I always saw the poverty and hunger that they must have suffered. Later on, when I was older and read Dickens, I used to see my mother in just the sort of Victorian squalor that his books described. My mother's feet were crooked from wearing shoes too small for her. Sometimes they lived on barley porridge. It seemed to me a very hard way to grow up, but at least in Vienna there were no pogroms, and no dangerous romantic Cossacks.

My mother fell when a small child and injured her knee, as a consequence of which she developed tuberculosis of the knee joint, a very painful and incurable condition. It meant that she could not walk properly, and spent no time free of pain. Her sisters used to push her around in an old pram and they took her everywhere. She was, for reasons of health, sent to stay in San Pilagio in Italy on the Adriatic for four months, in the summer of her ninth year. Quite how this came to be she does not know. She stayed in a convent. She tells of the nuns who used to sing softly whilst brushing her hair, a soothing soporific in the Italian summer heat. Her parents must not have known who ran the spa. It was here that my mother first came across Christianity in the form of the colourful, candlelit, song-filled Latin mass, which she attended every day like a good little Catholic Christian. She loved it! But her father did not, and when they found out they removed her, tearing her away from her first experience of a cheerful religion.

Such was my grandfather's devotion to his God that he would chant his prayers loudly and gratingly for hours on end, when my poor mother wanted to sleep in order to blot out her pain. On the one occasion that she begged him for silence he became exceedingly angry and prayed louder than ever.

My grandmother loved her children and did what she could for them, without antagonising the very strict habits of her husband's religious fervour. She arranged for my mother to go away on cures. She spent every summer in Italy, still with Christians, but was now forbidden to attend mass. They took her to Grado. Here she learnt swimming, which gave relief to the pain in her knee. My mother wore a calliper as a child and young woman.

My mother loved her sisters and brothers, especially her disabled brother, Moritz. Later, he was sent away, to be cared for and educated in a home in Silesia called Pilgramshain, one of the first anthroposophical curative homes for children with special needs. My grandmother must have held out for once against her husband's beliefs. This was a marvellous place, and Moritz was very happy there, coming home only for holidays. My mother, also at home for lengthy periods, found that she enjoyed looking after him. It was through Moritz that she met Dr Karl König, who became his doctor, a remarkable paediatrician, and the man who changed her life forever, bringing to it riches and adventures of which she never would have dreamed.

Though small in stature, he was an imposing man, grand in speech and large in gesture. He was extremely learned, especially in the field of medicine, and had made it his life's task to develop education and therapy for children with special needs. My mother was drawn to him and to the group of young men and women who were captivated by Dr König's sense of mission. They spent evenings studying the work of Rudolf Steiner, especially in connection with reincarnation and karma, no doubt attracted to this subject because of the uncertain times in which they lived. Dr König's father owned a shoe shop. As with many Jewish people, this was no bar to study and so the son, Karl, could easily move from the merchant class to the intelligentsia because of his extraordinary powers of thinking.

When my mother was seventeen she found a physician who could do something about her diseased knee, but it would entail a serious operation to stiffen the joint by removing parts of the knee that were affected by the TB. My mother, on hearing how much it would cost, agreed to the treatment but informed the doctor that she would have to work to raise the money. Would he accept payment by instalments? He was impressed by this young girl's determination and performed the surgery free of charge in the hospital. She made a good recovery and went to train as a children's nurse, or nanny, but her one leg was stiff and shorter than the other, its foot also smaller. All her life she had either to have her shoes specially made, or buy two pairs. But she no longer needed to wear the calliper.

My mother became nanny to Dr König's children. She was more than happy to continue her friendship with the exciting group of young people, students, doctors, dancers and photographers who collected in Dr König's home to study. My mother, though the only one of the group who was not an intellectual, enjoyed these meetings. Although most of the group were Jewish, through their study of anthroposophy they had become Christians. Dr König himself was a Jew by birth but a Christian by religion. My mother now converted and became a Christian too.

For her parents, this was a blow so great that they simply decided that it had not happened. In my fertile imagination, I saw them casting her off. She used to say that when she went home to visit them, they were so successful at ignoring her that she wondered if she really did exist and had to pinch herself for verification. I dramatised this too, and pictured them mourning her as a lost ghost, sent to haunt them and that they never spoke to her again. Her brothers and sisters, however, continued to meet with her. My mother loved her parents and was very aware of the hurt she had inflicted upon them by her embracing the new faith, but she could do no other than to follow her conscience. My mother's conscience was a source of strength for her, and as time delivered its blows, this was her greatest aid to survival.

When Hitler annexed Austria, life became hard. Jews were in danger of deportation and all became stateless. To gain a visa to leave for another country one needed a passport; but as a stateless Jew, one had no passport. My mother, having been born in Poland, was told by the Austrians to get a Polish passport, and by the Poles to get an Austrian one. Eventually she obtained a stateless passport from the Nazis in which she is named as 'Sarah'.

All Jewish women where given that name on their documents, just as all Jewish men were called Abraham by the Nazi overlords. She wanted to get permission to go to Holland. Dr König was sponsored by an unknown benefactor and went to England, as did others of the group. My mother thought to join them via Holland because she wanted to work in an anthroposophical home for children with special needs. But permission was refused, and at the last minute she heard that she had been sponsored by a family in England called the Wrigleys. Whenever she came to this part of her story, she would stop as though it was all boring after that.

But maybe she was remembering the voyage to Britain, the cold uncomfortable train journey, the fear of being stopped, and the overcrowded boat from Ostend. Did they stand and look back at the receding shores of Belgium? They must have wondered when, if ever, they would return to their homeland. Being dispossessed of land and nationality cannot be pleasant or secure. And what about the rest of her family? She must have known in what great danger they were. She must have wondered if she would ever see them again.

Her brothers and sisters suffered very differing fates. Aba roamed Europe all through the war, always in hiding and always one step ahead of incarceration in a concentration camp. His story is so bizarre it would take its own book to tell. In the end, he sat it out in Switzerland. Her two eldest sisters went as Zionists to Palestine just before the war began. One sister went to France, married a Frenchman and endured the war in hiding in the Vosges Mountains, the winters freezing them so badly that the baby who was born to them had ice on him in the mornings. But they survived. Another sister waited out the war in Switzerland with her brother, Aba, and then went to South America, to Peru. Moritz died before the war, thank God. My mother's youngest brother, Joseph, was a bright boy. They sent him to a yeshiva in Poland, and when the war broke out, following the age-old instinct of survival, my grandparents fled home to Brzozow, to join their youngest son. They could not have chosen a worse thing to do, and all three perished whilst trying to escape across the Carpathian Mountains. Were they shot at the border, or did they die in a concentration camp? Long after the war, my Uncle

Aba, whom we loved as much as did my mother, with his funny hand that had no fingers – a birth defect – traced the manner of their death, but could find no account of their very existence. They had simply vanished in the holocaust. My mother could therefore never tell us how or where they died.

My mother was utterly devoted to Dr König and the ideals that were alive in the group of enthusiasts around him. When still in Vienna, these inspired young people wanted so much to do something bright and true for a world entering one of the darkest periods in history. They resolved to found a community that would practise freedom of thought, equality of living, and brotherliness in economic matters. This threefold way of life was something they had learnt from the lectures of Rudolf Steiner, who proposed an entirely new political structure for Europe after the First World War was over. Unfortunately, the politicians of the day were unable to make such a huge shift in the leaden weight of government. Perhaps smaller circles were a better way to start the reform in any case. They wanted to practise his ideas and to do so with disadvantaged people in order to help humanity. Europe was about to go into a war against evil, and these displaced Jewish young people saw a similarity between their probably temporary plight, and the absolute and permanent situation that people with handicaps were subjected to in those days.

Dr König was a physician trained in homeopathy and with experience as a medical doctor for people with special needs. He had worked with Dr Ita Wegman, who pioneered curative education for children in need of special care, under the close supervision of Rudolf Steiner. This was in a time when good homes for the handicapped did not exist, never mind schools. They were shut up in large, grim institutions and often treated like animals, or less than animals. Rudolf Steiner, who was a visionary and an inspired reformer, contributed a great gift to the present day by raising public awareness of people with disabilities, not only as suffering human beings, but as individuals who have something to teach the rest of humanity. Dr König was dedicated to the spiritual aim of creating homes and schools and places of work for the misunderstood, deprived, second-class citizens of the world.

I loved it when my mother started talking about how

Camphill, my home, came into being. I knew from an early age that we were growing up differently from other families with children, but I thought it was much more interesting to live with different people and their funny ways than to live behind a closed door in a street. Sometimes I envied other families, but most of the time I was too busy having the time of my life to really think about the oddness of my home.

And so Camphill was first an ideal, and then a reality. One of its most fundamental principles was that those who wanted to join the community should be of any ability and any nationality. That no one should be prevented from living in a Camphill community for any other reason than lack of goodwill. As long as you were prepared to do anything and help out, without payment, or very much personal space and time, you could come to Camphill. If you wanted money, time off, and an easy life, then Camphill would never have suited you. The community was founded for human beings regardless of creed, colour, ability or nationality. It was to be a place where human beings could live with human beings and work together in freedom.

Those who had pledged themselves to help bring the ideal to birth eventually arrived in Britain, and Dr König set about writing letters and meeting people. Because of his extraordinary gift with disabled people, he was offered a temporary home in Kirkton House, near Williamston in Scotland, to start with one or two children with special needs. There the little group collected and something like a community was born. My mother, obliged by her sponsorship (and her conscience) to work for a year for the Wrigleys as a nanny, only visited when she had leave. She described this house as damp and cold, so cold that she did not take her clothes off in the winter at all and slept in her coat! What an odd thing it must have been for the dour Scots to have such a colourful and foreign group arrive in their midst. Most of them could hardly speak English and actually many of them never really learnt it very well at all.

Then the men were declared enemy aliens after the fiasco of Dunkirk, and were interned, one or two destined to meet my father in Canada and on the Isle of Man. The women were left behind, and whilst on their own were offered a beautiful, dry and warm house called Camphill, just outside Aberdeen. The money to buy it was lent to them by a branch of the Macmillan family. Their son had special needs and there was no room to care for him in Kirkton House. So the women packed up, not without misgivings, and wondering what their men would say afterwards, and moved into Camphill House. From here on the community grew to become a worldwide movement bearing the name of the original house and always working with people with special needs.

Here too was a point where my mother always stopped, and would sit for a minute, brooding on the Camphill Community and its destiny. As a little girl hearing this tale, I would think that there must have been a bit more excitement than my mother would tell me, and after some prodding about what it was really like in Nazi Vienna, she told us a story about it. She said that once, when she went home to see her family, even if they would not see her, the Nazi police called for her brother. She hid him behind the door and stood in front of it, telling them that they could just leave again, the anti-Christians that they were. And so they went. I could imagine her, small, thin, fair-haired and fierce, with her stiff leg and fearless face, and as I knew that one always did as she said, I had no difficulty in believing this tale. She also said that as she did not look Jewish, which was true, she could walk about safely and that she used to carry her Bible under her arm. How powerful is the word of God! I thought with glee.

But I could feel the fear and the anxiety when the permit to Holland was denied. Just think if it had been granted, we would say! None of us would have been born. I saw the passport that declared her stateless, all stamped with eagles and swastikas and calling her Sarah Gerstler. I knew my mother as Barbara Lipsker. The Lipsker was obvious, but when did Sarah go and Barbara appear and which name was correct?

My mother's given name was Sura Rivke, a very Jiddish name, though she was usually known as Sali, an Austrian appellation with which she was more comfortable. Only her religious father called her Surali. But when she became a Christian she changed it to Barbara, and when she obtained her British naturalisation she did so in the name of Barbara Lipsker. She said Sali had gone with the war, her Jewishness and her old life. Barbara was the person who stood at Dr König's side and helped to found Camphill. She was proud of the fact that she was very practical and that hard work and early rising did not disturb her. On the other hand, she seemed to be ashamed of her lack of education and always said she was not really a thinker, meaning, I suppose, an intellectual.

At the start of Camphill, this group of strong-minded individuals who argued over every principle pledged themselves to work for the handicapped, and in so doing, to give up their personal aspirations to fame and fortune. So the doctor became a farmer, the dancer did the laundry, and the richest of all was sent to plant potatoes, though wondering loudly why they had to be put into the ground in the spring, only to be dug up again in the autumn. The miracle of the loaves and fishes had not seeped through to him yet! They worked hard all day at menial jobs, and in the evenings, after the children had gone to bed, they studied. They read Steiner and worked hard at becoming good curative educators. In the mornings they rose at six, and arranged the day's tasks. Dr König, a hard but fair taskmaster, saw to it that no one shirked. But if you were truly in need, there was no better friend. The evening study was often my mother's undoing, but she made up for it with hard work during the day and was always a good organiser.

My mother's gift was her extraordinary morality. She had a lion's courage, and no matter what might occur she upheld the truth, shaming many into better behaviour or cleaner thoughts. She was warm and compassionate, but never sentimental. And she knew when things were true or a lie. You could trust my mother till the ends of the earth.

Barbara and Bernhard married on New Year's Eve. A year later my eldest sister was born, but only after another obstacle was thrown into my father's difficult destiny, and made a vast change in my mother's life.

Funnily enough, neither of them spoke much about their courting, and about what happened after they were married not much was said either. But from the little one could read between the lines, they were very happy together, except for the substantial presence of Dr König. Bearing in mind the remarkable intelligence and vivacity of my father, it can be easily understood that he and

Dr König fought. Two such personalities under one roof did not fit so very well. My father felt that Dr König was too demanding and too dictatorial. What Dr König thought no one will say.

There were others of the original group who felt the same as my father – not, I was led to understand, because they ganged up together, but because each had their own particular row they wanted to hoe, and the plants they saw growing were different from the crop that Dr König was dedicated to nurturing. A group left a few years after Camphill was founded, each to start their own type of curative educational establishments, or to teach in Waldorf schools, and amongst them were very close friends of my mother. She missed them greatly but would never have thought to desert the striving community that was Dr König's.

One could ask whether something so led from the top could be called a community, but my mother explained this as being necessary for the pioneering of a completely new social attempt. As the years passed, the strong leadership softened to group work, and today this involves even the newest and youngest members of the community, as well as those with special needs. But when crisis arose in my father's choice of a future, group work was still a dream, and Dr König was always very present and vocal with his demands.

My father was a teacher; he had discovered his true calling because the disaster that Hitler wrought all over Europe denied him the study he would otherwise have done. He wanted to teach in a Waldorf school as well as live in a community. He had, since his teacher's training, been looking for a school that would teach children from the heart, and in such a way that their developmental needs could be met naturally, without forcing the growing intellect. He used to say that Rudolf Steiner, the founder of the Waldorf School movement, understood children's educational needs, and that most children grow better and more intelligently if they are free to learn the things that interest them. If the teacher can discover this, then every child can become a professor, or a scientist, or an artist or even a workman, because they *love* learning. He appreciated the Waldorf approach for those very reasons. But people with special needs were not his vocation; nor was gardening. The sights and smells of the classroom beckoned with great force, and if this meant forgoing community living, then this was the necessary sacrifice that had to be made.

My mother wanted to continue with the adventure of Camphill. Dr König was her ideal, a man with force and character, wisdom and kindness, and with a mission. The person with special needs, particularly the child, tugged at my mother's heart. She wanted to help the community survive.

The discussions must have been painful. My mother, quiet and resourceful, and my father, boisterous and clever, had come up against an impossible problem. In the end my mother would have given in to my father's superior pressure; but God, or destiny, or some other agent stepped in and made the decision for them.

As an important part of the community-building endeavour, Dr König had started something unique and powerful. He had created what was called the Bible Evening. On Saturday nights, the members of the community met in a beautifully prepared room and ate a special festive meal together. As a small child, I imagined it to be something like the Last Supper, sombre and compelling and definitely very, very holy. It was intended to include profound and real substance, the conversation was to hold meaning, and Dr König, at first, but later other senior members, read a passage from the Bible and discoursed upon it, asking those present to contribute their own personal understanding of the passage. In such a fashion, they were to get to know each other deeply and spiritually. Individual ambitions could be discovered through daily life in the work that they shared and the social activities that they enjoyed. For the forming of a community that seeks to work, play and pray together, there could be nothing better than a formal occasion that bound all three aspects together. To this day, in Camphill communities worldwide, the Bible Evening can be experienced, but today anyone can go, and it nearly always includes adults with special needs. In the early days, however, the Bible Evening was precious, and one received an invitation to attend and could speak only if well prepared beforehand.

My mother loved going. My father came to dislike its formality and the dominance of Dr König's contribution. So one

Saturday night, shortly before they were going to leave for Ilkeston in Derbyshire, where my father had obtained employment as a class teacher in the small Waldorf School that had just started, my mother received an invitation to the Bible Evening. Knowing that my father hated this, she asked him at least to meet her afterwards. This meant finding a way to get from Camphill House to Heathcot House. My father had a bicycle. The brakes were broken. He borrowed another, and rode fast down the drive to the road at the foot of the short but steep hill. The brakes of the borrowed bicycle had gone too. He crashed into the fence at the bottom and bounced onto the road, under the wheels of a passing van that could not stop in time.

This is the story as my father tells it. My mother tells it differently. She said that they had resolved their differences well before the accident and did not connect the two events at all. She said that his brakes failed and he got run over, not the bit about the Saturday night Bible Evening disagreement. However, the story ended the same way. My father was seriously injured, his skull crushed and many bones broken. My mother was carrying their first child.

My father says he should have died. My mother says he would have died if it had not been for Dr König. My father does not remember any of these years. He suffered total amnesia and only gradually regained a part of his memory; but the years before and around his accident remained hearsay to him. He lay in a coma for three months, sometimes babbling in a strange language that sounded like Hebrew. As part of his rehabilitation, Dr König counselled him regularly in an attempt to help him to remember where he had been when unconscious for so long. My father used to say that this coma was a false initiation period, and that was why he could not remember anything. He said that he should have been able to control and master his near-death experience and that he failed. As a consequence, he held on to his great knowledge and sagacity, but lost the ability to apply it. Study he could manage, but the power to teach left him. He could talk about what he knew, but could no longer give a lecture. Any responsibility gave him a migraine.

But a remarkable change had taken place. Gone was the

critical, intellectual coldness of my father's Jewish brain. In its place was a man with a heart that warmed everyone who came across him, and a simplicity of Christian faith that was a lesson to everyone. He loved everyone, accepted everyone and treated all with warmth, humour and gentleness. My father was always a gentleman, honourable and true.

My mother was devastated by his accident. She sat day after day by his bedside, praying for his recovery and knitting for my unborn sister. She doesn't say much of this time. But when my father finally returned to the world of day, he did not remember her and had no interest in the fact that they were married. On release from hospital, he had to learn everything like a little baby. He was deaf, and could not control his movements properly. Walking and handling life's daily events returned to him by virtue of Dr König's medical care, but he did not recover his hearing. It was only then that we learned that he had been partially deaf from birth and so had acquired the art of lip-reading. This was a godsend that only his angel could have planned, because he could participate in conversation even now that both ears could not hear. We grew up speaking very, very clearly and precisely, but we did not have to slow down for him as long as he could see our faces.

Because of my father's disability, my parents went to live in a house outside the community. There my sister was born. And my father learnt to be a man as best as he could. He loved his little daughter. And he became a good and much loved father to all three of us. My mother was lonely. She wanted to live inside the community's space. So they went to live in Murtle House, my mother becoming the matron. Then my second sister was born.

My mother found life very strenuous. Murtle was the largest house in the community at the time. I have heard it said that at one time it housed sixty people. To attempt to run such a mammoth affair required a great deal of organisational talent and an awareness of people's needs. My mother found it very hard to combine it all with caring for a growing family. She accepted that all children need attention and saw no reason to care for those with special needs and thereby deprive her own. She gave us what we needed with the attitude that if you bring children into the world then it is your responsibility to look after them.

My eldest sister remembers sitting on the potty by the side of a little girl from another family. This girl was crying for her mother and so she said to her, 'Don't cry, *my* mother will look after you,' and wondered why this did not seem to comfort her at all! To us, our mother could make everything right in the world, and our father knew everything in the world. From being a quiet, shy and retiring sort of person, my mother had to learn to wear the trousers, so to speak. My father could not make decisions, could not remember wanting to leave Camphill and became dependent upon her for everything. Dr König saw her distress and banished her once again, first to the Garden Cottage in Heathcot. Here a foster-daughter joined us, Barbara, whose mother had died and whose father could not take care of her at that time. Then the family moved to Camphill Cottage, and finally to Heathcot Lodge, a very small gatehouse at the bottom of the drive to Heathcot House. Here I was born.

Actually, my mother gave birth to me in Aberdeen Royal Infirmary and the story goes (as she tells it) that she was in a filthy temper, the delivery suite was full and so she gave birth to me outside on a table. I saw her lying on our round, dark gate-legged dinner table and me popping out screaming blue murder! I was very good at that all my life, and my mother says it was all because she was so angry at the time of my birth! They had called my eldest sister Agnes Maria Barbara, so sonorous and grand. Agnes was a healthy Scots name, Maria as she was born in the twelve holy nights, and Barbara probably because they both loved the name. My second sister was not so easy to name. They could not agree. Finally they settled for Elizabeth Leonore, my mother wanting to call her Gertrude and my father absolutely forbidding it.

As for me, my mother said that my face told her my name – Martha – which is my first name on my birth certificate; but as she disliked it, they called me Veronika, and so I grew up with a forename that has never been used. Of course, we gave each other nicknames. Agnes became Agi, pronounced with a German 'A' which to English ears sounds like the 'U' in cup. Elizabeth became Leezy, since we used German vowels and the 'I' had to be lengthened. I became, for some obscure reason, Gony. My sister,

Agi, says that she was sitting brooding on the toilet, wanting me to have a nickname too, and she ran through my name by giving it fresh starting consonants and so came up with 'Gony'. Anyway, it stuck and I lost it only once I reached full adulthood, my sisters still using it to this day.

We were all three baptised in the Christian faith, my eldest sister having Dr König and Peter Roth as her godparents, and my second sister being given Mrs König and Arno Rode to accompany her through infancy and childhood. By the time I arrived, they had run out of powerful godparents, so I was given into the spiritual care of a woman of whom my mother was very fond. Maybe my name came through her because she was also called Veronica, though with a 'C'; but she died when I was very young and I only have a beautiful delicate turquoise and gold chain to remember her by. I do not, in truth, recall her at all. My other godparent was Thesi Baum, a strong and purposeful woman, who had a family of her own. I remember her low voice, and that she smelled of cigarettes. I was a bit afraid of her, and envied my sisters their godparents who hardly seemed to have any bearing on their lives. Except for Mrs König. She came and went throughout our early childhood and we had to call her Frau Doctor.

I cannot remember Heathcot Lodge, but I am told that my mother fitted us all into this tiny little cottage, including Barbara, who lived with us until she was six when her father married again and so could care for her once more. Barbara could scream as successfully as I could. I remember her dark hair and flashing smile, but little else. My early years are a blur of sounds, songs and flashes of houses and people. I do not remember the names of the people who later shared our home when we had moved, once again, to Camphill Lodge.

This little house, close to the River Dee at the foot of Camphill's back drive that connected to the road called Pitangulley's Brae, also had some people with special needs living in it, besides our family. I remember the front door, the little stream running beside it, and that we had a white rabbit called Peter. We ate our meals together. My very first memory is of a meal at the end of which I needed the bathroom. I was, of course, taken out to fulfil this necessity and when I came back, a disaster had struck. In Camphill, grace was spoken at the start of the meal and afterwards we took hands around the table and blessed the meal together, chanting, 'Blessing on the meal.'

They had, on this occasion, blessed the meal without me. The insult was so great that I screamed and to my joy, my mother interpreted my pain correctly and made everyone sit down to bless the meal again! My sisters have always maintained that I was spoilt. I only know how intensely grateful I am to my mother for understanding my very forceful nature and my entirely real desire always to be part of any community activity. I really loved it.

Being with people with special needs was not something that we thought about. We called them 'ill', because when there was something the matter with us, then we were ill, so we applied this rule across the board. They accepted us as we accepted them. Apparently I was very much beloved by an adolescent girl who had social problems. She used to carry me about and, having seen my father toss me up in the air and catch me, she did the same, but dropped me. My sisters liked to tell me this story to account for my fussiness, making it sound as if the fall had damaged my wits, something that they teased me about. Moreover, in Camphill Lodge lived another girl, who had word fixations. In the prayer that we said together, standing in a circle at the end of each day, were the words, 'and a smooth path below me.' Of course this line meant that the angel of God should grant this to the petitioner. But the poor girl would take this line as a trigger, and dive across the circle to grab me by the neck, shake me fiercely and demand, 'Veronika, say *below me*, say *below me*!'

I remember nothing of this strange event. But it must have been traumatic enough for my sisters to remember it. And in rest hours, later on, when we were bored, they liked to re-enact it, vying as to who would shriek the words and try to strangle me. I found this memory of theirs really quite entertaining in its dramatic tone.

The bedroom in the Lodge that we four shared, called the nursery, was a dark little room, and in it I first met the devil. We were ill and my mother said she would call the doctor, but what entered my sleepy vision as I woke from rest hour was a tall thin man, dressed in black, bending over my cot with a cold metal thing against my chest. I, predictably by now, did what I knew was sensible: I screamed! The Devil, properly frightened by the noise, fled. I met Dr Thomas Weihs many times thereafter, but never again mistook him for Satan and found him to be a very kind man.

It was whilst living in Camphill Lodge that I acquired my secondary nickname, aptly so called, because the boy who gave it to me was called Nicholas. He was older even than my eldest sister, and was much admired by us younger girls. Being the youngest meant that I was always struggling to keep up with the others, not only physically, but also mentally. I had to hurry to catch up with them. On one occasion, as on many, they used their superior agility to run away from me. They did not want me tagging along, a common experience until I arranged my own gang. Now I ran after them, my short legs aching with the effort, and Nick turned round, calling, 'Little pair of posh legs!' – an epithet that stuck unmercifully. I hated it, and so it became a hurtful weapon in my sisters' mouths, to be used when really wanting to insult me into tears.

I also acquired a pseudo-godfather. A young man came as co-worker to Camphill and we recognised each other, so to speak, even though I must have only been eighteen months, and we consequently became fast friends, entirely ignoring the age difference. I loved him dearly. He fed me in my high chair, and as I grew older, gave me much joy and laughter. Jens has remained an excellent friend to this day, and has been faithful in his adopted role of godparent.

One further memory I have of Camphill Lodge is of a white horse getting loose, and everyone going into a panic except my father, who made us stand still. Then quietly he talked to the frightened animal, which walked up to him confidently, and so was returned to his field. My father said that the animal was more frightened of us than we of him, and that no human being had the right to frighten dumb creatures as we had done, running after it like that. I learned my lesson well.

When I was about three, we moved to Heathcot House. Here we stayed until I was nine years of age. We had by now moved five times. Without the strong family identity that my mother was consciously creating, we might have been very confused and insecure. But she held us together, making the moves exciting and forward looking, never neglecting us in word, thought or deed. And she cared for my father in such a way that we admired and loved him, never seeing his handicap as he gradually learned to become a man again.

Chapter II

HEATHCOT

If you wanted to leave Aberdeen for the Highlands and Banchory, Ballater or Braemar, the royal seat of Balmoral, you had a choice of roads to take. You could take the North Deeside road which runs through a series of small villages, one of which is Bieldside, and you found first Newtondee, then Cairnlee, then Murtle and on reaching Milltimber, you had arrived at Camphill. These were all at one time large houses for the rich and mighty, probably small compared with what they might have been used to, but big by today's standard of housing. As the community grew in size by the admission of more and more children with special needs, so accommodation became a problem. The estates came on the market after the war with the fall in the fortunes of many, and with it an inability to pay servants.

Altogether, times were changing. To people wanting homes for children in need of special care, or boarding schools, such properties were a boon. Camphill had collected excellently supportive sponsors, and so it grew very quickly. One could walk along a path by the railway from Camphill, to Murtle, and from Murtle to Newtondee, or by way of the slope down to the river, along the Dee, and up again by the ferry road, or just simply along the top of the slope overlooking the river. Contact was exceedingly frequent and very good. The estates operated as one community in those early days.

Heathcot was the only house on the other side of the river. If you took the South Deeside road out of Aberdeen, your second choice to the royal holiday castle, you travelled through pretty countryside, whose large houses and estates were set well back from the road, until you came to the police station and just beyond it, in the scatter of houses and farms called Blairs, you took a small road leading up a hill and there was the Lodge, a curving drive and Heathcot House, set within a ring of mature beech trees. Now you were in Kincardineshire. A little further down the road was Blairs College, a priests' seminary. This set us children apart from the rest of our friends who lived in unromantic Aberdeenshire, a built-up suburb. They used blue double-decker buses to go to town, whilst we lived in the free and romantic countryside, in the wilds of Kincardineshire, and used a single-decker red coach to go into, and out of, town. We *knew* our bus drivers, whilst they rode in anonymity.

Heathcot House was large, cold and grey. Built of granite, it had a slate flagged hall floor, cold and uninviting. The house itself was large and interesting, with three staircases and endless corridors and hidden nooks and crannies. We had a small flat upstairs in the centre of the house and only shared it with one outside member of the family, who inhabited the room separating our nursery from a dormitory of children with special needs. It was one link from our flat to the rest of the house. Otherwise, you approached our rooms by a winding stair that also descended to the basement, in which were some of the former servants' quarters. Now they housed the kitchen, mending room, vegetable cellar, coal cellar, larder, sundry bedrooms for co-workers, and the laundry, which boasted a copper that had to be lit from underneath and steamed the place up most satisfactorily. There was also an ironing room.

Down in these interesting rooms ladies came to work. The washing ladies and the mending ladies were favourites of ours because they said we were so pretty and gave us sweets to eat. My being the youngest stood me in good stead. I got more treats than did my sisters, though they took care to remove them from me in case I became too spoilt! Usually they left me with one or two barley sugars, or a pear drop, the latter giving me blisters on my tongue. But they had no compunction in sending me ahead of them when they wanted more goodies.

At either end of the house were the dormitories, filled with children of all ages, many of them in wheelchairs. The co-workers often slept in these rooms, sharing them with the ill children, partly from lack of space and usually to afford the children natural security and care, as would a parent. Upstairs at the far end was the baby nursery, a lovely place to visit with my mother. She had become the matron of this huge house, which at its fullest was a home to forty people; but was nevertheless considered small compared to the other houses situated across the river.

We ate our meals in the large dining room and had a room called the Green Room, which was kept smart and beautiful, only to be used by us children on festive or formal occasions. We also had a treatment room, where one went when cut or bruised, and where the 'ill' children were seen in clinics by the doctors; and a massage room, of great fame to us staff children because of the equipment, which we played on until being told off and sent out. It was fun to swing along the pulleys attached to the ceiling, put there, no doubt, as an aid to those with physical disabilities to help them to learn to stand and walk.

Outside, the grounds and gardens were very neglected. There was so much to do for the ill children, and so few people to do it, that beautifying the grounds took second place. But for us children it was a paradise. We could play freely and unsupervised in acres of trees, shrubs and fields, corners of rhododendrons giving us their shelter and hiding us from the prying eyes of the grown-ups. We were, I believe, little savages, and my memory of freedom and fun is very strongly connected to the years that we lived in Heathcot.

The curved and gravelled area in front of the house had two exits, one to the left and one to the right. The left led down the drive to the Lodge, and out to the main road, where one caught the bus to town or to the bridge over the river and then one had to walk the rest of the way up to Camphill House. The other led to the back drive, probably formally the servants' entrance to the estate. The back drive went up and down the hill, down to the road, and up to Heathcot Farm, which did not belong to us and was guarded by two fierce and loud sheepdogs, and past the farm to the walled-in garden where my father worked.

There was a path under the circle of tall beeches, which could take a small child more safely to the garden, because it protected one from the dangerous dogs. Usually we took the path, unless we were in the mood to send a newcomer to run the gauntlet and prove his courage. Once in the garden, many pleasures were available. My father was not particularly strict and so we ate whatever we wanted, and whatever seemed nice. The garden was rather like the pictures by Beatrix Potter of the garden belonging to Mr McGregor in the book about Peter Rabbit. It had a high wall around it and we delighted in climbing onto the roof of the shed and so onto the top of the wall. Once up, we ran round it, picking the fruit from the trees that grew up it, or just playing games. It had a broad enough surface to keep us safe, and none of us ever fell off it. My mother worried, but my father said that if we fell, we would learn the danger, and if we did not fall, so much the better.

The smell of the turned earth as he dug the ground and the feel of the warm apples in my hand still return to bring back the essence of that garden. Here my father told his tales, and we used to sit and help him eat his second breakfast. A man called Bob helped him with his work. He had a robin (just like Mr McGregor), and it would hop one or two steps away from him as he dug his rows of earth. We pulled the potatoes and ate them raw, as well as the turnips, which we called neeps. Then came the nasty deworming treatment, which in those days meant, a soap enema. It never stopped us tasting the sweet gritty raw food.

The garden greenhouse had a peach tree growing in it. My father cultivated this treasure and guarded the fruit. We were not allowed to pick any peaches. They were for my mother. We knew that summer had arrived when we were allowed to go barefooted, and when my mother had a small, round, downy, hard peach sitting on her little table next to the wooden stool that bore her stiff leg when she sat in the blue armchair in her room. I knew better than to pinch that peach, though I often stole the chocolates that she kept in a little grey-blue lidded jar.

The 'we' that I shall continue to refer to are the children who grew up in and around Heathcot. There were several families who came and went in this large house, trying out community life and either loving it, which meant they moved on to their own house communities, or hating it, which meant that they left.

Many co-workers who came during and after the war were refugees from Hitler's regime. They were mostly German speaking, and though they spoke a peculiar form of English during the day, and always to the ill children, when alone or at night, they spoke German. We grew up without recognising there was any difference between the two languages. My parents spoke only German to Agi, wanting her to be bilingual, but her very first words after Mama and Dada were 'stop it', so they did and talked English with us.

Bedtimes were magic moments of stories and conversation. My father read to us from Grimm's *Märchen*, which we later understood to be *Grimm's Fairy Tales*. He read from a leather-bound book with dark black lettering, and sometimes from a fat black book with a paper and cardboard cover. The stories were of wolves, dragons, witches, princesses and princes, wise kings and foolish kings, clever young men and stupid ones. I think I was roughly five years old and had already learned to read a little, when I discovered to my amazement that there were two different languages being used. I discovered this fact because I could not read the leather-bound black writing from Grimm's *Märchen*. It was in Gothic script, and entirely illegible to me with my newfound skill. Thus did I realise that German and English looked different as well as sounding different, and that the Germans and the English really were separate nations!

This was more a corroboration of something obvious than a surprise, since we had a sort of cops-and-robbers game that was entitled 'Germans and English', and the outcome was always predictable. The English won and the Germans were executed. Usually we had imaginary Germans because no one wanted the role. We were all without doubt, English.

Bedtime stories were not always as healthy as the fairy tales of the brothers Grimm. My father told us tales of the Holocaust. He tried to disguise them in some fashion, making them human and historical, but I knew of concentration camps, of starvation, torture, the gas chambers, and the wholesale destruction of our Jewish past. It was so close to the war that the pictures of terror still appeared in the papers, and of cities devastated by bombs. I saw a photograph of a heap of skulls piled up on top of bones, next to a big pit beside a house with a high chimney, and I dreamed about it long afterwards. When the rubbish was being burnt, it sometimes had a particularly nasty smell and I imagined this was the smell of the ovens at Auschwitz. I knew the names of many camps: Birkenau, Chemnitz, Oranienburg, Ravensbrück, Treblinka and Maidenek. My father told us about the cattle wagons, the long trains that rolled at night over Germany from Holland, France, Belgium, Russia, Poland and Austria. Why were people put into animal carriages? He told us of medical experiments with live human beings. He said Hitler was trying to find out how to make the perfect Aryan. What was an Aryan? Certainly not a Jew. I found aeroplanes overhead always a little dangerous and dreamed of fire from the sky. Sometimes when he told his tales, I heard the noise of gunfire like claps and rolls of thunder. Electric storms have consequently always terrified me. Even now in my adulthood I dislike them, especially at night.

Hunger was something I understood less, but having seen pictures of starving louse-ridden concentration camp victims, I knew it was extremely painful and understood why we were taught to eat what was on our plates; not that the food we got was so terribly delicious. We were not rich in those early Camphill years, and food bulked out with milk sauces – milk being a good cheap source of nourishment, was common on our tables. Moreover, the vegetables were usually mashed, to meet the difficulties that physically disabled people have when chewing. I did not like the food at all, making a fuss at meals, so that I had to be sent out. Then my mother, taking pity on me, fed me bread and cheese in the kitchen. This was a wonderful way to get a bit of quality attention from her. Otherwise I was always having to share it with forty other people at a time. One part of me was jealous; another loved the large crowds of my childhood days.

Perhaps because of the tales that my father told, I suffered from nightmares. Waking up screaming was not an uncommon occurrence. My mother would come, soothing in her nightie, and take me into her bed. My parents had separate rooms. In principle, we were not allowed in our parents' beds, but a nightmare was something to be dealt with appropriately. She would cuddle me, whilst I spread myself out in the comfort of her arms. If the dream was terrible and would not leave me, she would tell me stories, of angels and helpers that guard the good in the world, and then I could sleep again, whilst she lay squashed on the edge of her bed.

Once or twice, I woke screaming before she had gone to bed. It must have happened on a Saturday night after Bible Evening, because her light was still on, draped with a red cloth that made the room glow, and she took me on her knee and fed me Bible Evening juice, holy and cool in my hot throat. I remember recommending it to the mother of a friend as a good way to chase away evil from him, because he too suffered from bad dreams. I strongly believed in its magic powers! His fear might have had more reality since he was a refugee and I only suffered by hearsay.

I loved the company of the ill children, and visiting their nurseries was always interesting. The nicest was the baby nursery. It was cool and quiet, and smelled of baby powder. The co-workers who cared for these tiny Down's babies, abandoned by their parents, were always the most beautiful in my eyes. They looked like Botticelli angels in their white aprons. And they sang to the babies. I loved that nursery very much and would go round peering into the cots with warmth and wonder.

Not all the co-workers were wonders of love and humanity. Not all of them had time to spare for the staff children. Some treated us as if we were not there at all! Some barely spoke to us. Some told us to go away whenever we appeared. Depending on how much time they had for us, our treatment of them was meted out. We could be very unhelpful, rude and sly, if we felt disregarded.

In the co-worker's room next to our nursery slept a variety of fortunate, or unfortunate people. We hosted Janet McGavin, a lovely lady who always spoke politely and was one of those who worked in the baby nursery. I felt that she was someone to treat politely in return and we gave her no trouble. Then there was Jürgen Hess, a violinist of no mean talent who later became quite famous. He gave us concerts at night and in the morning by practising his violin, and to him we gave no trouble either.

Renate König, the eldest daughter of Dr König, we admired fearfully. She was slight in build with long dark hair that she wore in a plait down her back. She was also, to my eyes, very beautiful. She was brave and true and cheerful and she was also a nurse. She gained my sister Leezy's undying devotion by paddling over the river in the winter without let or fear. We were only allowed to paddle across the river in the summer when the water was low and there could be no drowning.

Carlo Pietzner also had that room, and we gave him a lot of grief. He was tall and fair-haired, large in build and fancied himself as a lady's man. He was also very vain, but his saving grace was that he had a good sense of humour, at least when with other adults, and was of a very social nature, again when he was with other adults. He had no time for staff children and found us a nuisance. We made altogether too much noise. He would complain to our mother that we did not give him enough peace and that she should keep us quiet. So we stole his peppermints, and I cried loudly every evening, and we talked in the rest hour. My sisters would beg me not to cry because it would disturb Carlo, and they did not like it when he strode into our nursery to tell me off, but I cried anyway, and he would storm in and tell us to be quiet. My mother used to soothe him and say, 'Wait till you have your own children.'

Down in the basement, other co-workers resided. Some of them were nice, some less so. We liked those who were able to muck in with the work, and soon recognised the shirkers. Being country children, we despised the posh types, and make-up and high heels were not popular with us. One day a lady arrived from Holland with make-up, high heels *and* a tight skirt. This was really a bit too much! And she wore them even when working with the children. We longed to see her ordinary and clean faced. She did not like us at all, calling us 'the spoilt Lipsker brats' behind our backs. To get even, we released young frogs from the pond into her area window, and were happy to hear her yells as she fled from them, the frogs hopping over her room, even onto her bed. We did not make nice enemies. We also understood German so well that we knew when the co-workers were complaining and took a great delight in sitting silently until there might be a question, and then answering it in English. What horrid little spies we were!

But to those co-workers who treated us like intelligent and useful human beings we were very, very good. We helped them with the ill children, who responded well to us because we were their friends. We were willing to clean, wash dishes and do whatever we could to help a newcomer feel at home. We made many friends out of these displaced people who came and went. Their going was always sad, because we might never see them again. I learned when quite young that friends need not always live in the same part of the world as I did, but I missed them nevertheless.

Heathcot House was an ideal playground for children. The sweeping drive ended in a very large, curving, gravelled fronting before the main entrance. We loved to mark out hopscotch in the pebbles and skip with our ropes on this safe and spacious area. The lawn, which in more affluent times would have spread out towards the curve of beech trees that protected the gardens, was fenced in and provided a safe and grassy field for Ann Trier's ponies. In the centre of the field grew a rhododendron bush. In truth, it was *the* rhododendron of all rhododendrons!

Behind the house, the gravel ran round in a path and went past the area windows of the basement. Behind this ran the back lawn, neglected and full of nettles along the large and rambling hedge. The centre of that garden featured beautiful roses, and when the lawn was mowed one could see that they were dug into formal gardens of odd shapes. Down either side of the lawn stood stately Irish yew trees, pointing their branches to the sky – another magic place in which to play. Round the side of the house grew a row of young beech trees, excellent for practising before graduating to the real climbs of the mature trees.

In this place of freedom and adventure, my childhood stretched with play, play and still more play. We lived as one big, noisy, interesting and odd sort of family. The ill children were our friends, our sisters and brothers (though some of them had the strangest of habits), and the co-workers our uncles and aunts, some of whom were fun, others more strict, and some we actively disliked, as one does in any family. What sticks in my mind and my heart were the friends we had, and the friends we made. Every year new people arrived, some with their families, and then there were still more children to join our gang. At one point, I believe we were altogether fifteen staff children of varying ages and naughtiness.

The staff children played together all the time. Although the ill children were a part of my life, we could not always play with them. They had to do so many things in their time out of school. Many of them needed massage, extra tuition, feeding at the mealtimes, and a great deal of physical care. There were never enough co-workers to cover their needs so fully that there was also time for as much play as we more able children could organise. Sometimes we joined their therapeutic activities, drawing, painting and so on, but only when the nursery parents were our friends and saw the potential in us as helpers and companions. My eldest sister, Agi, was particularly useful because she often understood the children's poor speech better than the co-workers and could interpret what their needs and wishes might be. I just tagged along out of fascination.

I loved the wonderful aids that the co-workers made for them, such as wooden-handled spoons that a paraplegic – or spastic person, as we called them in those days – could feed themselves with. Each child had their own special spoon and fork, with their names engraved by a hot needle in the wood. Trying to eat with one of these gave me a feeling of how hard it was to have a twisted, rigid arm and hand. There were children who could write and draw with their toes or mouths! This was truly clever and amazing. When I tried to do the same, I found that it required a huge amount of patience and skill, of which I had neither. I admired them very much for their good nature and endurance. I wondered why God had made them as he did. So I asked my father. Questions like that were better asked of him, because he would tell us the truth, whereas my mother would tell us a long and complicated story in which we lost track of our original curiosity and were left with a somewhat unsatisfied feeling at the end.

My father's answer was that God made them as he did for us, to learn something about life and ourselves. As we were fortunate enough to be mobile and healthy, we could learn how to have love and pity for others who could not do as we did. We could appreciate all that they *could* do, and so see that all people are human, whatever way they come into the world. This was a very satisfactory answer indeed. I determined to love them a lot, which lasted only as long as that afternoon and then I forgot all about it.

Because our parents were so busy looking after the ill children, the bigger staff children looked after the younger ones – after a fashion, it is true; but they meted out justice and kept us all in order. We knew our place down the chain of command, and the bigger boys and girls knew their responsibilities. Sometimes rules were broken, as for instance with the tree houses.

The older boys, Chris Bould and a friend whose name I cannot remember, had built a very good tree house in the branches of one of the tallest beeches. It was also quite far away from the house, and had a most exciting rope ladder up which to climb. The ladder itself was not the attraction. It was the fact that one raised and lowered it by means of a rope that was hidden in one of the lower branches. We smaller children were not allowed in the big boys' tree hut. We had to content ourselves with dens on the ground. These could be very hidden and exciting too, because we played 'at house' in them and filled them with old carpets and broken bits of furniture in which our dolls could live a very satisfactory life indeed.

But the tree house was special. You could only get up with one of the big boys, and only on special occasions. It was like climbing up to the sky, and when you reached the safety of its wooden floor, you found it was not so safe because of the gaps between the boards. It was a bare and masculine place, with no frills and nothing interesting to play with. The fun lay in the fact that it was a forbidden place.

Other forbidden things were no less attractive, for example the pond that lay in the weedy, reedy backfield. Did it belong to us? I cannot remember, but I remember going there with bated breath because its edges were swampy, and I knew that one could sink and drown in the swamps and bogs of Scotland. Then the fairy folk would have you forever! Still, we went to the pond and made rafts out of planks and string. No one drowned, but maybe that was a miracle.

On walks of exploration, of which there were many, we came across the hidden menace of the electric fence. Fences were wires simply placed there for us to climb over. They were to deter the cows and horses, but to us human beings they were no barrier. However, there was that first fence that shocked us. We met it by accident. My friend, Paul Bould, made the discovery. He badly needed to pee, when suddenly he was hurled backwards onto his bottom as if by the hand of God. What had struck him down? Surely God could not have suddenly banned peeing outside? We always peed outside, unless our parents were with us. So that couldn't be the reason. Cautiously, he crawled towards the place where he had been aiming the stream of urine. He looked at the wet grass and then stood up, only to be thrown backwards once more. Then he realised that it was the fence. With trembling yet courageous hearts, we both took hold of the wire and felt the electric charge. We knew it was electricity because Pauly's scientific mind knew about batteries and our acute hearing picked up the 'tick, tick' of the electrical charge. It wasn't really so bad now that we knew what it was. It proved the greatest fun to introduce innocent friends to this adventure – fun for us, needless to say. Some of the less hardy children did not enjoy it nearly as much as we did.

Paul Bould is the other part of the 'we' of my childhood. We went everywhere together. We were inseparable. Life was unimaginable without him and all my memories of the years in Heathcot include him as closely as my body is mine. He had a round smiling face and an imagination that none could rival. He feared nothing, defended me staunchly, giggled infectiously, roared like a lion when hurt and was never without a new idea of what we might do on each new day. Boredom was a thing unheard of in his fertile imagination. On the rare occasions when he could not come out to play, my days were grey and dull.

The Bould family lived in the Garden Cottage, a small house built up against the wall of the garden in which my father worked. It was so small that it had only three rooms in which Reg and Molly and their five children lived. The family's arrival in Camphill was a great event because they were from England. They were not the usual displaced persons from Germany or Austria, and they were certainly not of Jewish origin. They all spoke such beautiful English that we were astounded. It was the first time I heard my mother tongue without an accent. I loved to hear them speak and revelled in the vowels. I don't think we could have spoken English properly without their influence.

Reg was a man to be admired. He had worked in an aircraft factory during the war, making planes to shoot down and bomb the enemy. This made him a hero in my eyes. And Molly was an excellent cook. The meals that we had eaten before she came were something to be forgotten as quickly as they were painfully consumed. But now we had interesting food to eat, like potatoes roasted, or mashed with milk, and cabbage that was still crisp instead of cooked till it resembled sauerkraut. Sometimes Pauly and I went to play in the kitchen and then we got to eat the leftovers, if we liked them. On one occasion, an apple lay on the scrubbed oak table in the centre of the vast flagged basement kitchen that was Molly's domain. Pauly asked for it and Molly answered, with a sigh, that it seemed to her that whatever he saw he wanted to have. Pauly, to my utter admiration, lifted up the milk churn lid that lay next to the desired fruit and covered it up, saying that he couldn't see it any more, so could he have it now? Needless to say, he got it, and we ran away to munch its sweetness outside on the steps of the house.

Sometimes when I went to visit the Boulds in their tiny cottage, Reg and Molly were talking at each other. It made me very uncomfortable. I was unused to quarrelling adults. The co-workers were always polite to each other, and my parents never seemed to fight. I did not really understand what it was all about. Molly seemed to be unhappy living in Heathcot and Reg wanted to stay. Another thing that amazed me about this English family was the way in which discipline was dealt out. A smack came very easily and I sometimes felt as if the boys were afraid of their father's wrath. I was never afraid of anybody. I was always sure that my parents were right, and if they were angry, it was certainly justified. I trusted my mother and father utterly and completely.

Later, the Boulds, who had lived first in Newtondee, and then in a Camphill community in Norway before coming to Heathcot, moved back to Newtondee, and I had to visit Pauly over the river. It was like wrenching my arm off to be parted from him. But I dare say such a large family in such a small house as the Garden Cottage would have made any wife bitter, and was probably the reason for their often stiff way of conversing with each other. Going back to Newtondee gave them the opportunity to live in a bigger house.

My eldest sister, Agi, played with Pauly's older sister, Lizzy. We found it highly amusing to have an Elizabeth in both families and knew which was which by the difference in the pronunciation of the nickname. I thought they were actually different names altogether, and only later realised that it was merely the difference between a German and English way of saying the vowel. Agi and Lizzy were 'best friends' and giggled probably as much as we did but about different, more grown-up things. We giggled mainly because life was something about which to giggle. Everything was so very interesting and around every corner was a potential, new adventure.

The ill children had a playground in which to play. It was not safe to leave them running free as we did. We loved that playground as much as they did. It had a swing on chains, on which you could swing as high as the sky, and Pauly once went right over before he fell off. He was so seriously winded that it took a lot of pushing and pulling on my part to get him upright, and when he took his first breath again, it sounded like a whistling train. His face had gone quite blue. But on his first breath came the irrepressible giggle! How I wanted to fly over the top too, but my courage (or foolhardiness) was never as great as his.

There was a red wooden see-saw in the playground. One of the tests which we ran for a new child to be admitted to our gang was to make him or her stand up on the one end, whilst one of us sat on the other end and bounced the plank as hard as we could, up and down, until they either fell off and cried, which meant failure to join us, or fell off and got up smiling. We allowed them in if they got up with a grimace, because we knew that it hurt a lot, but crying was not allowed in our savage childhood rules.

By passing this test, Hans Georg was admitted. He too is a feature of the Heathcot days, but more because through him I began to learn something about compassion. He was neither an ill child, nor quite the same as us. He needed a shepherd, and my heart was drawn to him, whilst my head and limbs were irritated by his slowness and lack of dexterity. Still, we allowed him to tag along, feeling very virtuous in our generosity and offering him a very rough kind of protection. Besides, he was really very useful when you needed a robber to catch, or Indians to our Cowboys.

The ill children had wheelchairs, but we had go-carts. We made them from old pram wheels, and Pauly's natural skill at invention did the rest. This inventiveness of his got us into trouble fairly regularly but it was always worth it. One of these occasions gave us the greatest go-cart of all time. One rest hour, he removed the wheels of two chairs and constructed a go-cart that for once had alignment instead of old buckled scrap metal. It went like the wind, down the front drive, turning the corners as smoothly as silk. We whizzed down, and trudged up again only to repeat the experience of speed. Unfortunately, one of the co-workers came to get the wheelchair for its owner and found it down on its seat, minus wheels and axles. There was, of course, an outcry and retribution fell swiftly. Pauly's father had a hard hand and my poor friend got it on his backside. My parents too were bitterly disappointed in me, a far harder punishment, I thought, than the merciful smack, where the pain dies away quite quickly. We had to spend the afternoon getting those wheelchairs properly reassembled.

Actually, some part of me had felt rather guilty about it all, even whilst we were having fun. I never thought how hurtful it might have been to the feelings of the children whose chairs we had appropriated. Pauly also made us guns out of bits of wood, elastic bands and paper pellets, and if you were skilled at shooting, they almost worked like machine guns! Many a moth or fly died from a hail of paper pellets from his gun.

Not all our games were played outside, though most of the wildest ones were kept for the overgrown park around Heathcot. Inside the house were just as many places that lent themselves to our vivid fantasy. The steps leading up to the house, with their gracious curves and strong Georgian pillars, were a favourite place to sit and chatter. From this vantage point, the entrances and exits of children and co-workers could be observed, and we had a word to say to everyone who passed us by. Sometimes the co-workers sat with us and chatted about this and that. I liked to know what was going on and sometimes passed on information to my mother, especially complaints. It made me angry when co-workers talked in German about my mother, the matron. I thought everyone loved her as much as I did, and was disappointed to find that some people did not see her in the same glorious light.

The hall flagstones were cold to our bare feet in the summer, grey and hard! Falling on one's knees hurt very much, so generally I walked over them carefully. The hall was not really a place to play, though we did sometimes try it out for hopscotch. It commanded too much respect in its gloom.

Our bedroom was up the middle winding stairs, and here we played very happily indeed. After lunch everyday we took a rest, which we called, naturally enough, 'rest hour'. We were supposed to sleep, or so the co-workers fondly imagined, but our mother knew that we played, sang songs and told stories to while away the time.

We each had our own corner in the room, and in my memory, it was big enough to house all our toys. My dolls were special friends and sometimes, if my sisters were so inclined, they threw them around the room, making me scream with fear that they might get hurt. My panic always brought my mother, or a co-worker. If it was my mother, peace was restored instantly. If it was a co-worker, it would depend on whether she saw what was really going on. Sometimes I got the punishment of extra rest hour, which I found rather hard to take.

Once, when my sister Leezy and I were recovering from some illness or other, we decided to wash our dolls. This was because the naughty creatures had been playing in the fireplace and were covered in soot. In the corner of our room, which we called 'the dollies' corner' and where their cradles and clothing were tidily laid out in baskets, there was also a Victorian fireplace, black and interesting. Sometimes, on very cold days when we were ill, my father would light it. What a way to go to sleep at night, with the wind howling and the coals glowing on the hearth!

But today, those glowing coals had caked our dolls with soot. So down we went to the bathroom, fetched water in a bucket and washed our babies. Oh, the disappointment! Being made of cloth and raw wool stuffing, they became lumpy and shrank out of recognition. My dismay was so loud that it fetched my mother, who pegged them out to dry and, by some miracle during the night, restored them almost to their former shape.

In our bedroom was a round table of dark oak on which we ate our family meals. These happened every Saturday night. We came home from whatever adventure, were bathed and ate supper – Mother, Father, Agi, Leezy and Gony – around the round table. Agi sat next to my father and I sat between Agi and my mother. Leezy, who was always a little afraid of my father, sat on my mother's right side, a trifle closer to her, so that we could have fitted in one more child between her and my father. That place was filled for a time by Barry Dent.

We sat companionably round the table and ate soft-boiled eggs, sardines, and drank cocoa. Chocolate was a rare treat, but cocoa we could have once a week for supper. Then we cleared away and my father told us stories. We read many books, mostly classics. Although my parents were not born in Britain, my mother had an unerring sense for a good book. She said she liked the smell of them. We had all the Dent Dutton series of children's classics; Dickens, Arthur Ransome, Andrew Lang's coloured Fairy Books, Louisa Alcott, and many others. But no Enid Blyton; my mother said that her books were cheap and nasty rubbish. We also never read comic books, or saw weekly comic papers. They too were considered common and even harmful to the growing child. Now I thank her from the bottom of my heart, because having foreign parents could have branded us; but our reading gave us standing with our peers as we moved from the shelter of community life into the world of boarding school and out into the wide, wide world.

The bathroom, in which we took our weekly bath, was small and airless. You had to go down one or two steps, and at night this could be a fearsome way, because when you had negotiated the dark corner and reached the bathroom, the bright light revealed great black beetles in the bath! I could barely tolerate them, but wetting the bed was not an option. Sometimes I lay awake suffering a full bladder rather than face those monsters, and then I woke in the early hours of the morning, having emptied it in a dream. How gentle and kind was my mother when such accidents happened. She never shouted or grumbled. Her soft hands soothed, she made up the bed with clean dry sheets and I slept the sleep of the protected child.

The softness and sureness of my mother's hands was a guide in uncertainty. When ill, she would stroke my forehead and sing softly in German with a little Austrian accent in the lilt of her voice. She always gave us her full attention when we needed her. Lying in bed with a fever was the most pleasant of times, because then we had our mother to ourselves. She would sit and sew, mend our clothes, fix our dolls, do the ironing, or tell us wonderful tales of fairies and knights and gentle ladies. Sometimes, when I was getting better, she would bring me her mending basket. What a mess! Buttons, threads, needles, all jumbled up, and the darning wool nicely knotted. It was a very satisfactory afternoon's game to tidy it all up, to sort and wind and tuck. Other times, she brought out her jewellery box. This too, needed sorting, with necklaces in one compartment, rings in another and the wonderful glittering brooches that she loved to wear. Like her taste in books, my mother despised anything that was not real gold or silver. Paste jewels were not to be found in her box of treasures. The feel of the cut amethysts and garnets, of which she was very fond, and the smoothness of the pearls and golden chains, were satisfaction unparalleled.

The bathroom with the big black beetles was not only a place to be feared. It was also a place for the most enormous fun. Those Saturday night baths were taken with at least two, if not three of us, in the water. Maybe we had scant hot water, maybe it was because we loved bathing together. The games we played left the bathroom flooded. My mother patiently dried us and cleaned up. I do not remember her complaining of the mess we made. One of our games was to place our feet inside plastic tooth mugs and then ballet dance on our toes round the edge of the bath till we fell into the hot water. We called it water skating. We also bought and sold water from the tap. One of us sat with two tooth mugs and offered 'hot, cold or warm?' The buyer then chose according to their bravery and received a shower from one or more of the mugs over their head. Cold was terrible in winter, and hot was pretty scalding. I usually chose warm, coward that I was.

We three girls had long brown hair, which we wore in plaits

down to our waists. Washing hair was a nightmare, and the brushing out of the snarls afterwards was exquisite torture. To save us the pain, my mother plaited it up when wet, so that in the morning it was wavy and easy to comb. She brushed it gently from the bottom to the top so that the tangles moved with a minimum of pain. Then she plaited it exactly in the same place behind the ear each morning, never making us feel uncomfortable. Leezy and I had natural curls, but Agi's hair was dark and straight.

We appreciated this devotion when she was away and a co-worker took us on to care for our needs. No one ever knew the exact place to start the plait, as did our mother. No doubt when she had to leave us she tried to choose someone we liked and respected, but this was not always as successful as it might have been.

There was the time of a smart English teacher, who decided once my mother's back was turned to re-educate the 'spoilt Lipsker brats'. She began with rest hour. My mother usually only closed the door, knowing that we would come out to use the lavatory. This woman locked us in, a mistake in her trust that she paid for because we sat on our beds and peed on them in protest. When she told us off, I cried most artistically and wailed that if she had not locked the door, we might have stayed clean and dry...

Her next attempt was to teach us table manners. At our family suppers, manners were very important, but we now treated her to burps and stuffing of mouths and no 'Please' or 'Thank you'. We were very glad when our mother came home again. So also, I dare say, was the unlucky English teacher.

But there were others who gave us a lovely time, and most of my memories of surrogate parenting are good ones. However, I always missed my mother greatly, even though my sisters took good care of me, on the whole.

My mother's room was a pleasure to visit. It was always tidy and smelled of lavender. In it was a blue armchair and from this we were given rare treats after rest hour. Because there was still rationing, we saw fruit very infrequently, but sometimes there would be an orange to be shared by us three. We sat on stools at her feet and she spooned out the segments equally in rotation round the circle of eager open mouths. How sweet an orange is when you get one per week! Fridays were barley sugar days; one for each of us, after rest hour. And Saturday was pocket money day. I remember getting 'thruppence' to spend on sweets, which we bought from the Ferry Lady by the river.

My father's room was smaller than my mother's. It had a low window out of which we climbed to play on a small balcony. What fun it was to lean over the railing and wait for a blind young man to pass underneath on his eternal walk round the house. As he strode beneath us, I am sorry to say that we tried very hard to spit on his head. I am equally happy to report that we invariably missed because the winds of Scotland were on the side of the righteous and blew our wet slime away. This same poor young man had to put up with quite a lot of teasing from us. We used to try to lure him into puddles on wet days. Dreamily, he would step right over them and walk on, dry footed. Secretly, I admired him very much. How did he know that there was a puddle to be avoided?

The balcony that saw our misdeeds gave access to the roof. We were expressly forbidden to climb it, and so we did so at every possible opportunity. Gripping the gutter, we ascended the tiled slope that could have dropped us three stories down to the gravelled path below, and clambered over the top to a marvellously secret, flat centre square. It was, as roofs were, a leaded place, and in the summer it got so hot that it burned our bare feet. It also melted to the touch. Sometimes we took my dollies and played 'at house', high up beneath the summer sky.

My parents were not the only couple who did not share a bedroom. Many of the early Camphill pioneers slept separately. Maybe it was because they took their meditative life rather seriously. All of them had certain times in the day during which they could not be disturbed. They called this private time 'working'. What an odd way to describe meditation! But that is what they did. And we would not dream of disturbing our mother or father, or any other co-worker, when they were 'working'. If a new and ignorant young co-worker came with a message, or the telephone rang, we would turn them away, saying that our parents were working. It was only as an adult that I finally understood the significance of the wording, when I began a meditative life myself and realised that 'work' is a very real way to describe such attempts.

I never saw my parents unclothed. On one memorable occasion, I entered my father's room when he was just getting out of bed. He wore an old-fashioned nightshirt with blue stripes. As he swung his legs out from under the eiderdown, I saw the dark hair on his limbs and was really quite shocked, averting my eyes from his loss of dignity. I was so embarrassed that I carried it round like a secret for months, brooding on his pale, dark-haired skin. My mother I sometimes saw in her underwear. This was serious stuff: woollen stockings, woollen vest and long-legged woollen knickers. She wore her suspender belt on top of this warm armour, and the suspenders fascinated me. I always wore leggings, as we called the tights of those days. They too were woollen, nice and warm in the cold wet Scottish winters. (My mother, to this day, wears long-sleeved Victorian nightdresses.) To my childish nose, they smelled of lavender, as did her white eiderdown, under which I crept when feeling scared at night.

Being scared at night was a feature of my childhood, and my sister Leezy knew how to make me terrified. Once, on an autumn day when the wind was up and the clouds hung almost to the ground, we went on an excursion to Dunnottar Castle at Stonehaven. Out in the raging waves, a bleak mountain rose, and on the top a threatening stone fortress brooded, gloomy and dark. We walked across a causeway to reach it. In the misery of rain and wind, a toothless warder appeared. He showed us round, down into the dungeons and the ruins of the old prison, telling us of those who had been tortured and starved to death for their faith, only a hundred years ago. He left us, then, to explore alone and whilst in a windowless cell, the door clanged shut, and keys rattled in the distance. Had I not been so terrified, I might have screamed, but then he reappeared, grinning evilly, not a tooth in his head, and opened the gate for us. All the way home, I trembled and shook.

Consequently, Leezy discovered a new game. Coaxingly, when the lights were out, and often on a windy night, she would invite me across the room to kiss her goodnight. On the first occasion, I was so pleased with the invitation, that I scampered over and kissed her. On my return journey to my cosy bed, when I was in the middle of the empty cold expanse of the darkened room, she whispered in a dire voice, 'Dunnottar Castle', whereupon I yelled as if the fiends were after me. Needless to say, Carlo appeared in wrath. I think I must have flown back into my bed, my sister's laughter loud in my ears. Periodically, she played this game, and because I loved her, I always fell for her soft manner and crossed the dark floor on her solemn promise that she would not tease, only to be let down as always.

Lying in our beds during boring rest hours, we amused ourselves by singing every song we knew. We loved to sing in harmony. My sisters, who were already at school in St John's School, knew a multitude of songs – folk songs, seasonal songs and religious festival songs. The school was attended by the ill children too, the first integrated school ever, of which Camphill was the pioneer. Dr König was truly an inspired man. Normal and special needs children sat side by side on benches behind desks and learned about the world, through maths, reading and writing, history and geography as in any school around the country, each according to their age and ability. My sisters' teachers loved to sing, and taught their classes many songs. In the Heathcot days, I was forbidden to join my more tuneful elders. They said I was too young to sing properly!

Sometimes we played another game. Camphill in my childhood had very few cars. Each one had a very distinctive engine noise. We liked to blow on the backs of our hands to imitate the sound, altering the clatter according to whom we imagined was driving. Then the listeners guessed who that might be. The few people who drove, did so each in their own way. Dr König made a sort of put-put sound. Carlo roared at speed. Thomas Weihs purred past, and Dr Lotte bumped and banged, racing the engine in the wrong gear till it screamed for the mercy that she never gave it.

The games we played were not always as nice as they should have been. Poor Hans Georg once nearly lost his life. At the end of some war game, it was decided to hang the enemy. So a rope was found and Hans Georg was strung up on the end of it. Then we all ran away, probably afraid of our own temerity. I was so frightened that I sneaked back and pulled him down, the interesting shade of blue that his face had acquired scaring me more than the thought of what the others might say at my treachery. The others came back, shouting and roaring that someone had freed the prisoner, and I did not dare confess to my guilt. But I was glad that I had rescued him, nevertheless. How cruel children can be, and how realistic their play can become!

One of our favourite places in which to spend the day was the large rhododendron bush in the front field. If you pushed your way into the centre, the ground consisted of dry, smooth dirt, and up above a ceiling of smooth waxen green leaves swayed and whispered. When it rained they protected as well as any roof, and if you climbed up the trunk and into the branches, the lightness of your childish body could lie cradled on the tangle of twigs and leaves and be lulled by the breeze into sleep. The blue sky of the summer was enchanting from such a vantage point. I used to lie and dream dreams, telling myself stories of boats and faraway countries.

In the inner clearing we made houses. We lived a life quite different from reality. Mr and Mrs Bould lived here, bringing up children and eating food like fried potatoes and tasty beef roasts. We ate imaginary ice cream and sweets and forgot the dining room where at least forty people sat, eating in various odd and often nauseating ways.

Round the back of the house, in the bushes surrounding the usually untended rose garden, my father put up a swing for me. It was a secret place, where the nettles grew high. You had to be brave to walk through them but once up and swinging, the world went away, and here too I dreamed my dreams. On one occasion, I was given permission to swing until time for bed. After a while, I thought that perhaps I should go in, and was met at the door by a furious mother. She declared this deserved a spanking, because I was at least an hour late. I assured her that I had been, as was allowed, on my swing. She stopped shouting, looked at me, and apologised for misjudging me. I was so deeply impressed by this, that a grown-up should say sorry to a child of eight years, that I vowed then and there, never to be too proud to apologise to a child. I hope that I have kept this promise.

We rarely went to town. The country was our home and we despised the townies who washed their apples before eating them. Getting lost could not happen to us out in nature, but once in a busy city, I felt very small and alone and feared losing my mother and father. I would cling to the security of a hand and follow very close to them. Once I saw a little girl step off the pavement into the road to avoid a passer-by. Her father took her roughly by the arm, turned her over, lifted her skirt and smacked her on her pink-knickered bottom, right there for all the world to see. I was appalled and thanked God that *my* parents were mine! My chastisements were never delivered in public but were treated with suitable dignity and privacy.

Going to town was not always a negative experience, however. We sometimes went into Fuller's and had our tea there. We sat upright on plush seats and beheld the snowy white linen tablecloth with awe and expectation. Then onto it was placed a tower of silver plates, laden with drop scones, bannocks, fairy cakes and cream cakes, and delicious lemon fizz filled our glasses. We seemed to be able to eat as much as we liked. The poverty of Heathcot rarely permitted us such a treat, but that made the occasions all the more thrilling.

Town meant new shoes. For dresses and suchlike, one did not need to go. They could be bought without trying on, and in any case, only Agi got new clothes. We wore them after she had grown out of them. It was a rare occasion that brought me a new dress unworn by someone else. But shoes had to be fitted. My mother's crooked toes were a testament to ill-fitting footwear and she was determined that our feet should be healthy and comfortable. We wore Start-rite shoes, the best that one could get. I often and loudly longed for red patent dancing shoes. I must admit that this was a wish never to be fulfilled and, like many other children before me, I declared that I would buy them for my own children as compensation for a deprived childhood dream. (However, just like others before me, when the time came, I bought my own children sensible shoes!)

Mostly, my mother went to town on her own, leaving us to the tender mercies of a co-worker or my father for the day. When she came home, she always brought us a little present, sweets, or a book to read. Once she left us to a visitor, a lady of whom I was deathly afraid. She was small and quick and rather fierce. For some forgotten reason, I was crying when my mother came home and I wanted to run to meet her. Many of the co-workers did not know what a normal child's reactions were. They tried to control us as they were taught by the customs of that day to control the ill children. So our temporary nanny tried to control me and fiercely ordered me to stop crying. Of course, I cried even louder, whereupon she put her hand over my mouth. This too, was standard practise when dealing with screaming ill children, and it always made me want to hit out at the co-workers on behalf of the apparently suffocating victims. Today, no one would do such a thing. But in those days one did not think twice about muffling a child's cry; and to give her her due, one could not accuse her of discrimination. She treated everybody in the same fierce manner. But in my case she got more than she bargained for, because I lost my temper and bit her hand very hard. I also did not stop crying and roared extra loudly until my mother finally arrived and rescued the situation, soothing us both down.

My mother used to have her clothes made for her because of her shortened right leg, which gave her a crooked figure. The first time I went with her to visit the dressmaker was an adventure indeed. The lady lived in a town house that smelled of damp and vaguely of cats and perfume. She had pins in her mouth and a tape measure around her neck that hung over her ample breasts, and in the corner of her workroom stood a rigid dead and naked body. I knew very well that it was made of plaster, but it looked quite lifelike, albeit headless. In the other corner of the room was a large dark oak cupboard and from it rumbled a man's voice, telling stories. I sat silent and mystified on a high stool, not daring to speak and waiting for my mother to tell this strange woman to let the man out. My mother, I realised, had exquisite manners. She did not refer to the dressmaker's strange habits and politely allowed herself to be fitted for a new dress, never even glancing in the direction of the invisible prisoner. Because she refrained from comment, so too, did I. But I wondered why this lady should need to keep a man locked up in a cupboard.

Some time later, I visited Heathcot Farm with my father, who protected me from the dogs, and there again I heard the same man's voice. This time it came from a brown wooden box on the sideboard of the farm kitchen. Now I felt brave enough to ask what this was. My father would tell me; he told me everything. And so he did. He explained at great length the magic and mystery of the wireless. I was fascinated and reported what I could remember to Pauly, who set about trying to make one. We did the tin cans on a string, and that worked, but only later did he try the crystal set. Reg knew how to make one. What magic the world held for us children!

It was in that same farmhouse kitchen that I first saw a television some time later. A new box had appeared with a glass screen and on it snow fell endlessly accompanied by voices and music. The farmer's wife asked me if I enjoyed the show, and I politely replied that it was very interesting. But secretly, I wondered why people stared at snow on a screen. It was much more fun to play in the real thing. Also, the snow was like round dots, and very boring. The next time she invited me in for a treat of television, I was amazed when suddenly the dots coalesced and a picture appeared that moved and showed me a funny kind of mouse who ran around in clothes. They called it 'Mickey Mouse'. I could not laugh at the antics because I was so amazed. I think I may have been four or five years old at the time.

Chapter III

THE ADVENTURE YEARS

Adventures seemed to be happening all the time. On Saturdays, the whole house had to be cleaned for Sunday, a very special day in the week. In order that this mammoth task could be undertaken reasonably efficiently when the total occupancy was at home, the ill children had a rest morning. With them safely off the floors, the cleaning could begin. There were, however, the staff children still to be thought of. As we grew older, we refused to stay in bed, so excursions were the thing to do. My eldest sister was in charge. She took care of us all, keeping order and seeing to our safety. We were dispatched with sandwiches, one spread with only butter, the other with cheese, plus hard-boiled eggs (one each), and a screw of salt. We took apples for sweetness but no drinks. An apple had to do till we found a stream from which to quench our thirst. This was the way we journeyed into the Scottish Highlands.

We took the Strachan bus from the bottom corner of the road where the postie set the parcels in the wall. He brought the letters on a bicycle, but the parcels were delivered on the bus and sat safely in the wall until someone collected them. No one ever stole them. The bus driver took our fare and we sat on the long seat at the back, all in a row. I remember other children coming too, but no one with any great clarity except a friend of Agi's called Heidi Kaerhahn. She too, had long plaits down to her bottom, but her hair was darkish blond and she usually wore a dirndl, the Austrian national dress. She looked the perfect *mädchen* and we were very fond of her.

We rode the bus, sometimes into Banchory, more often to Ballater, and got out at the green in the centre of the town. The bus driver would ask us on which bus we intended to return. Agi gave him the time and he promised to wait in case we were late.

On one occasion, I remember dashing headlong down the mountain into the square, seeing the miniature bus growing bigger as we approached, yelling at the tops of our voices for it to wait, which it always did. Then on the way home, tired and happy, and usually rather dirty, we sang every song we could remember. We sang in harmony, in part songs, in rounds and catches. We did not think about the people listening, until one day a lady got up just before her stop, lurched to the back and gave us a shilling for our lovely singing. We were so embarrassed that we could not sing any more!

Those outings in the Highlands were filled with joy and laughter, breathlessness and aching legs. I could never really keep up with the others and always seemed to be huffing and puffing behind them. We clambered over the hills, following sheep paths and enjoying the smell of the heather and the freshness of the bracken. When it rained, we wore windcheaters, as we called the anoraks of our day, and pulled up the hoods. We wore corduroy trousers and our oldest Start-rite shoes and were as happy as the sheep on the hillside. We knew we were safe and never got lost. We did, however, sometimes come home with scratches and bruises, and on one memorable occasion I came home really injured. We had been climbing up and up and came upon a barbed wire fence. This was a surprise, but not really an obstacle to the bigger ones. They rolled up a log and climbed over. I too, attempted the climb but my short legs could not quite make it, the log rolled as I frantically scrambled about and I fell, palms down, onto the barbs of the fence. Needless to say, they sank in and as I pulled free, they ripped my flesh off, down to the bones.

This made me roar with pain and brought Agi back to investigate. She bound up the tear with a dirty white handkerchief, one of my father's, and told me sternly not to make a fuss. The pain was really quite severe, and I could not stop crying. To cheer me up, she stuffed a banana, a special treat for that day, into my mouth to stop the din. This made me laugh through my tears. We just went on with the outing, my sore hands absolutely no deterrent to the others. When we got home, my mother soothed the pain with warm calendula lotion and bandaged me up, but not before I had had an interested and ghoulish look at the insides of my hand. I bear the perfect image of a barb from a wire fence on the fleshy palm of my hand to this day.

On hot summer days, we went to the seaside at the 'Brigg o'Don', where there was a lovely long sandy beach. We went on the Strachan bus again, into Aberdeen, and then on the tram, in which we always occupied the back seat. These visits to the sea were fun and exciting but also had their moments of terror. There was the time my mother's watch got lost. Agi was entrusted with this precious timepiece so that we would know when to get the bus home in time for our bath and family supper. Now it was gone, buried somewhere in the sand. My efficient sister placed us strategically round the area in which she hoped it lay hidden and instructed us to dig. By some miracle, we found it, still bravely ticking behind its stainless steel protection. I inherited that watch and promptly lost it whilst hitch-hiking to Galway on my first holiday without my parents. My mother, as a refugee, and infinitely more careful than I, had brought it all the way from Vienna.

It was on a summer's day at the beach that I first saw a naked man. We were playing at the water's edge, because none of us could really swim, when Leezy began to giggle. We looked at what was making her laugh and saw a man, supine in the sand dunes, without a stitch of clothing on him. At first, I only saw his curly hair and then I saw the hair of his body, and the flaccid penis surrounded by red curls. I thought, like my sisters, that this was hilarious. Our laughter woke him, but quite untroubled, he continued with his sunbathing.

I was far more embarrassed by the drunken man who patted me on the head and gave me 'thruppence' because I was so sweet. My sisters had it off me in no time, declaring that he had made a mistake and I was glad to be rid of it because it made me feel dirty, for some inexplicable reason.

Those excursions were so much fun. On wet Saturdays, we took our picnic up the hill behind the house and walked over the fields and up into low hillocks between Aberdeen and Stonehaven. We explored the lanes and farm tracks and stopped somewhere against a stonewall to eat our hard-boiled eggs and sandwiches, wet with raindrops. When we were by the sea, the eggs and sandwiches were sandy, whilst in the Highlands they tasted squashed and salty. But hunger is really and truly a great sauce, and we enjoyed our food immensely.

Coming home after the long day out, we entered a house that smelt of floor polish and lavender furniture polish, of hot water and soap. Sometimes, in my dressing gown, I accompanied my mother on her rounds, and smiled at the babies in their beds, enjoyed the bathed faces of the big children in their wheelchairs and tiptoed quietly through the nursery where the very ill children lay. James Embleton, whose head was bigger than his body, might sing a song to me in his high, pure voice. And everything was clean, fresh and beautiful.

Sometimes we were asked to pick the flowers for the vases that decorated the white Sunday tablecloths in the vast dining room. Then we went by the backfields to Ardoe House and stole the blooms that grew in the neglected and abandoned garden. We found cyclamens and begonias, daffodils and roses, depending on the season. We also gathered mushrooms in the autumn and brought them home to be checked for edibility. We were rarely wrong in our choices, using our noses to detect the good from the poisonous. Many of the co-workers, having lived by hook or by crook in wartime Germany, could recognise at a glance which ones could safely be eaten. We also loved picking blackberries, not paying any heed to scratches. That is, my sisters were brave. I hated the prickling thorns, but was very happy to take the credit for the buckets full of the dark sweet fruit. These were made into jam and juice for the winter.

Our favourite mushroom was the chanterelles, or *pfifferlingen*, as we called them. These tiny yellow delicacies could be found down the drive amongst the moss under the beeches. We picked them carefully, brought them home and selfishly refused to share them with anyone but our parents. They were so small that they could only go round the family if mixed with egg. So we ate them, scrambled in the frying pan, with butter and brown bread. What a treat!

It was on one such mushroom hunt that I lost a unique present. My mother had bought me a pair of white gym shoes for the summer. They were on my feet for the first time that fateful

Saturday. I went scrambling through the trees and stepped into a dark peaty bog. By the time I had extricated myself from the swamp, I was minus one gym shoe and had to hop home, crying bitterly. My tears softened my mother's heart, so I did not get the spanking that I expected, but I had only one white gym shoe to admire, which was no use to me at all. They were never replaced, either.

My sisters and I had one pink bicycle between the three of us. We had to take turns and did so very fairly. When I was eight, I fell off it onto my nose. I thought I would die from the pain and spent three days in bed with a raging temperature and arnica all over my face. When I arose, I saw that I would never look the same again. My nose had grown and it has stayed that way to this day.

Saturdays were great fun for us mobile children, but they were not less so for the ill children. They stayed in bed, but had pictures to draw, meals in their nurseries, and lots of attention, one to one as much as possible. Rest days were meant to be relaxing times. Lunch was always soup, which for many of them was a treat because they did not need to make the effort to chew. They had a bath and a hair wash, and their nails were cut. Then they had supper in bed, usually something nice like fresh white rolls with egg spread, or honey. Honey was a rare treat. What we saw every day on the table was its surrogate, golden syrup, which I found too sweet and cloying for my fussy taste buds. I remember those days as cosy and homely.

We always felt safe and loved. We knew we were cared for and could go anywhere in the world without let or hindrance. Perhaps because of our complete belief in the goodness of the world and its human beings, our trust was never broken. People were always kind to us wherever we went.

A good part of this great faith in God and humanity came to me through the institution of the Bible Evening. This event always ended the Saturday experience. We went to bed tired, clean and well fed in body and soul by the different food and the warmth of personal attention from our parents. We knew we had to settle and talk quietly if we could not sleep immediately, because the grown-ups were now preparing for the Bible Evening.

It deserved its capitals because I certainly saw it as the holiest of holy happenings in the week. It rated even above the Sunday service, because Dr König attended regularly, and everyone became very hushed and reverential about it.

Sometimes, I tiptoed out to go the bathroom, in order to feel the silence that pervaded the house as people sat in their rooms, bathed and still, to study the weekly gospel reading. They would walk, in their finery, the men in black suits with startlingly white shirt fronts and serious ties, and the ladies in long dresses, grey or blue or other such stately colours, their brooches, rings and necklaces gleaming and glittering. No one wore earrings, except Anke, who always looked like a duchess at the very least, her trained dancer's step, with toes slightly pointed outwards, lending her an elegance that was beautiful to see. Alix, too, looked elegant in her black dress, and smelt of cigarette smoke, beneath which lurked a subtle and slight perfume, mysterious and awe inspiring.

My mother and father would return from Bible Evening peaceful and glowing. I supposed they were blessed by Dr König and God. I loved to be awake when they came home, especially if I could invent a bad dream from which to be comforted. Then my mother took me to her room, sat me on her lap and fed me the coveted Bible Evening juice, and I could go safely to sleep, knowing that all was right with the world.

The Saturdays of my childhood had the feel of a mini-holiday. The real school holidays, however, made life very different altogether. Heathcot House was emptied out. Some children stayed there all the time, having no other home than this vast and friendly community, but many went home to their families on the Steiner Train, pronounced 'Steener' in the Aberdonian accent. This was laid on by British Rail for the many children who came up to Aberdeen from London in order to go to this strange school for the retarded. Transport day was very exciting. Early in the evening, the suitcases would stand outside in the porch, or inside in the hall, depending on the weather. Wheelchairs would be collapsed and bound up with a rope or straps. The buzz was wonderful and the leather and cardboard of the trunks smelled heavenly. Then a bus arrived and the children, plus their delighted escorts, would be loaded on to it and sent off, to be seen again after the holiday ended.

Once I went with my family on the 'Steener' train and it still ranks as one of the most thrilling adventures of my life. We too entered the bus, with our suitcases, to make the long trip to Austria. I was six years old and so excited that my tummy was filled with butterflies and I could hardly sit still or stop talking. We were going to see my mother's home country and pass through dreaded and feared Germany on our way.

We arrived in the station, driving through the grey granite streets of Aberdeen and decanted onto the platform – assorted baggage, children and grown-ups. To be an escort meant a free ride to London on the night train. One by one, we were invited to board and a guard in smart uniform showed everyone to their sleeper. We too were invited, and shown to a tiny mahogany cabin with red plush seats, which the guard miraculously unfolded to reveal four beds with white linen sheets and grey and red blankets. This was the first novelty. We usually slept under feather eiderdowns. Now I had my first try at sheets and blankets, the English way. How uncomfortable it was!

They were tight over my feet, and when I pulled them loose they fell off. I wanted to sleep on the top bunk, and won the fight by sheer persistence and fuss. My mother took one of the bottom bunks next to Leezy, whilst Agi also slept up top. Where my father spent the night I do not know, but there were only four beds so the ladies had them. A gentleman, said my father, always helps ladies first. A lady, he also used to say, never whistles. People in general, he used to add, never cut their potatoes with a knife. It is an insult to the cook. So, true to the gentleman's code, he let us have a comfortable night.

Sleeping with so much excitement inside me was not an easy state to achieve. I could hear the children and their night noises, the attendants passed up and down the corridor outside, and I felt the train slowing for every stop. I opened the curtains a crack and peered out at the lit-up stations, watching passengers come and go, and lay listening to the train travelling over the iron rails, on its way to London. '*Quarter to two, quarter to two, a-hurry, a-hurry, a-hurry, a-hurry*,' it said, as it sped down the map from north to south.

I wondered what England would be like. And where was Harley Street, where we were to spend the day and the next night before travelling on to Dover, catching a boat and then taking a train to Salzburg? I did eventually sleep, and woke early to watch dreamily as my mother lifted up the top of the corner table to lay bare the magic washbasin beneath its disguising lid. Then we got up and put on our clothes, having slept in our underwear, and washed, ate a sandwich for breakfast, and drank the milk the attendant brought. It tasted like poison. We were unused to pasteurised milk, and the boiled flavour disgusted me. But I was thirsty, so I drank it.

I knew we were in England when the cows turned brown and white and the houses became brick red. The grey and black beauty of Scotland had gone, and we were in the land of the Sassenach. It seemed boring and flat to me, very green and cultivated. I missed the savageness of the Scottish countryside.

London was vast, and cold. We took a black taxi to Harley Street, and the driver showed us St Paul's, the Houses of Parliament, where Guy Fawkes was caught, and I looked for his head on a pole. It was very disappointing to find London just like a bigger Aberdeen. I thought it might have had a few more castles and palaces. Buckingham Palace was very big, but it had no turrets, so it too was not as spectacular as I had imagined. But the guards that stood outside, so still and tall and grand, were everything that I could have hoped for. They made my blood rush with pride at the royal family's power.

My father took us to the zoo at Regent's Park and then we went to bed, all in one room in the house in Harley Street, which turned out to be a three-storied town house, very carpeted, velvet curtained and flowery wallpapered. We had soft-boiled eggs for breakfast, and toast and marmalade in silver dishes. I felt serious and posh as I ate with enjoyment. The train to Dover now felt familiar and less exciting. I had done an overnight train ride from Aberdeen, so the three hours or so to Dover were as nothing to my seasoned traveller's soul.

The boat to Ostend was another novelty. I did not like it at all, feeling sick and claustrophobic. Again, my father spent the night somewhere on the boat, leaving the cabin to the ladies. The following train journey I only vaguely remember, passing through bomb-damaged German towns, which made me feel sad and abandoned, like the Jews of the ghetto on their way to the camps, whom I imagined in their rows of terrified grime and hunger; and the picture-book German countryside, which to me meant the might of the Aryan race. The guards on the train frightened me in their uniform. A part of me expected a Nazi round every corner that the train rolled.

At Munich railway station, we lost my father. He alighted to buy a newspaper, a risk I thought highly unnecessary in hostile Germany, and when the train began to roll, he had still not come back. We saw him running across the platform and then I began to howl. He was gone, lost forever, to be swallowed up by a concentration camp! I absolutely hated this holiday we were supposed to be having! How could we enjoy it without my father? My sisters joined in the wailing, my mother trying frantically to calm us. My father had the tickets, the money. How would we manage? In the midst of the disaster, the compartment door opened and there he stood, grinning sheepishly. For the first time, I heard my mother shout at him. Apparently he had just hopped on the last carriage and walked up the train to find us.

The holiday in Austria was our first time abroad. I remember little of it, except that the farm had a wonderful hay barn, from the rafters of which we could, and did, jump onto the softness of the sweet dried grass. It felt like flying. I ate greengages for the first time and was party to the slaughter of a pig.

This was a terrible experience. As the farmer merrily caught the pig, it began to squeal in fear. I ran inside and buried myself under my feather eiderdown, but I could still hear the squeal that ended in a gurgle as its throat was cut. Then the smell of singed pig's hide crept under the door, and then, to cap it all, it began to sheet lightening and hurl thunder, bringing down a torrent of hot raindrops onto the farm. The trauma of it haunts me to this day and probably provided the real reason for my still having a slight fear of thunderstorms.

I found a wireless in the dining room of the pension. It had a crack in it, and the light shone through when it was switched on. I spent hours determined to see the little men inside. I knew that they must be there, because I could hear them, and now was my chance to catch them in the act. Needless to say, they always vanished when I got their stage into focus.

However, as Camphill was poor, most of our holidays were spent in Scotland, in little cottages, with no water and no amenities. We washed in the clear Highland water, and peed in the 'Wee Hoosie' built over the same stream. The trick was to wash and drink upstream from the 'Hoosie'. Being woken to the sound of sheep and the fresh smell of the heather haunts my memory as a dream of pleasure and delight. My mother cooked our meals, delicious potatoes and mushrooms, and fried eggs, all our favourite foods, which we rarely saw at home. My father read us stories, we went for walks and played on the hillside.

One holiday that we spent at Lochinver saw all three of us get very ill. I cannot imagine it was a great rest for our mother. In fact, the old Bedford Dormobile had to come and fetch us earlier than planned. Neither of my parents were able to drive, so we had no car in which to go and get medical help. We were always either driven, we walked, or used public transport. Another holiday that we took at a farm called Blackhill, near Inverness, was such a success that we went back there, Agi even going to stay with the farmer's family by herself for a week. They had sheepdogs that we loved to watch rounding up the sheep high up on the pastures, with only a whistle from the farmer to tell them what to do.

There were also the holidays when my mother went to the Movement Council. This was a dreaded time, because people moved after these meetings. My father said it was very aptly named, as was the Camphill Movement, because no one stayed in one place for very long. People went where they were needed, taking their dependents along with them, but usually without asking their leave. If Dr König said that another community or house had needs, you went, without a question. They were not issued as orders, these moves, but they were recognised as obviously wise choices.

During these days, group holidays were arranged for us and we went, together with the ill children who lived with us, to somewhere nice. Once we went up to Tomintoul, high up the mountains and stayed in a haunted cottage by the road. I remember the yellow raspberries that grew wild in the back garden, large and succulently sweet, and the dark kitchen of the farmhouse from which we daily fetched our milk. The woman had a magic dog. She could stand at her door and whistle to it. It ran up the mountain, a speck of black and white in the distance, and rounded up the sheep whilst she stayed snug at home.

We were too many to fit the beds that the cottage provided, so being the smallest, I slept between two chairs. This was not very comfortable, and so I lay awake at night, listening to the creaks of the old cottage ghost, as it slyly stepped from tread to tread, up and down the stairs. I was so petrified that I wet my bed every night.

A woman called Christl, of whom we were very fond, took us on this particular holiday, trying hard to give us a lovely time but not understanding my behaviour at all. I could not tell her about the ghost, as many small children find it hard to express their fears in words. I hated that holiday, longing for my mother to come home, and was so happy when the old brown petrol-smelling Bedford Dormobile came to pick us up again. Heathcot was home to me, and nothing else could be as good, except going somewhere with my mother. Then I could have loved a sheep shed in the Arctic.

It was not just holidays that were a mixed pleasure. The mealtimes in a dining room for sixty people brought their highs and lows too. We sat at long tables with benches at either side and a chair at each end in which sat the co-workers who presided. We children sat on the benches, trying to sit up straight and certainly never putting our elbows on the table. The children in wheelchairs had their own fixed place beside a co-worker, who could assist them as necessary. I found it very painful to sit opposite someone who ate as their disability dictated. The food was often sucked in and mouthed or tongued with accompanying noises that could not be controlled. I felt sickened and unable to enjoy my food, and ashamed of my inability to cope. But I was a small child and could not find the words to say what troubled me. I was supposed to set an example, and was clearly quite unequal to the challenge.

The only way out that my childish and angry little soul could find was to make a fuss at almost every meal. This was an unforgivable sin. Shouting and screaming, and worst of all, declaring loudly that one did not like the food, was unacceptable behaviour. We were growing up with people who had experienced starvation, and rationing was still a fact of life. Ungrateful behaviour such as I exhibited meant that I was sent out to stand in the passage outside the door until the meal was over. I used this ploy often and loudly because my mother, an understanding woman, always gave me food alone afterwards, in the kitchen. Not only did I get her all to myself, but I could eat without having to feel sick.

For a time, probably because we were such a large gang of staff children, we ate our meals separately in another dining room, which previously had been used for massage. This room had an old-fashioned dumb waiter that travelled up and down on a pulley system from the kitchen to the dining room. Its shaft was in the wall between the kitchen and the scullery, a dank and noisome place that smelt of old food and Sunlight soap. The lift had two shelves on which the food ascended and was filled with the dirty dishes after we had eaten, to be lowered for the ladies in the scullery to wash up. We loved that lift and played with it during our meals. Generally, those mealtimes were raucous and disorderly. We behaved like pigs and had great fun, but the free-for-all hilarity was stopped by some sensible parent who must have seen how our manners were rapidly deteriorating. Funnily enough, although we all had such a good time, none of us were sad when that privilege was withdrawn. I know I sometimes felt a bit anxious about the disrespectful way in which these times were handled, and it was a relief to have them curtailed.

The lift, which we so enjoyed, proved to be the painful downfall of Chris Bould, who happened to be emptying a jug of milk down the shaft just as Gertrud Meir, a strong-minded and fearful woman for whom we had a huge respect, was leaning through the hatch that its ascent had created, in order to place a cooking pot into the scullery. The downpour caused a shout of anger, Chris disappeared as though a spell had been cast, but retribution found him in the shape of Reg in a fury. Chris was very quiet for a few days afterwards. We had much better and safer fun with that lift by lying on the shelves and being hauled up and down; but this happened between meals, rather than during them.

I think I must have been about five years old when we contracted the whooping cough. We all got it, one after the other, including the ill children. For those with Down's syndrome, this was no joke. They were very ill indeed and needed a great deal of care and attention. As we Lipsker children were quarantined, Marisha and Margaret joined us in our sickbeds. Marisha was not a beautiful little girl, but she had beautiful black hair and blue eyes and she longed to be a princess. She was meticulous and fussy and we loved her very much. She had come to Camphill as a small baby, abandoned but still bearing the magnificent surname of Turtzanski. I loved saying her name, it sounded rich and strange.

Margaret Eadie had been born in Scotland. She too came very young and her blond hair and impish smile were her greatest charms. Marisha was in Leezy's class and Margaret in mine. We were happy together, coughing, whooping and vomiting. Because we lost so much weight, we were given special food, all the things we liked best, and were coaxed to eat these magnificent feasts in the nursery. We could only go outside during the official mealtimes because then everybody was safely out of infection's way, in the dining room. Heathcot gardens were ours to do as we willed. The fresh air felt wonderful after the stuffy nursery confinement. The illness brought a satisfactory consequence in that it made my mother stay with us most of the time, and I did not want it to end. However, it did end after some weeks; the girls returned to their own nurseries, and we were told that we were better. I tried to keep the cough and whoop alive for as long as I could, but eventually it disappeared.

It was somewhere around this time that Barry Dent joined our family. He was a small fair-haired boy with a cheeky smile and stick legs and arms. He had a wonderful disability, as far as I was concerned, because his elbows were frozen and he could not straighten them at all. This made his movements odd and puppet-like. He had a great sense of humour, could giggle uncontrollably, and was a little monkey. I loved him very much and enjoyed his naughtiness, except for the fact that he could not listen to the stories that we loved to hear. I dreaded my father's anger with him at bedtime, when he was trying to settle us and Barry would disrupt not only the story but also the prayer. Somehow, my father could not accept him. I think that we were supposed to be fostering him, probably because Dr König prescribed family life as the curative approach to his deprived little soul. We children accepted him, but our father found him an intrusion and could not manage the challenging behaviour that he displayed. So he moved out into another nursery after some time, and I missed him a lot. He had become my brother, and his absence left a hole in my life. I did, however, continue to meet him every day in school, because he was in my class.

One of the finest pleasures of my childhood was Ann Trier's horses. Ann came to Camphill, as a widow with two small children, Sally and Charles, and her name then was Gairdner. She was slight, elegant and very, very quiet. I found it restful to be with her, and loved her English voice, even more than the Boulds' slightly coarser accent. She married again, this time to a German man called Hans-Jürgen, and so acquired a foreign surname. She gave birth to Christopher, and later when I left Camphill in Scotland, and moved to Botton in Yorkshire, we met again and became close friends, although he was a few years younger than me.

Ann and her family lived in the Garage Cottage, in an upstairs flat over the maintenance workshop. I loved that house – its upstairs, because it was furnished in an English fashion and so was different; and its downstairs because Bill, who ran the workshop, was a craftsman who let me watch him. I used to perch up on a high stool, smelling the wood shavings, the glue and the varnish, and gaze in admiration as he mended and made chairs, beds, cupboards and tables. Next to watching my father dig, I found joinery almost as mesmerising.

It was upstairs in the Garage Cottage that I ate yoghurt for the first time. I thought it was cream cheese, a milk pudding I was very familiar with, but this milky substance was more delicious than anything I had ever tasted. We had pudding for supper every day, sometimes nice, sometimes nasty, but never, other than ice cream, had I tasted a dish so wonderful. I had three helpings. I did not know its name and so could not ask for it again, and it was only at the age of sixteen, when I visited Agi, who was then living in Holland, that I found that exquisite flavour once more.

The horses that we loved to ride were called Lee and Don. They were actually ponies, and very well behaved. Ann taught us how to master the art of horse riding and we rode bareback until we could control the animal with our knees. Only then did we graduate to a saddle. What fun it was to ride like mad round the field in front of the house! Next we were permitted to ride the lanes and up the hill. Only then were we allowed to ride in the forests. The feeling of freedom, and yet companionship, was never so strong as when Leezy and I rode out together. She was big enough for Don, and I rode Lee, who was a bit temperamental and loved to head madly for the nearest low branch in order to sweep her rider off her back. Once you knew that trick, you just lay down on her neck and the branch passed over harmlessly. However, she was clever and would then lower her head very suddenly, making it very easy to slide off her. But if you kept your head and held on to the reins, she would stop the moment you hit the ground, sniff you in sympathy and laugh down her superior nostrils. It was never a dull ride with Lee. Don, bigger and more sedate, led the way, and Lee followed meekly, once all the preliminaries had been duly attended to. The ill children too, had riding lessons, which later developed into quite a sophisticated riding therapy. It was Ann Trier who first showed how therapeutic horses could be for people with disabilities.

With the coming of the ponies, I discovered the wonders of the smithy. A short way along the main road was the post office and smithy of Blair's village, just opposite Blairs College. The post office was dark and not very interesting. The smithy, in contrast, was a place of magic, heat, noise and smells of burnt metal and hoofs. The smith was a large, fat man with a very red face that got redder when he bent down to lift up the horses fore or hind leg, and he wore the traditional leather apron. He had huge muscles and gobbled up white bread sandwiches in one gulp, just as the wolf gobbled Little Red Riding-Hood in the fairy tale. He had a broad Scots accent and walked slowly and mindfully. When we took the horses to him, he chattered and grunted and I did not understand a word he spoke. He held the ponies by the nose, examined their teeth, walked round them and lifted up one hoof at a time, to poke and scratch at them with a bent metal pick. Then he would leave them standing patiently, and begin to make the shoe.

The iron was heated in the furnace, which a boy blew up hot by turning a wheel, and the sparks flew up, as the smith hammered the hot iron on the anvil. He hammered in a particular rhythm, one sharp hard blow, and two shorter softer taps, repeating this till the shoe glimmered. Then one last blast of heat and he stuck the red hot metal into a cast-iron tub of water, where it hissed and cooled into shape. This done, he filed it smooth with a rasp and then heated it, just enough to sear the now raised hoof that rested over his bent knee. The smell of burning was terrible and thrilling. I was amazed that the horse stood still for such treatment. The smith hammered in the nails with their square heads and clipped off the protruding ends. Then he varnished the hoofs so that they shone. Both horses seemed to walk a lot taller after their visit to the smithy, as though proud of their new shoes. Sometimes I visited on my own, just to sit and watch the nails and shoes being prepared. Like many smiths, this man also serviced cars, and later when horses were no longer a means of transport, his shop became a garage. But in my day he still looked after the carthorses and ponies of the neighbouring farmers.

When I was six, school began. I had already taught myself to read out of sheer envy of my sisters, who lay snug in rest hour and entertained themselves silently with books. I learnt it from the Woodbines cigarette packet, then from the Players cigarettes, and followed on with *The Tale of Peter Rabbit* by Beatrix Potter. I knew it by heart and studied the patterns and hieroglyphics until I could make out 'and' and 'the', which Leezy showed to me. Somehow I could see that these patterns of shapes that were letter were related differently in different spaces, and one day it clicked and I could read. I promptly picked up my favourite book, *Heidi*, by Johanna Spyri, in the Dent Dutton series, and read it from cover to cover, to my mother's horror, as she believed unquestioningly in the Steiner approach to education. This method says that a child should not learn to read or write till it has started losing its milk teeth. My father, with more common sense, said that if I had taught myself, then I was ready for it.

The first day of school was very memorable. I had to dress properly in a dress, no longer able to wear my corduroys all the time. I wore a Liberty bodice made of rough cream flannel with two suspenders to hold up my woollen stockings. This meant that the backs of my thighs were coldly exposed to the wooden seats and the icy winds. I pulled over this horror a pair of thick cotton knickers with a pocket in them to hold my handkerchief. They were called gym knickers and they were always falling down, as well as being no use as a receptacle for hankies. Whoever thought that a proper little girl like me would lift her skirt to blow her nose! I just sniffed inelegantly in defiance. They fell down because I had no waist and was a very wriggly child at best. With polished shoes and a warm coat on that late September morning, and with a leather satchel on my back, I was dispatched to the Garage Cottage, the upstairs attic of which had been turned into classrooms.

I remember our classroom vividly, but not because of the lessons. It sits in my memory as the place where, for the first time I was cruel, deliberately, to one of the ill children. Because the room had a sloping ceiling, being up in the attic, the edges were straightened with plywood boards that created useful storage spaces. An adult could stand upright at either end of these cupboards but in the middle the sloping roof descended and so it was closed off as being useless. One wet break, we discovered that there was a gap, and if you crawled through you entered a warm, dark and thrilling place. Hiding in there meant that Ella, our teacher, had to look for you, and whilst she was out searching, you could reappear, to the delight of the other naughty classmates. Knowing that Margaret Eadie was afraid of the dark, we pushed her in and closed the cupboard door on her. Ella came in to hear a ghostly moan from inside the wall. We found this hilariously funny, but Margaret was, indeed, terrified and wet herself with fright. Ella was justifiably furious with us. No one owned up, so I said that I had done it and took the blame for the others, mostly because I was ashamed of my cruelty. Part of me had enjoyed the joke with the others, but a greater part, I am happy to admit, did not like such practical jokes at all.

Leezy and Agi crossed the river Dee to school in Murtle, and I went to school, for the first year, in Heathcot. The lessons ran one into the other, but I can recall the mood, smells and sounds quite vividly. I loved it. I loved my teacher, Ella, whose skill in singing and recorder playing delighted me. She told wonderful stories and showed us how the letters came about. I remember a swan becoming the number two. First we saw a beautiful drawing on the blackboard of a white swan sailing over a lake. We heard a story about it that I do not remember very well, except that the swan was joined by its mate and so there were two swans. Somehow, by some magic, each day the shape of the bird became more and more symbolically drawn on the blackboard, until there were two squiggly lines and I saw that they made the number 2, drawn twice over where the two swans had been. A giant became the letter 'G' when he sat with his head on his knees, and a king became 'K' with his foot forward and a sword in his hand. That 'A' was an apple was really true for me, and 'B' was the bridge, the one over the Dee, which you had to cross over to get to Camphill House from Heathcot House.

Coming back from my first day of school, I was greeted by my mother with a huge coloured cone made of shiny paper and filled with oranges, barley sugars and hazelnut chocolate. This followed a German tradition that a child returning from their first school day should be rewarded with sweets and cakes and celebrated as though it were a birthday. I ate them all as fast as I could before my sisters could get them off me.

Most of my school years were a pleasure, but none were so magical as those first three years in St John's School. I moved classrooms a few times, first to Murtle estate, where classes were held in old army huts. Mine was next door to Leezy's and I could hear her teacher, Friedwart, doing battle with some very naughty boys. We were meek and mild in our class, very quiet and well behaved compared to her classmates. I loved the stories that she told about her day at school, and gobbled up every song she ever sang that Friedwart taught her. The actual subjects were less memorable, though I found that when I finally went to boarding school, I was well ahead of all the other children in my class except in French. Obviously, we had no French co-workers in Camphill in those days. My German, of course, was excellent!

From Murtle, my class moved to Camphill. Visiting that classroom today, I find that the smell is exactly the same as when I sat there, hair plaited and neatly dressed. In my class was my friend Pauly, Hans Georg, Johanna van der Stok and Vincent Smalley. Margaret Eadie, Barry Dent and assorted other ill children surrounded me in warmth and friendship. We had the main lesson together as a class in the morning, where the important subjects like stories, letters, numbers and farming, geography, Bible study and so on were established. Then, after break, we split up into ability groups for the three R's. Also the afternoon lessons were taught in groups, though these consisted of art, craft and handwork subjects.

With adult hindsight, I realise that the way the groups were divided was not according to ability alone. The staff children were grouped together for the second lessons. Two of them might have benefited much more from being with slower children because they were dyslexic, but they were staff children so they came with us. Pauly had great difficulty in remembering and forming letters, though numbers were easy for him. Johanna, whom we called Hanneke, never learned to read properly, right through her schooling. Both these children moved on to boarding school with me, but Hanneke left aged fourteen, and Pauly too, left early. Hans Georg was a bit slow but always thorough in his work. Vincent Smalley was well able to keep up with me, so at least I had one friend for competition, as well as Dominic Poole, who was certainly as able in his lessons as I was, but never very forthcoming, being rather shy.

I loved tests, finding them an exciting challenge. I loved being asked to read out loud, and I loved recounting the previous day's lessons to the class. What I failed to understand was that I could not be that privileged person every day. Others had to be given the opportunity too. So whenever a question was asked, I blurted out the answer in my eagerness to learn, and forgot to hold up my hand to be asked to speak. Ella told me, nicely at first, to wait, but eventually her voice got sharper and sharper, and then she would send me out in exasperation. I could not understand her at all. Why was I being excluded for giving the right answer? But I accepted it, because she always let me take a book with me into the draughty lobby, so that the punishment passed very pleasantly. Probably separating me from the class was the only way to get the rest to contribute and memorise, without their becoming dependent on my speed and capability.

I used to do Pauly's and Hanneke's homework for them. This was discovered by Ella, who wisely, applauded me on my helpfulness, and suggested that rather than doing it for them, I should help them to learn their sums, or spellings. We spent many interesting afternoons at this task. It even became a weapon for me, at one stage. Perhaps because I was so quick and smart, Hanneke took a dislike to me. She was a very pretty girl with rather persuasive ways, and she somehow succeeded in making me unpopular with my friends. This was a novel experience for me. I was used to shouting the loudest, having the second best ideas for games, next to Pauly, who was undoubtedly the leader in this field, and being by far the most clever. Suddenly, none of my friends would play with me and they called me nasty names. They ran away when I came by. Even Pauly, with a sheepish grin, deserted me when Hanneke came to play.

I cried a great deal over this, and pondered my revenge until I hit upon withholding my superior brain from them. I refused to help them with their homework. It took two days of red crosses in their homework books for them to come round to acknowledging their need for me. But it left a bitter taste in my mouth. Was I only liked for what they could get? It was, however, a very chastening experience. All at once, I knew what it must be like to be Hans Georg, or even more serious, to be Judith, who could not speak and was often ignored by us brighter folk. I looked at their lives with fresh eyes and a kinder heart.

Break times were fun and games. When I was younger, I had attended the kindergarten in Murtle House. It was a vague time of ring games, nursery rhymes, of which I knew a million by heart, and dressing up in Wendy houses, or playing outside under the trees. The only distinct memory I have of the kindergarten relates to the breaks. We were seated around a low table and given a glass of milk and a piece of bread and marmalade. I detested milk unless it was icy cold and tasteless. I disliked it so much that I could not touch it if it had been in contact with anyone else's mouth, not even Pauly's, from whom I could have eaten anything, even pre-chewed. I could not drink it from a glass that someone else had used, and I could not lick it off a spoon that had been near someone else, not even from my mother, whom I loved so very much. Was it my Jewish heritage coming to light instinctively? Anyway, at kindergarten, the milk was always at room temperature, and we had to drink up because it was good for us. It made me choke and I had to hold my breath to swallow down.

The idea of giving small children marmalade with bits of peel that is large and tough, is a weird one. Children like bland and sweet fruits, and marmalade, with its bittersweet taste, was quite shocking. We called the peel 'sticks' and thought that they should have been taken out. Because I could not eat them, I gouged them out with my finger and surreptitiously stuck them under the table. One day this was discovered and the teacher, whose name I have forgotten, perhaps because we had a series of them, made me wash them off. This was a hard and humiliating work, the offending bits being old and well dried from years of children finding the same way out.

Break times at school were so different. We played outside, all together, and found a million things to do like hopscotch, ball games and skipping games, all of which we played in a fiercely competitive manner. Having poor eyesight (which remained undiagnosed) I always lost these games. Sometimes we huddled in groups and shared bits about our lessons. If the weather was wet, we still went out. I remember an autistic boy in Leezy's class being fascinated by the enormous black slugs that teemed among the Scottish hills. Many migrated to the path outside our classrooms. One day we dared him to eat one, and he did. I admired him fearfully, thinking that this took real courage and endurance.

Another boy, David Nailor, was also much to be admired. He too was in Leezy's class and walked with two crutches, his legs thin and useless beneath his strong muscular torso and arms. He used to swing along like nobody's business, quite undeterred by his disability. He had a lovely cockney voice and always seemed to be laughing and defiant. I liked to run very fast and challenge him to keep up, which was silly of me because he could go so much faster on his crutches than my little pair of posh legs ever could do.

In the summer, once my class had moved to the army huts that had been donated to Camphill to be used by St John's School, we went to school across the river, using the ferry. This meant walking down the drive, along the main road and then down the Ferry Road. There was Bella, the Ferry Lady, and tied to a wooden jetty was her boat. Because of the swiftness of the current, it was secured to a rope that was tied to a pole on either bank of the river. Bella would hold it steady for us as we clambered in, satchels on our backs and windcheaters over our arms. Then she untied it and poled us across.

We either walked along the bank between the gorse bushes and weeds, up the slope and fearfully through the 'jungle way', an overgrown stretch of the path that my sister Leezy found terrifying, and then into Murtle, or, if for some reason we were visiting Newtondee, we ascended the Ferry Road straight up on the other side of the river. The ill children went to school in their own grounds, or were transported by the inevitable Bedford Dormobile that rattled and banged but did its job.

Coming home from school, we reached the ferry and called loudly to Bella, who came out, poled across and returned with us in her boat. Bella was known to us as the Ferry Lady. She had white hair and twinkling eyes and she kept a tea shop in the corrugated iron-roofed shed on the Heathcot side of the ferry. Inside were treasures such as marshmallows, bubblegum, gobstoppers, lemon sherbet, liquorice shoelaces, sugar cigarettes and lemonade. She also sold snowballs, a marshmallow cake covered with chocolate and rolled in desiccated coconut, of which we were especially fond. Sometimes, when we had a farthing to spare, we could buy the coconut that fell off them. She would sweep them up into a paper bag and hand them over with a smile. Then a wet forefinger poked delightedly into the bag and emerged with coconut adhering to its tip, to be licked off with pleasure.

She also sold ice cream on hot days, in a cone, or between two wafers. These cost 'thruppence', the total amount of my irregular pocket money. Some children got sixpence every week. My mother gave me money on a need-to-have basis, which seemed always to be at her discretion, not really meeting my need at all! I could have used thruppence twice a day when Bella's tea shop was open. In order to remedy this unfair lack, I took to looking in her little wooden pot that sat on her desk and into which she carelessly tossed loose pennies. A penny went a long way in those days. You could get a gobstopper, a shoelace, a small screw of lemon sherbet with a straw up which to suck it, and three sugar cigarettes. There were other combinations for a penny but this was my favourite. My mother never commented on the disappearance of those pennies. I wonder where she thought they went? When I asked to go down to the ferry, she usually let me go. A broad-minded woman, was my mother.

Sometimes, when we came home from school on a hot summer's afternoon, we would pass courting couples lying on the soft grass between the gorse bushes, clutching each other in passion, and on occasions actually in the midst of sexual intercourse. We would stand still to watch the gyrating heaves of their buttocks, disturbing them with our noisy attempts at silence that broke into uncontrolled giggles. They looked so very funny and uncomfortably inelegant with legs in the air and knickers round their knees. I hardly really understood what was happening. I merely observed that it did. On occasion, the man – or boy – would erupt out of the embrace and roar at us with frustrated fury as his lady tried frantically to cover herself up again. Then we would run as fast as we could, calling Bella in our panic, which stopped the hunter in his tracks.

When the autumn came, the river rose, and we could no longer use the ferry until the late spring floods had died back. Bella shut up shop and was seen no more unless we made a rare visit to the roadside cottages on the North Deeside road in Bieldside, which was where she lived. We had to travel to school in a more conventional way. We took the red Strachan bus to the bridge below Camphill House and walked up the road. Alternatively, we took the old Bedford Dormobile to Murtle House, or we crossed over the Shakin Brigga. This last was forbidden because the shaking was caused by the river's changing bed that undermined the bridge's foundations. It shook because it was a suspension bridge, and some of the ropes were snapped and others rather loose. It was a dangerous route to take. If you stopped in the middle and bounced only a tiny bit, the whole thing swayed and trembled very satisfactorily for daring children. It gave us a cheap thrill. Leezy, the bravest of us all, often used this route to travel to and from Newtondee when visiting her friend, Celia Poole. The Pooles were another English family who had joined Camphill: Richard and Mary and their three children. Nicholas was in Agi's class, Celia in Leezy's class, and Dominic in my class.

Sometimes, we walked down to the road to wait for the bus to school and a friendly farmer passed by on his tractor, with a cart behind. He slowed down and allowed us to hold on to the back of the trailer, to run like the wind to the bridge at Camphill. This was exciting too, and also probably very unsafe, but such good fun. We would arrive breathless and red cheeked in our classrooms, all ready for a day's work. The Bedford Dormobile was my least favourite mode of transport because it stank of petrol and made me very carsick.

In the summer, we ran about in bare feet and light cotton dresses. The summer began when my mother said so. My father used to quote, 'Ne'er cast a clout till May is out' at us, but I didn't really want to wait that long. On the first warm spring day in May, I would start begging to discard my shoes and go on and on until permission was given. We used to love to lie under the cherry tree at the side of the playground in front of Heathcot House, eating bread and dripping for break, whilst the sun beat down on our heads and the wind lightly blew up the soft cotton skirts. On Sundays in summer, we wore our dirndls and had our hair loose, curly and free.

The ill children also, loved the summer warmth, basking outside in their wheelchairs with bare skinny cramped arms more relaxed in the heat. The boys wore shorts and also soaked up the sun through their white-skinned legs and knobbly knees. On really hot days, they were taken out of their wheelchairs to lie on the soft green grass and roll about with glee. Their guttural shouts were fun for us to hear and we would roll with them like puppies.

On hot Saturdays, we might go down to the ferry for a picnic, wheelchairs and all. We would spread tartan blankets on the ground, take off our socks and shoes, and paddle in the cold, cold water. The ill children were lifted in, to squeal with delight at the unfamiliar and stimulating feel of the soft Highland river water. Then we picnicked on the inevitable brown bread sandwiches and hard-boiled eggs, and drank the delicious lemonade bought from Bella as a special treat. We would walk home hot, tired, replete and happy, helping to push the now heavy wheelchairs up the hill. That is, my sisters helped. I usually fussed that I was too tired and got away with it, much to their disgust. Sometimes it was an advantage to be one of the youngest.

In winter we were not allowed to paddle or swim in the deep river. But my sister Leezy once did the bravest thing I could imagine. She wanted to come home from school and there were no transports running, so she walked down to the ferry in its winter sleep, took off her shoes and stockings, tucked her school dress into her knickers, and waded over. The icy water came up her shivering thighs and over her bottom, wetting her knickers. Her daring stemmed from a great admiration for Renate König, who performed this dangerous feat on her rare free days, when she would cross over to visit her grandparents in Newtondee Lodge.

Dr König had brought his elderly parents to live with him, and they occupied two small upstairs and two tiny downstairs rooms in one half of the Gate Lodge. They were bent and tiny, Grandfather König thin and drawn, and Grandmother König round and smiling. They spoke Austrian and were, to my childish eyes, just the way grandparents should be. I had none of my own and secretly wished that they might belong to me, but never voiced this to anyone, feeling it was a bit strange to want someone else's relatives for my own.

Coming home after school we went to play on the path around Heathcot that ran under the mature beeches. Directly opposite the house, it was banked up beside a stream and in the bank were mysterious holes, made perhaps by rabbits, the bigger holes being home to foxes or badgers. In the summer evenings, when we were allowed go to bed later, you could see the rabbits come out to play on the soft moss beneath the beeches. We used to build houses for fairies in the tree roots and leave bits of bread for the rabbits. The houses made from bark, sticks and leaves were often disturbed the next day, so we knew that the fairies were grateful for our attention. The trees themselves were marvellous to climb. We would clamber right to the top and enjoy the swaying that the wind created in the autumn days. We would each choose our own tree and race to the top to shout across to each other from the leafy crowns. In the winter, it was more scary to climb the bare branches because then you could look down a long dizzying way to the ground. From the top, you could look out over Heathcot House and admire its strength and solidity. I never thought that anything bad could happen to me, and I certainly never dreamed that it might not remain my home forever.

Chapter IV

DISBANDING HEATHCOT

Most of those magnificent trees survived the Great Storm of 1953, possibly because they grew in a circle and so protected each other. That storm is strong in my memory because it was the first and only time that I experienced free flying. I was on my way home from the Garage Cottage where I had been visiting Ann, when a gust of wind came round the corner and lifted me off my feet. Had it not been for the handy door handle that I clutched frantically at the side of the house, I might have landed heaven knows where. Breathless and thrilled, I ran into the house to tell everyone about flying with the wind, and my sisters laughed at me, not believing a word. But the wind rose, stronger and stronger. Carlo came in, as breathless as I had been, some hours later, to recount how he had barely missed being crushed by a falling tree as he drove home up the drive.

From that moment on, for three days, no one left the house. The wind raged, night and day, howling round the great house and we watched in awe as the trees around us snapped and fell, great giants that they were. As I stood staring out of the window halfway up the green nursery stairs, a huge and stately fir tree teetered and slowly dropped onto the corner of the house. I imagined the prickly bough running right through the window past my head, and I screamed in fear and delight. What an adventure that would have been! Then we would have had to sweep up the broken glass that lay on the floor under the window. Once the storm had died down, we became aware of the havoc it had wrought. We heard of Holland, flooded over, of boats that had sunk, of forests that lay ruined, like matchsticks, and flooded towns with roofless houses. The whole of Europe was battered and bruised.

In our own little world, the forest that we used to ride in was pulped and lay flattened with one lonely tree left standing in the centre. Some of the big beeches had fallen. Not many had gone, but one tree that we could never climb because of the way the branches grew now lay on its side, and for months afterwards we climbed it triumphantly as it lay in the moss halfway down the drive. We built houses in the roots and had a wonderful new den in which to create a fantasy home. Some trees had fallen over the road, so we could not go to school until they had been shifted.

But Heathcot House stood firm, unruffled by nature's forces, a safe home to so many people. And by and large, the ring of trees that encircled and protected it stood firm too. So our life continued as always, though the way to school now took us past bare roadsides, where lorries came and picked up the good and worthwhile fallen trunks, and others came to collect the debris to be pulped for paper, said my father, or to be made still smaller into matchsticks. Maybe the matches that my father used for lighting his pipe might now come from one of the trees that the wind had brought low with its might and power.

The yew trees that guarded the back garden stood firmly like soldiers on either side of the rose beds. Co-workers used to sit there on sunny days, enjoying the peacefulness and the sweet smell of the blooms. When the weeds were high and neglected, we used the grassy parts to play 'piggy doctors'. We knew very well that grown-ups would not understand nor appreciate the exploration that we undertook of each other's bodies. Not having any brothers, I found Pauly's privates fascinating, and so we happily poked and felt each other without any real sexuality, except that it afforded a faint pleasure. And the yew trees silently watched us, giving a warm sensation of security and timelessness. We felt embraced by and safe within our surroundings.

When I was nine years old, a momentous decision was taken in the Movement Council. There had been rumours that Heathcot was a big house, that maybe it was too big, that it needed repairs – and where could we find the money? It seemed the owners wanted to sell, and Camphill did not have the money to buy it and besides, as it stood alone on the south side of the river, it was too far away to keep. Whatever the rumours said, I did not listen. Heathcot was my home, so how could it belong to anyone else but to me and my friends and family? But the Movement Council thought otherwise, and my mother came home to break the news that Heathcot was to be given up. Not only was my home to be taken from me, but we were going to move from Camphill in Scotland to Botton Hall in Yorkshire. We were going to go and live in England!

I could not really believe all this horrible information. However, gradually people started to move out. Families left to live in Newtondee, or Camphill estate, to Murtle or Cairnlee. One by one the ill children left for other houses, or left Camphill altogether. Places were opening up for those we called 'spastic', where there were better physical aids than we had. I could not imagine that they could offer a nicer home, and pitied the children as they were driven away. Would they have such wonderful times as our Christmases and Easters were? Would they sit round a huge St John's fire, and picnic and eat as much ice cream as they liked, the way we did at midsummer festivals? Would the Dragon fight against St Michael and be forever defeated for at least one more year, as happened every September in Heathcot House?

The seasonal celebrations were an integral part of my life. I counted the year by them and looked forward to the next as soon as one had passed. Sometimes we went to Murtle and celebrated all together with the whole community. Sometimes we had smaller festivities in each estate, or people came from the other estates to Heathcot to mark the season. All our festivals were Christian in their essence, but we were happy to steal stories, plays, games and traditions from any country in the world. So, as new co-workers came from more and more countries to live our community way of life, new traditions entered our scope and practice.

Christmas was done in a very German way. There was no Santa Claus. On Christmas Eve, bathed and excited, but very, very quiet, we stood or sat like angels in the cold grey flagged hall and waited breathlessly for the light. From either end of the passages it would start to glimmer, and then get steadily brighter. Shimmering shadows were cast on the walls as angels, who were really two co-workers dressed in their Christmas finery, appeared at both entrances to the hall. In their hands they carried a tray of lighted candles skirted with fronds of silver and gold shiny paper, and each child was given one to hold. Then we went in procession, singing, 'O come, all ye faithful', the candles flickering madly and the shadows dodging around, down the passage to the Green Room. This was a stately room, only for grown-ups and festivals.

In the Green Room, a long table was set with gleaming candles that shone, dressed in silver and gold paper skirts, like the ones that we held in our fists. We each planted our candle at the place set for us and then sang more Christmas carols, said a special grace and ate a delicious meal of baked fish, potato salad and other green salads, with trifle at the end.

However, before we could eat such a feast as this was, the Christmas tree was lit for the first time. It was dressed with candles, three red at the top and the rest white. It carried red paper roses, copper signs and symbols mysterious and holy, and shining bright red apples that weighted the branches so that the candles stood straight in their silvery holders. Ceremoniously, the angels who had brought us our lights lit each candle one by one as music was played on the lyre, and a choir sang holy songs in exquisite harmony. We sat around this gracious and compelling Christmas tree, which reached in its majesty right to the ceiling, every afternoon for the duration of the twelve holy nights of Christmas.

After such a wonderful banquet, bedtime was especially quiet and pent with held breath till the morning when the Christ Child would be born. We went to breakfast in the Green Room, with candles and singing, and ate stollen, a specially prepared German Christmas bread filled with raisins, nuts and almonds, and covered with butter and icing sugar. We ate this, thinly sliced because it was so rich, with thick butter and honey – the real thing, not golden syrup. We wore our new Christmas dresses and had a very special Christmas service. We went to dinner excited, and enjoyed the roast chicken, roast potato, sweet-and-sour red cabbage and apple sauce. We had ice cream or smooth and creamy cream cheese for pudding, with fresh fruit salad, deliciously sweet. During the Christmas time, we were allowed to eat as many tangerines as we liked.

Then a rest hour was taken, and after this, at long last, we lined up in the hall and walked, or were wheeled, agonisingly slowly into the Green Room once more. There, on long benches and little tables were set out, in proper order, each child's Christmas presents. They were gifts from teachers, friends, parents and people we knew. Father Christmas was not in the picture at all in our Camphill community tradition. We sat down at our own pile and waited until we were allowed to begin unwrapping. Then the excitement erupted, as it would for any small child, and glee and joy made a delightful din in that gracious room. Nursery parents helped those children who needed help, but I needed none. I only wanted to have my parents close by to admire what I had received. We ran about, swapped presents and shared our toys with each other. Then we had a picnic supper and went to bed satisfied, full and joyous. Our parents, both together for once, settled us with carols and stories, and so the lovely candlelit days began.

Each morning we had carol singing, and in the afternoons a puppet show, or a little mime, or a story or a concert were performed for us. The puppet shows were of fairy tales or legends, and the drama too, so that our childish minds could see pictures of the meaning of the festival. Concerts, which we had throughout the year, were always of classical composers. I could sing pieces by Mozart, Bach or Beethoven alongside the folk songs that we learned in school. Many of the people who came to Camphill in those early years were musicians and artists of one kind or another. The richness seemed never ending, and ill children as well as staff children relished the culture and were quiet when it was good, and noisy when it was bad quality entertainment. We were great amateur art critics! At New Year, we sailed little walnut boats that carried lighted cake candles across a tin tub, and as we gently blew our boat across, it would land on the other side near a paper hooked over the edge of the basin. It was opened and inside was written your own personal fortune for the coming year. What magic!

On the last of the twelve days of Christmas, the Three Kings came, dressed in red, blue and green with copper gifts for Mary and Joseph, who took them along with them to Egypt, and the great Kings undressed the Holy Tree, accompanied by sad and solemn music, and carried it out to be kept safe for another year, leaving the dried and pungent-smelling needles all over the passage and hall floor. Where did they and the tree go? I used to search diligently and secretly, trying to find the skeleton of Christmas, but it was gone, to reappear miraculously as fuel for the midsummer fire, which we celebrated on 24 June as St John's Day.

What a very different festival that was! The candles of the dark December days were now a huge bonfire in the height of the summer sun, searing us with its mighty flames and sending sparks up to the sky. We usually gathered on Murtle slope behind the house, the whole community singing, and creating a celebration with the twelve signs of the zodiac and the seven planets that were portrayed in eurythmy in a huge circular mystery drama.

Then we picnicked and played games, such as sack racing, egg-and-spoon racing, wheelbarrow racing and other competitive but hugely enjoyable outdoor fun. Every one played together and the winner was given a chocolate or sweet of some kind. Sometimes a staff child won, but the award was always given to the nearest ill child who had done well. This I found very unfair, not recognising any real difference between us. I felt, probably quite justifiably, that the winner was the winner, no matter who they were. Later, as times moved on, those games were more fairly set up so that ability competed with equal ability. But in my day, many a prize did I sadly and enviously watch disappear down an ill child's eager throat. At the end of the afternoon, we had ice cream in cones, as many as we liked. This was the only time that I can remember when we were ever allowed seconds of a treat.

Coming from Heathcot to Murtle, meant travelling in hired buses, and going home, I remember feeling rather sick from all the goodies and having a stomach ache from the cold ice cream. But it was always worth it.

Easter brought hidden joy. The events of Holy Week were sombre and fearful. We saw puppet shows and some serious plays, and had extra religion lessons. The house grew more and more quiet, the flowers disappeared from the tables and bedroom, and all became still. On Good Friday, we stopped singing, we sowed seeds in the ground and painted hollow eggshells with bright and spring-like pictures. Then, on Easter morning we rose very early, before sunrise, and walked quietly up the hill to watch the sun rise. It came up, brightly shining, and then we sang glorious Easter carols all the way home to a breakfast of coloured hard-boiled eggs and an Easter loaf, which was a crown made up of plaited white-bread dough and glazed with egg yolk to make it a golden brown.

The Green Room was decorated, as was the rest of the house with painted eggs, hung up on spring-greened branches in vases with daffodils and other flowers. Little vases made from eggshells, painted and buttered to make them waterproof, were filled with violets and primroses. The beauty was abundant. Christ had indeed risen! After the service, we went to see whether the Easter rabbit had been, and he hadn't so we went home disappointed. But after rest hour, we gathered in the hall and went in procession singing praises to the Risen Christ, and lo and behold, sometime during that quiet hour, the rabbit had come and left huge chocolate eggs, and little nests of dried-up grass and moss, full of sugar eggs coloured like the wild bird's clutches. We ran hither and thither and collected them, sharing them with those in wheelchairs, who pointed out their finds for us to pick up. We ate till we were sick, for once without reprimand.

Michaelmas, the autumn festival, came by with wind and weather. We saw plays about the archangel Michael and the Dragon, about brave St George, or courageous Perseus, who slew Medusa and killed the Dragon to free the maiden. We went out harvesting and made an altar of all the ripe fruits and vegetables, singing songs about the bounty of the earth. This was the festival for a royal banquet that we called the Michaelmas Meal. We all gathered, Sunday dressed, in a hall with tables set as for a feast. We sang, ate vegetable stew and brown baked rolls, and had apple cake for dessert. In between, we sat silent, the whole community, and heard the Bible story from the Revelations, of Michael defeating Lucifer, and the Mother, who was with Child and who fled into the wilderness in fear of the Dragon.

This was the main seasonal cross of the year. In between came Advent, with its wreath of fir branches decked with four candles, one to be lit each week until Christmas. On the first Advent Sunday, we went to the Advent garden. We were brought into a room which was so dark that only the large candle in the centre drove the gloom away. We sat whilst soft lyres played Christmas carols and we all sang very quietly to their accompaniment. A story about seeking and finding the light was recounted in the mysterious sweet-smelling mossy dimness. Then, one by one, children were invited to walk round a spiral of moss that lay hidden in the darkness. They were each given an apple, in which had been wedged an unlighted candle. In the centre of the spiralling path stood the large candle, on a rock. From its flame, each child singly lit his or her candle and returned from the centre to the periphery with a small flame. Along the way, the light was planted in the dark moss, and thus the crystals that lay hidden there were revealed. They twinkled as the path of little flames became brighter and brighter, until, at the end of the festival, the spiral of moss had become a glittering path of light. All the time we sang softly. Walking the Advent garden was quite challenging. You could get lost when turning round after lighting your candle. Moreover, the candle flame might go out if you walked back too hurriedly. We held our breath as we watched our friends struggling on their way in, and smiling or grimacing with concentrated energy on their way out. Some went in wheelchairs, others were helped to walk, and we staff children strode through, boldly and confidently. The babies from the baby nursery were carried into the garden and came out beaming, sometimes crying as their apple and candle were planted on their way.

We had beautiful Advent calendars and opened a window each day. They were made from coloured tissue paper and each picture told a story. We opened one in the morning before breakfast, starting with the youngest child, and going up to the eldest. Sometimes this did not work out quite fairly, but there would always be next year to balance it again. During Advent, we had concerts, stories, and the visit of St Nicholas. Unlike the Dutch saint, who comes with fun, laughter and presents, the German St Nicholas is a stern and just man. He has a servant called Knecht Rupprecht who carries a switch of birch twigs and a sack on his back. We all had to gather in the Green Room for this painful occasion. That is, I certainly found it so, because St Nicholas came in, sat on a throne and opened a huge book. From it, he would read out each child's good and bad deeds. Depending on the balance of honour and sinfulness, you either got an orange or a piece of coal. I dreaded this yearly judgement, always making sure to be very good coming up to the fateful 6 December. One year, a boy called Roald was called up, his sins were read, and a stern Saint Nicholas gazed at him. He stood still, waiting for his good deeds to sound out. There was only one. St Nicholas, after a long pause, at last told Knecht Rupprecht to give him an orange. I was vastly relieved because I felt that this ill boy could hardly do better than he did. Roald looked at the orange, went to the back of the room, turned and with great force aimed the orange at St Nicholas, who had to duck as it flew by. I was thrilled at the boy's bravery and wished I had the similar cheek!

We saw a special play on Christmas Eve for the whole community in Murtle Hall. (The old front hall no longer exists, having been gutted for more bedroom space. Murtle Hall nowadays is a large and strangely shaped addition to the side of the gracious Georgian house of my childhood.) This was a play about Adam and Eve, Moses and Elias and the Patriarchs, who call on the Messiah to come. And he came from the Archangels of God, brought by Gabriel and accompanied by a host of small angels, who were us children dressed in white angel garments like nighties. Two lucky children were then chosen to seek for Mary and Joseph, who were hidden within the audience, and bring them to the place where the Christ Child could be born, under the Christmas tree. It was known as the *Community Play*. As part of the play, the Christmas tree for the community was first lighted, a flame from its majestic holiness being brought home carefully, to light each child's own candle. A flame from this special tree then brought the light to our own Christmas tree at home.

Carnival, in February, was hilarious. Here we dressed up and made up funny stories and the grown-ups made fun of themselves, showing us a side that we did not often see in their busy lives. We picnicked in the Green Room and had a great time together.

The ten days between Ascension and Whitsun were another long celebration. Each day we went out and did some gardening and practised a fairy tale, which we performed on Whitsunday, outside, to celebrate the spring. Often the play was done by the co-workers, but sometimes they needed fairies and we could join in.

May Day meant appointing the most beautiful girl to be the May Queen. A long procession of flower girls and beautiful maidens competed for this place. Once my sister, Leezy, was given the honour. I knew that she was more beautiful than I was, but my heart was sore with envy and pride, all mixed up together. Another time, a girl in a wheelchair won, called Nan. I saw her beauty behind her twisted face in the glorious smile that showed her delight and pleasure.

There were other smaller festivals that also came and went, but they are too numerous to recount. We seemed to go from preparing one festival to another all through the year. Birthdays were celebrations of the birthday child. You were woken with singing and a lighted candle surrounded by the flowers of your season, and feasted and spoilt all day, getting your presents only at supper time, with a cake and a party. There seemed to be a birthday almost every day, and grown-ups and children alike received this preferential treatment on their day.

I wondered fearfully, as I digested the news of Heathcot's demise, if all this light and colour and music would die with it. Could any other place be as rich and beautiful? I began to walk about the house and grounds remembering events, people and things as though already in mourning. The children were disappearing, the furniture was going too, to be seen in another house and used by other people. Our bedrooms were still intact, thank God, and our mother, who kept them shining and homely until the last day when we would finally leave too. Gradually Heathcot House was growing bare and sad.

I saw my first film with all the ill children on a grand Heathcot House outing to Aberdeen on the day of Queen Elizabeth's Coronation. Cinema was frowned on as not being real culture, but the Coronation of the Queen of England, the generous hostess who had taken in all the refugees that made up Camphill, was something not to be missed. First, however, we acted it out for ourselves. Richard Poole wrote, composed and choreographed a historically accurate play of all the kings and queens and battles and victories that went to make the present kingdom possible. Classes and groups of children played out their roles. We saw King Alfred burn the cakes. We saw William the Conqueror kiss the ground of England. We saw Robin Hood and his Merry Men. We saw the Welsh beaten by the English. We saw the battle at Agincourt. We saw Joan of Arc trounce the English. We saw the Boston Tea Party and so on. The whole community rang to the sound of the songs that were written for the occasion. The Coronation Pageant, which we all took part in, was magnificent! And then we saw the real thing on screen. We saw Princess Elizabeth with Prince Philip at her side, crowned magnificently in colour and glory. She looked small and gracious and so very, very serious. I thought it might not be the greatest fun, after all, to become a queen. I was overawed and silent in the face of such majesty, pomp and circumstance, and very, very proud to be born British.

Now I wondered about going to live in England and leaving the Scottish hills and heather behind. We used to go to the Royal Highland Gathering every September to see the games and the dancing. We would hire buses to take us there. I would lie in my bed the night before and pray for good weather. I did not make any fuss about getting dressed on the day of the excursion, but I did wish that I was really and truly Scottish and could be entitled to wear a kilt.

We would gather outside on the porch steps and watch as the bus, smelly and grinding, wound its way up the drive. Then the ill children were carefully lifted in and settled, and their chairs folded up and put in the side of the bus. We sat and bounced our way to Braemar. The field for the Games was huge. At one side was the raised platform and canopy for the royal family. In front was a stage on which the dances were performed. The one that I loved best was the dance over swords. They glittered in the autumn sun, and the kilts flashed over them with scything legs nimbly skipping. Tossing the caber was interesting, but the real excitement came with the pipe bands. They would skirl their way round the field and stirred my blood to unbearable heights of passion. I loved wandering about in between acts and finding lone pipers walking up and down, filling their pipes with air. No wonder they sounded so agonising, considering that the bags were made from sheep's stomachs. The pain of the dying animal was audible in the tones, the laments more moving than the battle songs.

The greatest moment came when the royal family arrived. We all stood and sang the national anthem and then tried to get as close as we could to see the Prince and Princess. I told myself many a tale in bed at night after the Highland Gathering, of how I saved their lives and they were grateful to me forever and made me a duchess, at least! The royal family came to Scotland, so why did I need to go to England? Scotland was by far the best part of Britain in which to live, and that was why they spent their summers here in the North. But to England I was to be banished, and if the Queen and the Prince and Princess could live there for most of the year, then so could I.

I started wandering aimlessly through the empty great house. I carried my dolls around with me, the two I loved most, called Annabel and Benjamin. They were my children, and they too had to say goodbye to their old home. Down in the basement we found empty echoing rooms, one still smelling of ironing, where the ladies who came in daily had worked. The mending room had a red-knobbed dressmaker's pin lying in one corner of the bare floor. I picked it up and stuck it into Annabel's bodice as a brooch. I thought of the many sweets and chats that I had had in that room. The wash house bore a faint fragrance of hot soap suds, and along the wall stood a big square laundry hamper with HEATHCOT painted on it in green capital letters. I still have that hamper and use it for storing the clothes that need mending, because my mother took it with her as a serviceable travelling trunk, and it was so well made that it has remained as sound as when new.

The coal cellar had its visit. I showed it to Benjamin as a warning. It had been a place that we were forbidden to play in for obvious reasons. I remembered with glee a unique Sunday when some careless grown-up had neglected to replace the lid on the delivery hole. This was where the shute went into the cellar from the road's surface, and where the coalmen, in their black leather-patched donkey jackets, emptied the sacks of coal that they heaved onto their shoulders from the back of the coal lorry. There had been a delivery just the day before. Temptation proved greater than wisdom. We forgot the rules, and jumped into the hole to slide down the coal. What fun it was! But it ended, as all the best games seemed to do, with a spanking. This was really not surprising, considering that I, at least, was wearing a white dress, all nice and neat after the Sunday service.

The vegetable larder had been given to us as a playroom, and we used it to perform our own staff children's productions. It was literally a cellar, smelling damply of old turnips and rotten potatoes. I vaguely remember a black earthen floor and dirty whitewashed walls, but this may be merely poetic licence. I was considered too young to act in the plays that the others scripted and so cannot recall this cellar as well as other parts of the basement. We scrubbed it and some helpful male co-worker installed an electric light. The bigger boys strung up rope and we were allowed into the ragbag for cloths and old curtains from which to make a backdrop and stage curtains. What we used for lighting I cannot remember. In order to seat the audience for a performance, we fetched chairs and stools from the kitchen.

We saw so many theatre productions acted by the co-workers that we too, wanted to try. At Christmas there were all the plays about the birth of the baby Jesus. These were traditional Austrian mystery plays, beautifully translated into rhyme and song and, as we saw the same ones every year, we knew them by heart. We staged our own version of them, enjoying the rehearsals and taking it very seriously. Adam and Eve and the Devil were fun to play and to watch. Dressing up as an angel was greatly coveted by all the girls.

The Christmas nativity play was my first and last attempt at acting of my own free will. In fact, I made such a fuss to be in it that they had to write a part specially for me. These plays were usually done by the older staff children and I, apparently, was deemed too young for a real part, until my nagging made them fit me in. So they divided the announcing angel's role into two parts. The first, which was my role, was to announce the content of the play and ask forgiveness and silence of the audience. The second angelic role was deemed too holy and responsible for me as it announced the birth of the baby Jesus to Mary praying in the Temple. It apparently called for an actress with long blond hair. We saw all angels as blond and beautiful, which could not be said of my dark-haired rotundity.

The day of the performance came. We whispered and giggled, a bit hysterically, as our parents descended the basement stairs at the appointed time, to watch our acting talents. I was dressed correctly in a long white garment and my dark hair ran in waves down my back. With my eyes still smarting a little from the fierce brushing my sister Agi had given my tangled locks, I went on stage. To my horror and shame, I could not remember my words, not a hint of what I was meant to say stirring in my paralysed brain. I stood, red-hot with misery, and then burst into loud sobs. My mother rescued me, took me on her lap, and the play proceeded without my dramatic contribution. I never asked again to be in one of our little dramas, hating the school plays that I was forced to act in, but finding later on, as I grew older, that I enjoyed writing and directing them. Maybe the many plays that I watched my friends create and produce had a lasting influence on me.

From the winding stairs that led down from our nursery to the basement, you had to pass through a door and then along a grey passage to the area exit and some stairs that ran up beside the coal shute to the side of the house. You would then come out onto a path that passed the pram shed. Here were stored the wheelchairs and babies' prams, the place where we got the wheels for our ill-fated go-carts. It was a lovely place to play because it had a flat roof that could be reached by climbing a young beech tree beside it. We used to play on the roof and used it as another test for would-be gang members. If you were brave enough, you jumped off it. It was an exhilarating way down, onto the gravel below. Some children never passed this trial of courage.

The half-grown beech trees were the scene of a lesson well learned. We used to climb up the first and easiest, and then pass from tree to tree down the row until we reached the pram shed. It was great fun if you had the daring and were not afraid of falling. Sometimes the branches that you had to use were so thin, they bent almost double as you sat or stood on them. One day, halfway across, I lost my nerve. I could neither go forward nor backwards, up nor down. I just sat there, frozen. What caused this loss of courage I do not know. Pauly was shocked. Never before had I failed to keep up with his challenges. He tried to persuade me to get down, or to move on. But I was stuck, utterly and forever. I began to cry miserably. Finally, Pauly ran off to fetch my father. He came, and stood and looked at me, stuck in the tree. He said, mildly, that if I could get up, I could get down, and if I could get up and not down, then I should not get up at all. It was foolish, he said, to take on something that you could not finish. Then he went away again. I was up that tree for what seemed hours, really scared that he would never come back, but he did, of course, and with a ladder to rescue me.

My father could teach a lesson very well. Once we found his pipe lying on the bench in the garden shed. Pauly took it away, into the bushes that hid one of our dens, and smoked it furiously. He said it was lovely, but he didn't look very well and swayed a bit when he went to return it, empty of tobacco and full of ash. My father said nothing, but I saw that he had seen us sneak it back. I wondered why he wasn't cross. That evening retribution hit like a stone. During holiday times, we had something called 'grown-up supper'. These were a treat beyond imagining. You got dill pickles, cream cheese, fried potatoes, bacon, mushrooms, ice cream, all the foods that we rarely saw. Best of all, you got meat to chew, not minced to make it easy to swallow. We were allowed to go to these feasts if we were good. They happened at seven in the evening, an hour that usually saw us already in bed, hearing the stories and books read to us by my father.

On that fateful day of the pipe smoking, we were allowed to stay up late and eat with the grown-ups. We sat down to the lovely food, smelling the sweet and savoury sauces, and my mouth watered at the sight of the fried potatoes done in butter and dripping. Pauly's face went green; he coughed and then vomited all over those so delicious fries. What a commotion! He had to go to bed, and we did not get the lovely supper. My father said quietly, when he met us the next day, that maybe Pauly should leave smoking to the grown-ups. We slunk away, chastened and determined never to touch tobacco again. But I was glad that my father did not tell Reg or Molly, because Pauly would have been very soundly spanked. I loved my father very, very much.

There were so many things to remember. As I walked about aimlessly and sadly I thought of the times that Pauly and I built new dens, or houses. Every thick bush or empty shed became a potential home. Between the wall and the beech hedge that ran along the road to Heathcot Farm and ended at the Garage Cottage was a perfectly shaped space in which to erect a hut. We found bits of old carpet and broken stools and thus set up home. There could be, of course, no toilet, and so we had to pee outside. This was nothing new. We found it a waste of good playtime to go indoors to the toilet at the best of times. I envied Pauly's ability to stand up whilst delivering a stream of hot liquid at any target that he chose. I was forced to pull down my pants to squat and spray a cascade, perhaps onto a leaf, or a stone, which consequently wetted my shoes. Sometimes I tried the standing way, desperately arching my hips to aim as accurately as he did, but with no great success. The shoes were simply wetter than ever and it ran all down my legs. Pauly would giggle delightedly, happy to be the winner.

During these last days, I took a walk to the garden. It lay neglected and full of weeds. I pulled up a few and then gave up. The peach tree stood in the green house looking sad and wintry in the weak autumn sun. I wondered who would get the first peach now that my father would no longer be tending it. Would there be a peach tree in Botton village? The garden shed was empty and only a cardboard box lay on the floor. I sat on it and remembered the stories my father told us over a mug of very strong black tea brewed by Bob. It was here that I heard how not everyone who came to Camphill in the early days agreed with Dr König's community building methods. My sister Leezy's godfather left because he could not work with Dr König. So did others, who went, some to Edinburgh, and some to England to start their own brand of community. But all of them continued working with special needs people. This was a common call, which led to the founding of many homes for the handicapped in the late Forties.

It was in the garden, at elevenses, that my father told us a story about the shortest marriage in history. A lady whom we deeply respected lived in Camphill House. She was courted by a man called Dickie, pronounced 'Deekee' in my father's Germanic accent, a name that made us snort with laughter. How could any respectable man be called by the name we gave to little boy's privates? Trying to keep our faces straight, we begged him to continue. Well, he said, they got married. I imagined the woman's large round body with her high bosom, dressed in a wedding gown, and wearing a veil and flowers. All the brides that I had seen in Camphill weddings were wreathed with the flowers of the season. Somehow, the picture of this severe lady crowned with a flowery wreath did not really gel. Dickie I could not imagine, because I had never seen him, but I thought he must have been rather small and skinny. My father went on to say how, late on the wedding night, he came into the house to make the breakfast porridge. This had been my father's job as long as I could remember. He used to mix up the oats with water and salt and put the pot into the Aga. In the morning, there was the steamy porridge ready for us to eat.

So, as was his custom, he came into the house to fulfil his duty and found Dickie lying sad and lonely, on the sitting-room sofa. Actually, there was no sofa that I can remember in Camphill. We always had upright and proper singular armchairs. No one was expected to loll about! But in my imagination, Dickie lay on a sofa. His wife of one night had thrown him out. I wondered why she did that. My father said that he was dressed in a striped nightshirt, and that she had locked the door on him so that he could not get his clothes. My father said this with a distinct twinkle in his eyes behind his round spectacles. Bob would snort as though choking on his sandwich, which he ate as do all labourers, chewing fast and throwing away the crusts. So Dickie came home with my father and borrowed some clothes. He left Camphill. I thought he must have done it in the borrowed clothes, which he must have held up with a leather belt (my father was fat and the imagined Dickie was thin), drifting quietly away in the 'Steener' Train. I found it a very funny and very sad story. My mother was not at all pleased with my father for telling us this tale. But she too said that not all her friends could be happy in Camphill. Everyone had to follow their own destiny.

I walked round the perimeter of the garden, eyeing the wall, and finding no heart to climb it without Pauly. He had gone already, some time before, to Newtondee to live in the bungalow. I used to go to stay with him for weekends. Molly had a baby girl called Veronica. I was convinced that she was called after me and was very proud to hold her. Sometimes, Molly let me feed her with a bottle. I loved the feel of the warm baby in my arms. We played with the Newtondee boys – big lads with loud voices from Portsmouth or London, who could tell hundreds of dirty jokes, rarely repeating one. I learned them off by heart, but did not really understand them properly. The language was coarse, and I did not know what 'fuck' meant, but I knew that it was not a word that I should ask my parents about. It was dirty and therefore a secret. But the forbidden is always attractive, and we used to ask them to tell us more. We hid in the bushes to do so, and sometimes we were asked to show them our bottoms. I did not like this so much, and usually ran away rather than oblige this request. But the thrill remained and I both dreaded and was drawn to these teenagers with emotional problems. The danger was addictive.

Playing on the roof of the house was another dangerous game, and now, as I gazed up the three storeys of Heathcot, I wondered if I dared go up alone. I took Benjamin and Annabel upstairs and out through my father's bedroom window onto the balcony, but had lost the heart to do the climb, missing the daring of my friends that had carried me through so many risky adventures. Besides, I was afraid to lose my dolls, and the thought of seeing them fall all the way to the path below made my stomach churn. I was so lonely in those last few weeks that my dolls had almost come to life in my too vivid imagination.

Inside the house I walked from room to room, telling my dolls how lovely it had been. I visited the massage room, with its pulleys still attached to the ceiling, but the ropes were gone. We had had so much fun, swinging from them and being shot across the room.

Upstairs, I sat down on the steps of the red-carpeted passage leading to my parents' bedrooms. This passage had been the scene of so many flights of fantasy. Halfway up was a large walk-in wardrobe in which my mother hung her clothes. Lavender sachets hung from the coat hangers. Her clothes made wonderful dressing up material. She allowed us to use them, but on one occasion we went seriously out of line. In the back hung her holy service-holder's dress, of dove grey, fine wool material, and we knew this was not to be played with. However, it would have made such a gracious wedding gown and I longed to try it out.

Weddings were common. People met each other on coming to Camphill. They got to know each other thoroughly and quickly, and after the war, men were in short supply. There were, at that time, at least three women to every man in Camphill. So weddings were not infrequent and were an excuse for yet another celebration. We would all dress in our Sunday finery and go to the wedding service, which was usually held in the chapel, either in Camphill estate, Newtondee, or Heathcot. I only remember two of these events, that of the marriage of Christof and Alona, and the other, which was the wedding of Taco and Ita.

The priest of the Christian Community came to officiate. The chapel smelled of incense and felt more holy than ever. We sat in rows, the family of the bride and groom in the front row. Down the aisle walked the couple to be, in a long dress and suit, flanked by their witnesses. We did not call these people best man and woman, but wedding witnesses. Words were spoken and exchanged in ritual, and the witnesses were asked to watch over the marriage. It was solemn and short, with lovely music.

When I heard the Bible story of the Kingly Wedding, which was read every year during the time of Michaelmas, I saw the fabled feast as it was done in Camphill weddings. I imagined that we were the guests from the highways and byways because we were so odd and varied and strange with all our different ways of being. When it came to the part of being cast out, I used to feel a small shiver down my back. Could I maybe be the person who was not dressed correctly? I used to be very fussy about what I wore to a wedding, just in case it might happen to me.

Both these couples were not only handsome and gallant, but

we liked them as co-workers and had fun with them. They were young and fresh and full of humour. Christof sang and played the lyre like dream. Alona was as beautiful as a princess. Taco's humour was such fun, and Ita's smile brought out the sun. After a wedding service, the whole community had a feast and sang, danced and made merry till bedtime.

Of course, not so long after a wedding, there would be a christening. This too, was a community happening and everyone attended. Sometimes the baby cried, sometimes not. I was fascinated by the words that the priest spoke because they made so little sense to me. He would dip his finger in ash, salt and water and anoint the baby, who usually howled on being touched. Then after the ceremony there would be juice and cake for all, and we could all gaze at the baby and admire it. This was usually the first time you saw the newborn. It was customary to keep the baby inside and close to the mother for the first six weeks. Only gradually was an infant brought into contact with other people. It was allowed to grow gradually into the world.

There came that fateful moment when we had witnessed yet another wedding – co-workers always seemed to be getting married and having their babies christened – and so Pauly and I were to be married for the sixth time. We often felt compelled to act out the events that influenced our lives, and holiness was a bit stressful sometimes, because we always had to be so good and set an example to the ill children. For this particular marriage, he had found a beautiful brass curtain ring that shone like gold and was dressed up in my father's white shirt and tie. His round smiling face shone with glee and excitement and naughtiness. Not to be outshone, I ransacked my mother's wardrobe and emerged wearing her holy dress and some of her heavy jewellery. Arm in arm, we walked slowly to the steps where probably Hanneke, who loved play-acting as much as we did, stood as priest. It was a lovely wedding that ended, once again in the inevitable spanking. Not only had we dirtied my father's Sunday shirt, but I had actually dared to take my mother's grey dress. It was rare that I disobeyed her; it was just that on this occasion temptation was far too great.

On another wet afternoon, we decided to christen the cat.

Monty was a favourite playmate of ours. She, or he (we never really knew which) was soft, fat and placid. She allowed us to take the most enormous liberties, and always came when we called. We dressed her up in a doll's white nightie, and a frilly doll's bonnet. She looked as sweet as only a baby can. Pauly and I, as fond parents, held her firmly whilst Leezy got the water ready. The baby behaved as all other babies. She squirmed and yelled a bit and we reached the part of the wetting without too many scratches. But the water was the final insult. Just as Leezy, the priest, was naming her correctly, if a little unimaginatively, as Monty, she, or more probably he, leapt out of my arms and ran helter-skelter down the stairs, dragging the white nightie most elegantly behind her. She escaped through the sash window, the one that had once crushed my fingers, and raced off with us all in hot pursuit. She ran into the back garden and up a yew tree; the branches ridding her of the christening dress. We never, however, found the bonnet, and Monty was quite hard to coax upstairs after that.

House pets were not generally tolerated in the early years of Camphill. Maybe this was the Jewish ancestry still at work. There were no dogs allowed because, it was said (and has since been proved incorrect), that people with special needs are afraid of them. Some are; but then, so are some ordinary people. However, there were a few cats roaming in and outside the houses, a necessary evil to keep down the mice. We had Monty, as already described, and we also had Sheeky, probably actually called Cheeky, but with so much German in the air, the mispronunciation stuck fast. Sheeky was white and fluffy and sly, not the sort of cat to play with or take liberties with. One morning, my mother woke us with a mischievous smile, announcing that Sheeky had had her kittens in the linen cupboard beside the green nursery's bathroom. We were delighted, and I got into my clothes for once without a fuss. My mother accompanying us, in case a co-worker should reprimand us for being out of place at that time of the morning, we hurried to see the kittens. There she was, warm and snug and purring, with her blind and rat-like litter sucking sleepily. My mother burst into laughter till the tears came. She then explained that it was April Fool's Day and that she had been well and truly caught out. She had invented the surprise, or so she thought. But the cat got the better of her. We dutifully laughed with her, but I thought this was just to be expected of my mother, considering the fact that she was so little partial to a joke.

For one of her birthdays, my sister was given a canary bird in a cage. She loved it, and it sang like a nightingale. Whenever I heard the story of the Emperor and the Nightingale, by Hans Andersen, I thought of that canary, yellow, fat and sweet. Sometimes in rest hour, Agi let it out to stretch its wings, but one day she left the window open. It made straight for the fresh air and as we panicked, my sister slammed the sash down, unfortunately catching and squashing the poor little thing. We cried and screamed, but it was too late. To lessen our genuine grief, we arranged a magnificent funeral, carrying the bird on a rhododendron leaf and burying it with tears and singing.

Weddings and christenings we knew off by heart. But we also performed meaningful funeral services, with Bible and bell and solemn faces. Usually we buried snails, flies and wasps or bees, but once we buried a rat that we found under the pram shed. It stank rather a lot, and so we actually had to dig a real grave, which was very satisfactory. Pauly made a beautiful cross to mark the spot. On days when I was sad and lonely, I loved to visit the graveyard that we made behind the pram shed.

The red passage was a place for silent times too. We used to sit on the steps and tell each other serious stories about life and death and suffering. If there was no one to play with, this was the place where I nursed my dolls and told them the tales that came into my head. Sometimes, Pauly and I would lie on our bellies, one at each end of the red carpet, and roll huge, heavy, grey and pink granite balls to each other, enjoying the clack that they made when they accidentally hit each other. Their smooth cool surfaces enchanted us, as did their weight and majesty as they silently traversed the passage from end to end. We got them from my mother's room, where many enchanting and beautiful things could be found. As long as we were careful, we could play with her precious things.

Mostly we played these quiet games during meetings. The co-workers seemed to spend a lot of time in such gatherings. You could not disturb a meeting, it was almost as holy as the Bible Evening or the service. Only in an emergency could you knock on the door and call your mother or father. Sometimes I hated those hours where no question could receive an answer. We waited less or more patiently for the grown-ups to emerge from the Green Room, and depending on the expressions on their faces we judged whether or not to make the request. Sometimes it was better to go away quietly and wait for a better time to beg for a sweetie. We knew that Camphill was a community and that decisions could only be made by everybody together, except when Dr König or Frau Doctor came, and then definite orders were given, which they expected to be obeyed. Dr König knew what he wanted! We staff children were sensitive to the grown-ups' moods and to their way of life and noticed perhaps more than they gave us credit for.

Turning right from the steps you came to the bathroom, of black-beetle fame, and the bedroom that had been home to so many co-workers. This had also at one time been the sickroom, when Janet McGavin was the nurse, and also when Renate König lived in Heathcot. The ill children shared the room with the nurse when they were really poorly so that they could receive the proper care and be thoroughly spoilt. Being ill in Camphill was a pleasure in those days. You got special food and lots of attention, no matter who you were, staff child, ill child or co-worker. We had a Turkish boy, whose name was Keshav, and he loved to drink. By accident he got hold of a bottle of bleach and drank it all. The acid burnt him right down into his stomach. He would have died but for the medical treatment from Dr Hans Heinrich Engel, I think, who administered to him. He came to sleep in the sickroom, and had to drink buckets of milk, the only thing that would water and feed him. It was fascinating, in a morbid kind of way, to ask him to open his mouth so that we could see the blisters.

Down the two steps and along the short passage to the stairs, you passed first the broom cupboard and then the linen cupboard. These were places of ill repute, the broom cupboard because it was home to mice and was also very dark and smelly, and the linen cupboards because, besides the lovely clean smelling sheets that were kept there, it was also home to a witch. None of us had ever met her, because when you went in, naturally you switched on the light, and, as she was mortally afraid of its rays, she vanished as fast as she could. But all of us heard her. We made up stories in rest hour, enjoying the cheap thrill that it gave us. We were sure that we were the only family in the world that had a witch living so close by to them. She rumbled and roared and hissed all day and all night. She lived behind the water tanks, which were protected by a grille so that she could never actually get out – which was lucky, because who knows what she might have done to us all!

Sometimes, again on wet afternoons, we played in the linen cupboard. It had a sink and a square wire basket not unlike an oddly shaped tea egg, in which a bar of soap lay. If you ran the sink full and swished the wire basket about, it made excellent soapsuds. Sometimes I grated the bar of soap and the bits floated interestingly in the suds. We called it soup, and fed it to our dollies. Feeding our dolls was a great game. We could go down to the kitchen and get dry cocoa powder, white sugar and raisins. We brought the goodies up to the nursery and mixed the cocoa powder with water and sugar. The raisins were added and a feast was had by all. It was only when I was in a silly mood that we fed the soap soup to our babies, forcing them to eat up, as we sometimes saw the co-workers do to the ill children, telling them that it was good for them.

Eating up was a big issue. If you did not like what was in front of you, this was very hard. I hated horseradish sauce, but it was said to be good for preventing colds so we often had it on our bread. It made me feel nauseous. My mother, thankfully, never made me eat it; but once, when she was away, my father insisted that I consume a whole piece of brown bread with the sauce spread over it. The bread was often dry and hard, because baking was not done every day. It was a really traumatic and horrible experience for me. After that, I wondered if all the ill children liked it, or if, like me, they detested it, but could not say so.

Leaving the linen cupboard, you either went downstairs or back towards our nursery and past the dreaded broom cupboard, a dark and worrisome place. I did not like getting up in the mornings, always wanting to lie a little longer and actively and loudly protesting at all the clothes that my mother saw fit to dress me in. I was always too hot and disliked the bulkiness of the woollen and thick cotton clothing that I had to wear. Sometimes I would make such a terrible fuss that she would bundle me, clothes and all, into the broom cupboard and lock the door after me, saying that I could only come out once properly dressed.

How fast I made it into those hateful clothes! I was deathly afraid that my dear sister Leezy might turn off the light, the switch being outside the cupboard. Once in the dark, the mice might come out, probably – nay, almost certainly – aiming to nibble my bare feet. The fusses that I could produce were quite spectacular and I do not blame my mother for this treatment. Even at the time, I knew that I deserved the punishment and I am not a bit afraid of the dark, as one could be forgiven for thinking might be the result of such treatment. My mother's love surrounded me, and the warmth of the co-workers and the community celebrations sustained me all through my naughty childhood.

Going downstairs, round the oddly shaped steps, I saw in my mind's eye Dr König coming up to meet me. I stopped to tell Annabel and Benjamin of this encounter, which was truly memorable. Most of us staff children avoided him because the grown-ups held him in such esteem that it placed a barrier around him beyond which we dared not go. However, meeting him face to face made it impossible to ignore him. My mother, who was accompanying me, told me to say good morning to Herr Doctor. I found that I could not. I simply *could not* bow down and worship. I rarely said 'Good morning' and shook hands with any other grown-up. Why should I do this for him? I stood stock-still and stubborn. I could feel my mother's shame and fury, and yet I could not give in. I waited for the wrath of God to strike, but instead Dr König chuckled and said, in German, '*Lass sie doch*', and went past with such a twinkle of collusion and understanding in his eyes that I thought I could love him ever after. This was a great man who understood children, especially loud, bold girls like me.

Hans Heinrich Engel, on the other hand, had less empathy with our pridefulness. He used to collect the post from the shelf at the bottom of our stairs and would seem to lie in wait for us in the mornings. We used to dread the confrontation of absolutely *having* to shake his hand and say 'Good morning' to him. Why, we grumbled, did he deserve more respect than our parents? We never were asked to shake *their* hands.

The only occasions where we allowed hand holding were on walks and in the service on Sunday. We thought that the continental handshake was very un-British. We had learned this from the English families that came to live in Heathcot. The service, however, was another matter. Shaking hands belonged to the ritual and was perfectly all right.

Sundays were lovely days with something special happening in the afternoons, and extra nice food for lunch and white bread rolls for supper. There was a white cloth spread over the tables and the flowers that we had stolen from other people's gardens graced the dining room. After a breakfast of white bread and honey, we went upstairs and waited quietly in our nursery till it was time to go to the service.

The service differed according to the ages of children. Until the age of fourteen, you went to the children's service. Then you went to the youth service. And the adults went to the *Opferfeier*. I imagined this German word to depict some special fire that blew up brighter and brighter flames and cleansed the souls of the co-workers. Mostly the *Opferfeier* was an early morning affair. We heard our parents rising and leaving the house for the chapel. We were all very quiet on early service days because we knew that it was something holy.

The children's service was actually only twenty minutes in length but it felt much longer to me because I had to be good and sit quietly. We sat in silence in the lobby until we went in to the chapel itself, and were then placed in rows, the staff children between the ill children, either to help them or to separate us so that we could not talk or giggle.

We walked in a crocodile to the chapel, which was an asbestos hut beside the house. Inside was silence, the light shining mauve through the silky purple curtains. We went in, one by one, and then the service began. We stood in rows before an altar covered in a deep red cloth with seven candles burning in carved wooden candlesticks. The service holder stood tall before the seven lights and then turned to speak the words of the service to us. Though this personage was often my mother, I somehow did not feel a kinship to her. She was, in her grey service dress, a person separate and awesome to me. I found it all holy and solemn and awe inspiring, but agony to my aching legs because we had to stand all the way through. I used to wriggle and move my weight from one leg to the other. Invariable, afterwards, a co-worker would feel inspired to tell me off, saying that I had set a bad example. I hated these reprimands, feeling that I was also a child and could not be expected always to be good. The ill children, however, were able to sit. I envied them, forgetting that they sat all the time, being in wheelchairs.

The service holder would come round and ask us to seek God and we would reply that we would seek Him. I used to wonder where God was, and how I could seek Him, but I thought that probably someone, like my father, would tell me how to seek Him all in good time. The Bible was read as part of the service and I loved the sonorous sound of the old English, not always understanding the whole story but revelling in the sounds and pictures. I particularly loved the bits from the Revelations, and the parables. They were so very bloodthirsty and righteous and my strong little soul loved the passion, drama and justice.

I was so glad to run out when it was over that I always forgot to ask the important question, so that every service I had to ponder anew on how to seek God. Sometimes, when we had to wait before the service, I sat next to Roger, and I dreaded this because he ruminated all through the service and the smell of chewed vomit was appalling. Altogether, there were times when being with the ill children was hard to bear. Some things simply were not fair, and telling me that I was a staff child and therefore very lucky to be healthy did not always make it right.

There were other times when I felt very fortunate to be a staff child, such as going on excursions, being allowed to stay up late, and most important of all, having my mother and father with me all the time. When something went wrong for the ill children, they could not run for help to their parents, as I could. At such times I pitied them greatly and was thankful to be who I was.

With the imminent demise of Heathcot, I could enter the chapel without having to fear retribution for being where I was not meant to be. The purple curtains had gone. The windows were clear and the mauve walls looked faintly drab and discoloured without the warm light. The grey floor was stained and dreary and all the magic and holy atmosphere had gone from that room. It was just a blank space. I told Annabel and Benjamin about the service and wished it was all as it had been, before the Movement Council spoilt it all.

We ate, during those last days, in loneliness in the kitchen. My mother was staying behind, like the captain of a sinking ship, to clear up and clean-up (with Anke's help), so that nothing would be left behind and that Heathcot would be vacated in an orderly fashion for the new owners to take over – or so I thought. And then I heard that it was to be demolished and only the cellar would be kept so that the new owners could grow mushrooms in them! I felt hot with anger, fear and shock. Never would I be able to behold my home again. It would be gone forever. I wished Dr König would die, just like Mögens.

Mögens was a young co-worker from Denmark, with a wife and two children. He must have contracted some illness or other and he died in Heathcot House. It was a strange day, very quiet and grey. I came across my mother crying, a thing grown-ups did not do, and this alarmed me very much. If, when you died, you went to heaven as we were told, why was everybody sad and crying? Why weren't they happy for Mögens who was going to finally find the answer to my question of how to seek God? Wasn't he going to meet Him at last?

I went down the passage to find his wife. She too, was crying, so I crept away, still puzzled. I heard someone say that the coffin was to be carried out to the chapel and all the children should stay in their rooms. So I hid behind a curtain in the passage and saw them carry the coffin out, catching a glimpse of Mögens' white serious face as the body went by. It looked peaceful and calm, and that comforted me. I thought the grown-ups were very strange about it all. But I understood that his children were sad. They missed him, he had been a very nice man and we all liked him very much.

Now Heathcot House itself would suffer a kind of death. I hated it all and went outside to look at the yew trees. I no longer wanted to climb them as we had done when we were all together. We used to scramble through the thicket of prickly branches up to the top and lie upon them, up high and invisible, cradled in the light and air of the sky. You could hide there very well from grown-ups who might want you to do something that you didn't want to do.

I began to remember bad things about Dr König. I remembered that he was a small man, that he could not drive very well, that everyone always had to do what he wanted. I thought about him and his wife, Frau Doctor, as she was called by everyone. Mrs König was godmother to my sister, Leezy. Though I did not like her very much, I think that she must have been a great support to my mother, who looked up to her and loved her. She was a great lady, not tall, but imposing. She always wore flowing grey skirts and pink silk blouses that moved in such a way that they gave her an air of sailing along as she walked, just like a matron in a hospital; and she was, like the matrons of old, very demanding towards the co-workers whom she taught. She used to visit us quite often and was always asking us how much we had learned, and whether we had grown up. I always felt that she was criticising my mother. I tried to keep out of her way whenever she was in Heathcot. She used to go round the house and instruct my mother, as though she still wasn't perfect, even though I knew that she really was.

Sometimes Frau Doctor was invited to Saturday supper with us. I dreaded these meals. She would talk to us in a patronising tone that no one else ever used with us. She asked us if we had learned our manners and inspected us, looking at our nails and hair. I really wondered how my mother could have chosen her to be a godmother, but when I thought of how mean Leezy could be sometimes, I felt a bit better. Although I loved my sister very much and we usually had good fun together, I was also a little afraid of her because she was so often right, and was also really *good*. She was thin and pretty and smart, but very, very shy, and this gave the impression to the uninitiated that she was also in need of delicate handling. I, however, knew how clever she was and how she could invent hilarious games that we played during rest hour. She was an excellent mimic and could make fascinating sounds that had us in stitches.

Frau Doctor was the cause of our losing the pet name that we had for our mother. We used to call her 'Munner', pronouncing the 'u' as in pudding. This probably arose through baby language when trying to say *Mutter*. I do not remember calling my father *Vater*, but we must have done so at one time, before the Boulds came and anglicised us. We were attached to the name 'Munner'. One day, on one of her more bossy visits in the summer, she took us aside and told us that we were too old for such silly names and should now call our mother correctly as *Mutter*. We protested for several rest hours, the occasions that my over-responsible eldest sister, Agi, made good use of, to try to persuade us to follow these dreadful instructions. Frau Doctor had done her work well, by telling Agi that it would be the best present that we could give to our mother, whose birthday was coming up shortly. After a lot of tears and moans, we agreed, but settled for 'Mother' as the correct name, and in order to establish some independence and freedom from Frau Doctor's dominance. So my mother became English and, in some strange fashion, slightly more remote from me through the change of name.

On the very last day of Heathcot, I went into every nook and cranny that I could manage, clutching my dolls to me in pain and deprivation. My sisters were not there, Leezy had moved to Newtondee already, to board with her friend, Celia, so that she could finish the school year in St John's School. My sister, Agi, had left for boarding school. We all knew that once a staff child turned ten years old, they would go away to school. This was because we were getting ahead of the ill children and needed a different approach from the curative education that imbued Camphill. The school chosen by the co-workers for their children was a Waldorf school called Wynstones, a good school, but far away in Gloucestershire. It had a hostel for those who required boarding facilities, but because Camphill was not appreciated by everyone, the staff children needed a place in which to live. Dr König's approach to the philosophy of Rudolf Steiner was not the usual one, and the rest of the Anthroposophical Society shunned him, finding him not to their taste. So he looked for, and found a manor house across the River Severn, which Mrs König took on to run as a hostel for the Camphill staff children. My sister Agi was one of the first batch of children to live there during the term time. She would come home for holidays, wearing a uniform, her hair cut short so that she could manage it by herself, with great stories of the fun they had and the soft gentle climate of the West Country. I longed to go to that school too, but I was too young. Being only nine years old, I would have to wait a further year.

My sister Leezy was going to live with her best friend, Celia, in Newtondee. Although she had passed the magic age to go away to school, she was extremely shy and vulnerable when away from the security of the family and Camphill. Moreover, her teacher, Friedwart, was so good and stable that she begged to stay on in St John's School. Agi's teacher had changed twice and this was probably why she was happy to board. So Leezy was allowed to stay on and had a good home to live in.

It was October, the dark winter of Scotland just beginning. My parents were going ahead of us to Botton village in Yorkshire, a place that I had read about in *The Secret Garden*, a book that I loved very much. Maybe Yorkshire would be all right, even if it was in England. But I was not going to go there until the Christmas holidays. I was going to board with Erika in Camphill House. I liked her but was not so sure about living with her. She had no family, was a single woman, and had a very, very German accent. Would she try to educate me like so many other people had done? Would she tell me stories at night? I ran down the beech path, looking at the rabbit holes that were empty and dry, and felt just as empty and abandoned.

Dr König, that great little man, had betrayed me. My life was ruined and I was very, very afraid. Now, hearing my mother call me, I walked back to the house, looked at it long and fiercely, and tried to fix it so strongly in my memory that no matter what would happen, I would be able to reconstruct it the moment I wanted to.

I can see now, as an adult, that giving up Heathcot was a sensible thing to do. It was in fact not a sound house, and would have needed an enormous amount of work and money to make into a home free from damp. It had served its purpose. All the other communities were on the other side of the river. New places were being started in England, such as Botton Hall, Thornbury Park and the Sheiling School. Strength and commitment would have been needed to keep Heathcot going, as well as money and co-workers. Glencraig, in Ireland, had started and there was talk of a community in America. How much could this remarkable group of pioneers carry? It was hard for me to accept and to find some understanding for the loss of Heathcot. I was too young to appreciate these aspects, but it had to happen to help the growth of the Camphill Movement.

The old Bedford Dormobile stood in front of the porch. We were piled into it with a suitcase for me and things for my parents. It drove to Camphill House and I was left alone there after a couple of days. My parents, with all our luggage, left for England. I sat on my bed in the room that I would share for the next three months, a screen dividing me from Erika's bed, and tried not to cry. Sally, the nurse at Camphill House, came to invite me out of my retreat, and I began a different life, meeting challenges and experiences all by myself, without the strength that our close-knit family had given to me for the first nine years of my life.

Chapter V
ABANDONMENT

Camphill House was to be my home for the next three months. The glass front doors were narrow and usually only one stood open, making it a serious threshold to cross, especially if someone was entering as you were exiting. One person always had to wait for the other. No one could rush in and out, shouting lustily, as we had done at home in Heathcot House. One entered Camphill House decorously. The very small entrance had two doors on either side; one went into a cloakroom, the other a sort of office. Then a mahogany door led into the actual hall. The smell of that space haunts me, not because it was unpleasant but because it was so distinctive – a mixture of wax polish and lino flooring and cooked cabbage is the best way to describe it. I caught that aroma later on at another time in my life, and it instantly brought back the hard lump of homesickness that now formed at the back of my throat.

The hallway led to many rooms, the library on the right with its grand mahogany door, as were all the doors in the house, and a dormitory lay beyond the dark wood directly opposite the front door. On the left, a beautiful staircase rose up and turned sharply to the right to open onto another hallway above. From this great landing, doors went off at every angle, leading to dormitories and Dr König's special wing over the kitchen. The banisters of those stairs invited sliding down. In Heathcot, the green nursery staircase had been our haunt on rainy days. You could walk up the outside of the stairs, dangerously treading between the bars and holding deliciously tightly to the banister rail, to climb over at the top, looking down for the deepest thrill, and then sliding at maximum speed all the way down, round the bend at the landing and reaching the bottom with a huge screeching grip of the hands so as not to fall off. The bravest went the fastest and only braked at the last second. I always had to brake early, to be jeered at by everybody except Pauly, who never teased me.

The stairs in Camphill House had broad rails and a very broad banister and the incline was less steep, so you could not rush down quite as fast, even if you would have wanted to. But I had no one to play this game with and, moreover, I instinctively guessed that in the house where Dr König lived, this delightful pastime would not be met with approval. I never slid down them, only looked and regretted.

The dining room was smaller than Heathcot's, but just as many people ate there. The meals were quiet and unexciting. The scullery divided the dining room from the kitchen and smelled as every scullery smells, of old food and faintly of vomit. The kitchen was a lovely room – not down in the basement as I was used to, but looking out over the River Dee, which ran slowly and comfortingly in its accustomed bed.

I was now going to sleep in a strange bed and be cared for by someone whom I did not yet know very well. Why my mother chose her, I do not know, but maybe it was because she offered to help out. I had nothing against Erika, but I did not know her and therefore felt very apprehensive and insecure about the whole thing. However, children did as their parents told them and I had always been obedient to my mother because she had never been unfair or untrustworthy. She was always there for me, even when she had to go to meetings, because I always knew where she was, and this gave me great confidence. Now I could not imagine where she had gone, could not picture the Yorkshire moors and could not see in my mind's eye the rooms and passages and gardens that were Botton Hall in England. My parents had gone to somewhere unimaginable to my untravelled frame of mind.

I thought about the ill children in their dormitories, parted from their parents for months at a time. Co-workers often shared a room, either with another co-worker, or slept in the dormitories with their children. This was because there was so little space and also because it meant that the children were properly cared for. Many of them were epileptic and needed night care. Some were so restless that they would not stay in their beds. Others had never learned to sleep properly. Sometimes the dormitory parent slept with the bed up against the child's bed for reassurance and security.

Now I was going to experience living with a co-worker. My bed had a screen around it, and at night Erika left a bedside lamp burning because she went to bed so much later than I did and did not want to disturb me. I would get used to sleeping, the light shining through the mauve-pink curtains and flickering weirdly. Erika would come in to undress, her shadow moving gently. She always left on her bra, pulling her nightdress over it. I found this odd, wondering if it could be very comfortable. (I had rarely seen a bra, only when watching a nursing mother would I catch a glimpse of the white cotton, carefully tucked under the sensible cotton blouse.) She would unfasten her hair from its bun at the nape of her neck and brush it. I wondered about that too. I went to sleep with my hair plaited to prevent the collection of knots that would otherwise cause me pain in the morning. Finally, she would get into her bed and sleep, her breath softly snoring in a gentle rhythm.

Told to go to bed on that first night, I took off my clothes and looked at my underwear. Not finding a laundry basket in which to put them, I carefully folded them and laid them on the chair by my bed. I washed my hands and face and lay under the eiderdown, wondering if I would have a bath on Saturday, as was my custom. I missed my mother dreadfully and lay there waiting for a story. Erika came in with a lighted candle and told me to sit up and say my prayers, which I did, the hard lump forming more firmly in my throat. No bedtime story ever arrived, but I learned to read my own, finding books on the shelf in Sally's room. It was my introduction to Enid Blyton.

In the morning, I woke to discover that I had wet my bed. Girls of nine years old did not wet their beds. Unable to tell Erika, I got dressed in yesterday's clothes and carefully made my bed, hoping that she would deal with the sheets. She did nothing, and that night I went to bed in the damp sheets, feeling lost and afraid. Had she not smelled the sour smell? On and off throughout my time in Camphill House, I wet the bed, and never did she seem to notice. The sheets were changed every week, but never in between.

The hard lump was there to stay. It lifted a little when I accompanied Sally on her nursing rounds. She let me watch her administer the medicines and took me with her on her visits to the dispensary. This wooden hut was ruled by Schwester Juliana, a stately lady with iron-grey hair rolled tightly in a bun. Whenever I thought of nuns, I remembered Schwester Juliana, in her mauve-pink long dress and starched white apron, with the stiff long cotton headdress over her scraped-back hair. She had a kindly smile and allowed me to sit on a high stool and see how the medicines were made. The room was scented with herbs and extracts and tinctures. She would grind things up with a pestle and mortar and pour the contents into brown bottles, carefully labelled with exotic names that I could not read. Then she gave these potions to Sally.

Sally was my lifeline and her kindness sustained me. Dr König too proved to be kind and made me feel a little less lonely. He lived in Camphill House, being privileged to have two very small rooms, one his bedroom and one his library. Alix, who was his secretary, also lived in the house. Frau Doctor and the children lived in The Grange, in Gloucestershire, and rarely came up to Scotland. Dr König afforded me one of the few pleasures of those months. I was allowed to bring him his breakfast. This did not happen every day, because he often travelled, leaving the house in his black suit with his black hat perched on his large bald head, followed by Alix, elegant as always in a long grey mackintosh, her black hair rolled in a sausage at the nape of her neck. They drove off in his black doctor's Austin, driven by Alix or Thomas Weihs.

Most of the ladies wore their hair in buns, a sensible solution because long hair worn loose would have got in their way. They wore tweed skirts or woollen gathered pinafores and white cotton blouses with puffy long sleeves. Woollen stockings and sensible laced up shoes adorned their legs and feet. The men mostly wore corduroy trousers and knitted jerseys, and suits on Saturday nights and Sundays. The colours were grey or brown and very, very conventional. In all this sombreness, beautiful jewellery was worn by the ladies. Apparently Dr König approved of this journey into finery. He said that adornment made one human and a step above the animal, which does not decorate. Brooches of coloured gemstones were extremely popular, and I loved to look at the different shapes and settings that people wore pinned at the throat of their severe white blouses. Nobody ever wore artificial stones or costume jewellery. Everything was real: gems, silver, and gold. Necklaces too were quite common, usually a pendant, again from cut crystals, or gemstones. The green of emerald, the purple of amethyst and the pale yellow of the cairngorm were beautiful to behold.

Pearls were not worn, being said to bring bad luck. My mother had a lovely delicate very antique pearl necklace, the tiny seed pearls strung in a lacy pattern. She used to wear it sometimes, but she said she did not like to do so very often because she had worn it on the night my father had his accident and it made her superstitious. One day, a child who was visiting our nursery upstairs in Heathcot tore it off her neck. The pearls scattered and fell between the gaps in the floorboards. They could not be recovered. I used to think that one day, when someone in the future dug up the remains of Heathcot, they might find these tiny treasures and wonder who had brought seed pearls to Scotland so many years ago.

Rings, necklaces and brooches were to be seen on the ladies of Camphill, but earrings and bracelets were rarely displayed. Many of the women had little holes in their ears, but they remained empty. My mother had pierced ears, but she said that earrings were barbaric and only pagan heathens wore them. My father said that you might as well wear beautiful golden neckbands as did a tribe in Africa, who stretched their women's necks by adding a ring every year. They considered this beauty. But, he used to say, as punishment for wrongdoing, the rings would be removed and then the neck would hang down and suffocate the victim. This horrified me. Why, I asked, would people do things like that to make their women beautiful? Did it not hurt them? Ah, answered my father with a twinkle, women have always suffered in the service of beauty. Did not the Chinese bind the feet of babies to keep them small forever? They tottered about as elegant adults on tiny, tiny feet. And surely it hurt them very much. But, he continued, look at the high heels and tight clothes that fashionable women wore today in the West. Weren't they also uncomfortable?

So, he concluded, women will go through great discomfort to look beautiful! I found this flawed logic, but could never quite work out where he went wrong in his argument.

But Dr König approved of jewellery and so I could admire the wonderful variety. He himself was always dressed in a suit and I do not remember ever seeing him in his shirtsleeves, or in any state of disarray. I used to hang around the kitchen when he was at home, hoping to take him his breakfast. This was a real treat. A tray was laid with a white napkin, and a plate and egg cup. When all was ready, I carefully carried the tray up the narrow stairs to his rooms, squeezing past the bookshelves that lined the walls, making a long narrow barrier down the middle of the floor, Alix hovering in the background for fear of accidents. Once the tray was placed before him, Dr König would shake out his white napkin and tuck it into his waistcoat. Then he would hand me the knife. Taking careful aim, I sliced off the top of his egg, whereupon he smiled and I left his presence, satisfied.

An epidemic of chicken pox struck almost everyone down. In those days, this was a serious illness, and children and grown-ups alike suffered, lying in bed with the distinctive golden blisters on their skin. Having succumbed as a very young baby, I was immune. Apparently, I had had about three spots, whilst my sisters were covered with blisters and sores, which I envied mightily. Leezy had a few scars as proof, which she loved to show us when we compared tales of suffering. I lost out on that front, having only the barbed wire marks of which to boast about. Sally enlisted me to help her with the nursing, because there were so few people still up and about, and because I was often tagging along behind her.

I remember sitting beside a sick child and holding the thermometer so that he would not loosen it from under his arm. It fascinated me, this business of taking someone's temperature. Depending on the state of the child, the glass rod was placed in the mouth (for staff and staff children), in the bottom (for the very ill children) and under the arm for those with a middling disability. I was not allowed to help when the thermometer was used rectally or orally, only when under the arm. I carried trays of food to those on the mend, helping those who needed me by staying with them and chatting whilst they ate. I helped making the beds, and loved dusting the room, whilst Sally swept and made everything cosy and comfortable. Washing the easier children with a face cloth and wiping them tenderly with a towel was nice to do and gave me a warm feeling inside. I told stories to those who could speak, making them up as I went along, feeling grown up and powerfully in charge. I carried buckets for those who needed to vomit. This was awful because I invariably wanted to join in, heaving and retching as I carried the bucket downstairs again to be emptied and washed. During those wonderful days, the hard lump melted and I forgot to be homesick.

Nowadays, giving such responsibility to a nine-year-old child would be considered madness, but I loved it. I loved being needed, feeling that in this crisis I was no longer an unwanted staff child but a reliable member of Camphill House. However, people recovered and life went back to normal, the hard lump in my throat returning to choke me again. I retreated to the swing, under the tall and beautiful exotic trees that grew on the once gracious lawn, to swing and swing and swing until I touched the sky, singing softly under my breath and forgetting my loneliness in flight.

School was a boon. I went every weekday, meeting my friends again and loving the lessons that were taught. Ella had gone, replaced by her sister, Nora. Their voices and manner were so alike that I hardly noticed the exchange and went on learning as much as I could with my usual enthusiasm. But outside school hours I had no one to play with. My friends went home to their various houses in the rambling country estates of Newtondee and Murtle, and no one thought to take me over to visit them. So I wandered about and swung on the swing, or followed Sally like a lost puppy.

Because I was lonely, I began to visit the dormitories. I cannot remember who the children were or who their dormitory parents were either, but I do remember that there were very few people in wheelchairs and very few children who could speak. I started to help the dormitory parents, washing, dressing and feeding the children, like a little grown-up. To be allowed to do this was a great kindness shown to me by the co-workers and lifted the lump just a little bit. But I did not feel that the children were my friends; they were strangers, and not the people that I had grown up with.

The young co-workers have become a faceless, nameless stream of enthusiastic Germans in my memory. People came and went, some nice, some not so nice. I remember their clothes as being colourful and flowing. The girls wore dresses or skirts, long and gathered. Some wore a dirndl, the Austrian national dress, very attractive and feminine. I loved to watch them walk, their hips swaying slightly. I wished I could look like them, but in my dirndl with the tubby shape that I had acquired this seemed hard to do. They wore sandals, or sensible lace-up shoes. None of them wore trousers or jeans, except on excursions. For such occasions, even the older co-workers appeared in their flannels, or corduroys, with windcheaters, usually pale blue or grey gaberdine. The few young men who came to Camphill were often shy and remain in the background of my memory.

One dormitory sticks out, however. I used to love going upstairs to the room that looked out over the river. Here there was warmth and homeliness. The beds were always properly made, the woven heather-blue covers spread tidily, and the rug in the centre with a table on it always seemed to invite me to sit down. There was a vase of flowers of the season placed in the centre of the table, and around this I and the children drew pictures and played games like dominoes or ludo. The dormitory parent, a pretty girl with longish soft brown hair that she wore in plaits and wound round her head, had a soft voice and held my hand kindly when I accompanied her on walks with the children. The atmosphere reminded me, in the nicest way, of my own nursery in Heathcot and it warmed the coldness around my heart. I wish I could remember her name and thank her for her friendship! She had some very wild boys in her group, but she never shouted at them or seemed flustered and disorderly. She placidly picked up chairs and set things right again after a stormy scene.

My teeth now began to hurt me, so Erika sent me to the dentist. This was a disaster. When only five years old, I had attended the dentist for the first time. He found it necessary to extract a tooth. I sat in the leather chair, sliding a little and probably squirming a lot, whilst he poked and prodded my gums and teeth. I do not remember much very clearly, but I remember the rubber mask over my face, my mother's hand holding me tightly and the extraordinary sweet sickly smell of the gas. I remember hearing someone giggling hysterically in a very high voice and the feeling of being dragged forwards and held down, both at the same time. Then I was violently sick into a bucket and screamed most awfully and furiously whilst doing so. We went home in the stinking Dormobile, and I continued being sick most of the way. In my mouth there was a bloody gap where a back tooth had been before. This was exciting to show to Pauly the next day when I felt better. Forever after, to this day, when I taste a rum toffee, the taste and smell of the gas comes back to me.

Erika told me where I could get the bus and gave me a shilling for the fare and sent me off. Since the infamous tooth pulling, I had been to the dentist once or twice with my mother, who sat beside me and held my hand whilst the drill ground its noisy slow way into the tooth and the filling tasted of hot spicey cloves. Needless to say, it was never a pain-free experience, but afterwards, the dentist would give us a shiny new penny, with which we went out and bought sweets!

The dentist had a big black dog, of which I was mortally afraid. Now I walked up Pitangulley's Brae and crossed the road to catch the bus. It was the Bluebird bus, not my friendly red Strachan bus of the South Deeside road. I sat on the seat, my legs dangling uncomfortably, the plush covers irritating and rubbing my bare thighs. I thought of the black dog. When you rang the doorbell, it barked fiercely and the nurse in her white coat opened the door, holding the monster firmly by the collar. I was very scared of dogs and would cross the road rather than pass one by.

The dental surgery was one of many grey granite town houses built in a square. On leaving the surgery, I always got lost, having to walk right round the square before I could find the road again, but I could always arrive safely, unfortunately. Trembling, I attended this torture, without complaint, every week for what seemed the whole of my stay with Erika. The waiting room was dark, and filled with large armchairs in which I felt lost and smothered, and very intimidated. There were shiny magazines to read and I loved the *Illustrated London News*. Sometimes there were pictures of the royal family, sometimes of wars and disasters, often reports on the aftermath of the Second World War. I looked at the pictures and trembled, feeling ever so slightly sick and cold. Then I was called in to sit upright and rigid in the leather seat, and my mouth was dragged open till I thought it would split. The dentist pumped the drill with his foot, I think. Anyway, it ground slowly and gratingly into my tooth and smelled like burning bones. He drilled and filled every one of my back teeth, and today I wonder if this was strictly necessary, or if the man knew that a child cannot judge and so used me to earn his fee. I dreaded the bus ride and still do not like to travel in this manner.

When I got back to Camphill House, I used the swing and its height as a way of escape. However, in any other context, heights became a problem for me. I found to my shame that I could no longer climb trees without fear. I would get as far as a few branches up and then freeze, fearing to look down and knowing that there was no one who might rescue me. I stopped that game and was glad that Pauly was not there to witness my cowardice. He had left with his family for England and I missed his warm giggle desperately. Mostly, I tried not to think too much about him. My safe childhood was falling away from me so fast that I could not really keep up. I wanted to cry but the lump in my throat prevented the tears. Though Erika was never unkind, she was also never aware of my real needs. She expected me to be independent, to be normal and capable, and I felt that though perhaps I should be all that and more, I really only wanted my parents and my friend Pauly and could not at this point in time have either. The co-workers around me did their best, I am sure, because I do not remember active unkindness; but the absolute assurance of understanding was lacking and I did not even try to tell anyone what I felt because I knew it to be hopeless.

I tried hard to remember things that had pleased me, but I could only think of the Vienna Boys' Choir when they came to Aberdeen and my mother and father took us to hear them sing. They stood in rows, their faces scrubbed and their hair as neat as could be, in their white shirts and loden suits with stag's horn buttons. They sang like a choir of angels and I was entranced. Sometimes, when we had a Sunday afternoon concert, their voices would sound again in the lieder that a co-worker sung, often accompanied by the lyre.

During that winter in Camphill, there must have been the usual festivals but I do not remember them at all. The days simply passed by, each one bringing me the hope that this was the day my mother would come to fetch me, and not daring to ask if this were so. No one seemed to feel the need to tell me when she actually *would* come; I just existed from day to day in a quiet and hopeless state of expectation that was never satisfied.

One day, without warning, my father came to visit. He had come to collect some things of ours that still had not arrived in Botton. I suppose my mother wrote to tell me, but I do not remember, nor do I remember any telephone calls. The phone was very expensive and was not used for chatting, only for business. So my father suddenly arrived, his eyes twinkling, the familiar smell of his Three Nuns tobacco bringing the hard lump right up to the surface. Because I knew that he would not cope, I did not let it dissolve into tears, but they were very near the surface all the time of his short stay. He took me to see my sister Leezy in Newtondee. We went up Pitangulley's Brae and he told me why it had such a funny name.

He said that in the olden days, halfway up the hill that we were climbing to catch the bus, was a pit filled with lime. At the top of the hill was the gallows tree. Here robbers and thieves were hanged by their necks and danced the Tyburn Jig. I wondered what that was and why anyone would want to dance whilst dying. After they were dead, he said, their bodies were flung into the pit and covered with the lime, making them all white in my horrified imagination. That was why it was called 'pit and gallows brae' which became Pitangulley's Brae in the vernacular of Milltimber.

We caught the bus and got out at the roadside cottage and walked to Newtondee Lodge where Leezy lived with Celia and her family. We had such a lovely time, and the hard lump stayed away for a few hours. I asked Leezy if she might visit me, but she said that she did not like Camphill House. So that was that. It never occurred to me to ask whether I could visit her. This would mean going on the bus alone and I was so afraid of that, perhaps because of the dreaded dental visits.

After my father had left again the drabness descended once more. I wondered if my mother would ever fetch me, and the days passed very slowly indeed. I had seen how happy Leezy was. She had a story every night in bed, and proper meals together with Celia. They went down to the river to play. Her hair was plaited in the right way, with the plaits just behind her ear. My plaits began in front of my ears. I had not learned to do my hair by myself, and Erika impatiently sorted it out for me, sometimes before, sometimes after breakfast. I always felt ashamed to go to morning prayer unkempt. I envied my sister very much and the loneliness got deeper and more melancholic.

The day came when I was invited to spend the weekend with my godmother, Thesi. I was very excited and looked forward to being in a proper family again. She lived in the roadside cottage with Alex, her husband and her three children, Christofer, Angela, and Hans. I did not really know the two boys, and Angela, pronounced with a hard 'g', had never been part of our gang in Heathcot. We found her alien and did not let her join us. Now I wanted to love them, and hoped that they might adopt me, in case my mother really forgot to fetch me.

The longed-for bonding was not to be. The boys were loud and teased me, and Thesi always had a cigarette in her hand or mouth so that she smelled smoky and I could not get near her. Alex did not talk very much and Angela smiled shyly at me. I had to sleep in a bed squashed up near hers and the door was left open so that the light shone in onto my face at night. The room smelled of cigarette smoke and unmade beds and the window was always closed. At night, as a treat, we each got a piece of chocolate, black and bitter. It made me very thirsty.

The worst part of that terrible weekend was Saturday supper. We ate together with the big boys and had apple purée with bits of core floating in it. I could not force it past the hard lump that was by now my permanent companion and found myself vomiting all over the table. The undigested food shot out of my mouth in a great arc. I had the most awful shooting pains in my head. With hindsight, I recognise that I must have had a migraine. I often had headaches and stomach aches as a child.

Back in Camphill House once more, I was grateful for Erika's unintentional neglect. At least I could do what I liked and have fresh air around me. I used to walk down to the river by myself and sit on the bank, not daring to paddle because the flow was too fast at the bend below the house, and dream of Heathcot, now reduced to its foundations, with mushrooms growing in the cellars that had seen so much fun and games. I dreamed it still stood and that at any minute my father would call me to come home, and hold my hand in his callused palm as we walked from garden to home and supper upstairs with only the family.

I wondered how my sister, Agi, could bear to be away from home for a whole term at a time. She loved her school at Wynstones and did not appear to be homesick at all. But she was so much older, all of four years, and she had Sally and Rosie and Christine to keep her company, just as Leezy had Celia. I had lost my companion and did not believe that I could ever find such a friend as Pauly again.

I began to have very unpleasant memories, which sometimes gave me nightmares. When I wanted to think about Heathcot, I saw the little body and large head of James Embleton, screaming with fear and perhaps pain whilst an inexperienced dormitory parent picked him up without supporting his head. I thought his neck would break and ran to hold it up, only to be told off for getting in the way.

I saw a co-worker hitting one of the more difficult children on his bare bottom with a hairbrush. I saw it through the window one Saturday afternoon when he was just out of his bath and was dancing around naked in his room. He too was screaming and jumping up and down. I was so angry that I ran to my mother and told her. She said I should be quiet, but her face was very, very stern and red spots appeared on her cheeks, so that I knew she was angry too. This gave me great satisfaction. The co-worker, needless to say, left rather suddenly.

The long and arduous meals in Heathcot dining room came back to haunt me. Sometimes, whilst talking to another grown-up, the co-worker would put spoonful after spoonful into the child's mouth until they almost choked and the food spilled out, only to be spooned up again and shoved right back in. It made me want to vomit to see the poor child having to eat half-digested, overcooked cabbage. Sometimes I protested loudly, criticising this lack of proper care, and then I was sent out for being rude to a grown-up. I found this very unfair and unjust. Sometimes, children were forced to eat, even when it was clear that they were either full, or did not like the food at all. I swore that when I would have children I would never do this, and I am happy to say that I have kept this promise.

Mealtimes in Camphill House were equally long and protracted affairs. I sat quietly, behaving myself and choking down food that tasted dull and unrewarding in the absence of my mother. For breakfast we ate porridge. This was something that I hated, especially when it was wheaten. The husks never got soft and they stuck in my throat, next to the lump of misery that was now a familiar companion, and would not go down, making me cough and retch. Moreover, the lumps of porridge were horrible to chew. The oats or wheat that burst out of them were dry and bitter. There was always either too much or too little salt in it. I tried to push the lumps onto the edge of my plate. At home in Heathcot, when the porridge was lumpy, we were allowed to fish them out. But now I had to eat them all up!

Probably because of the lack of money, nice things were always scarce. When we had hard-boiled eggs in a curry sauce (which I hated for its spicy taste), we only got half an egg per person, heavily covered in the inevitable milky white sauce, and coloured yellow with curry powder tasting vaguely like sulphur. The rice was sticky and tasteless. We had lumpy semolina, a fruit pudding thickened with cornflour and tasting faintly of redcurrants which was called *Rote Grütze*, and this was perhaps my least favourite. It refused to slide down, whatever I did to make it disappear. I loved potatoes, in any shape or form, but we ate them only rarely. On Saturdays we had soup, which in my memory seemed to contain all the leftovers of the week! We did not have meat very often and the fat and gristle were impossible to swallow. I was allowed, thank God, to leave this at the side of my plate. I missed the grown-up suppers terribly and I missed my mother's cooking.

One of my best memories of our family holidays is the food that we were able to enjoy. We watched our mother standing over the stove and preparing semolina pudding that tasted like heaven. She would whisk the milk whilst it boiled up and then she dusted the semolina grains into the hot liquid, whisking briskly all the time. Then, whilst it gently bubbled and simmered, she vigorously stirred it so that when we came to eat it, with cinnamon sugar sprinkled over it, there was absolutely no skin and it tasted creamy and pure. She made mashed potatoes with warm milk and butter floating on top. The meat was tender and without any fat on it. My father would make the porridge for breakfast, which for once I could eat and enjoy, not a lump to be found in it, and sometimes covered with black treacle. We had fresh lettuce and fresh fruit for pudding, sometimes even a whole orange each!

The only thing about the food on holiday that I could complain about was in connection with eggs. I had an absolute passion for soft-boiled eggs, and I wanted to eat more than one. But my mother said eggs were bad for you and you only needed one a week. So that was that. I wanted to eat the egg all by itself, but she said we had to eat it with bread, one bite of bread, one bite of egg. And that was that, too. As a result, I cannot eat egg without bread, and I never put salt on it! This was another thing to be taken in measure. Too much salt was not good and there should be enough of it in the food from the cooking, she always said. This was true when my mother cooked but not always so when other people prepared our food. But you would not have found salt and pepper on the dining-room table in those early years of Camphill.

Because of the fact that so many children could not eat properly by themselves, very often at the end of the meal, when we all took hands round the table to bless what we had eaten, the co-workers took the ill children by the wrist as we all said, 'Blessing on the meal.' At the beginning, after grace, this was said too, but the hands were clean because it was a rule to wash them before collecting quietly outside the dining room door to enter only when peace had been established. Sitting safely beside my mother at home in Heathcot House, I watched the little indignity of having the wrist shaken firmly, and was glad that I always had my mother's hand to hold. Now, in Camphill House, I found quite often that my wrist was taken. It was humiliating and galling, both at the same time. I felt what perhaps some of the ill children might have felt, and like them, was unable to say anything in protest. My self-esteem shrank every time this happened.

But I loved the little silences that went with the mealtimes and I loved the graces that were said. Partly it was the security of the ritual, partly it was because they were mysterious and did not always make sense to me. The words were clear but the meaning obscure.

> The bread is not our food.
> What feeds us in the bread,
> Is God's eternal word,
> Is spirit and is life.

This was the grace most commonly said. I wondered why it said that the bread was not our food? We ate it, it was comforting and filled me up, so why was it not our food? How could God's eternal word be our food? I had never heard Him speak, so I could not really answer this question at all. But I liked to think about this astonishing riddle. The Sunday grace was longer and more majestic:

> The plant seeds are quickening in the night of the earth;
> The green herbs are sprouting in the might of the air;
> All fruit is ripening in the power of the sun.
> So quickens the soul in the shrine of the heart;
> So blossoms spirit power in the light of the world;
> Thus ripens man's strength in the glory of God.

I loved the simplicity and the glory of that grace but could not understand any of its meaning. I thought that this was quite right and good. It was just like the Bible, holy and mystifying. I wondered if the ill children understood what was said, but I doubted it because there was so much that they could not understand and which they accepted without complaint, like the boy who could write with a pencil between his toes and the co-workers would stop him, saying that he was not allowed to do this because he would not learn to write properly with his hands. I found this not only unfair but also intolerable, and complained loudly and vociferously to my mother about it. She only told me not to fuss.

I wished, in those miserable days in Camphill House, that we were a normal family, living in a house in a street and going to a normal school with normal children. I wanted my mother and my father and a little cosy house with no other people in it. School was also becoming a part of my nightmare. I was getting bored. The lessons were going too slowly and I was spending more and more time outside the classroom, no longer allowed to take my book with me. I had lost my old teacher, who left to get married, and Nora was less tolerant of my interruptions than had been her sister, Ella.

I shared a desk with a girl called Judith Cohen. We shared more than a desk; we also shared a guilty secret. Judith had black straight soft hair and a white-skinned complexion. She was beautiful and could sing with the voice of an angel. But she could not say a word and did not vocalise other than in a singing hum. Sometimes, when bored with the slow stories, I would take her hand, spread the fingers out on the desktop and press my thumbnail on the quick of her fingernails, one by one, watching her face as she opened her eyes wide with pain, the tears starting. But she never uttered a sound, and so no one ever knew how I tortured her. I did this for two reasons. Because it gave me a sense of power and because she used to wet herself. The urine ran down the middle of the bench that we shared and wet my knickers too. I hated her for it and wanted to dominate. After some time, I began to feel sick when sitting next to her. I wanted to stop this awful game but did not know how. I was trapped in my own cruelty and just wanted to go home and have my mother put everything right. My world was all wrong.

Then one day, I do not know how, I became aware of my strength. I became conscious of a feeling of the control that power can give and I knew that I could no longer hurt anyone. I knew that if one has the power to do evil, one also has the power to do good. This was a hugely overwhelming recognition and it did not come as a thought, but as an experience. At last I was able to stop. I loved Judith with a fervour that could not be explained and I no longer minded the warm wetness that spread out into my clothing during the lessons.

I found reading from the blackboard a problem. I wanted to sit in the front row of desks because then it was easier, but Nora told me not to fuss. When I said I could not read what she had written, she just told me to try harder. I attempted to explain that though I could read it, I could not see the writing properly. Again, she told me not to fuss, and did not move me to the front row. It never occurred to either of us that perhaps my eyesight was at fault. But I often wondered about the paintings that I loved to sit and look at in the big books in the library of Camphill House. Here painters painted trees with tiny leaves on them, each one exquisitely formed, and yet the landscape was seen from a great distance. To me, trees were green, differentiated only by their various shades. Singling out leaves one by one had to be done close up. I loved to touch things, using my hands to extend what my eyes only saw in larger outline. I did not tell this to anyone because I had no knowledge of any other way than the way that I saw the world, and no one ever questioned my clumsiness, thinking that when they pointed out individual stars, which I could not see, that I was simply not concentrating, or looking in the wrong direction.

I began bitterly to resent the feeling that being a staff child seemed to mean being a second-class citizen. The ill children got everything, the front desks in school, the care and concern, the attention and the time, all of which I felt I needed too. I was only a child and without my parents, and I wanted someone to notice me and love me. I also wanted someone to love, but Erika was too remote, Sally hardly ever had the time and my sister Leezy seemed to have forgotten about me. I didn't even have anyone to be naughty with! I remembered the go-carts that we had made and now understood why the grown-ups were so angry. We had taken the mobility away from the wheelchair children. I was secretly glad that we had done it, and at the same time felt guilty for doing it.

Even those people whom I admired had shown their feet of clay. I thought about Renate who, shortly before we left Heathcot, met me at the door when coming in from playing, grabbed me by my plaits and pulled them sharply, making my eyes water fiercely. She shouted at me for having given Hans Georg the knife and now he had seriously cut himself. I looked at her in bewilderment. What knife? I had simply been playing out on my swing. She called me a liar, and I could not make her believe that I was innocent of hurting him. He must have told her that I did it, because he was too afraid to confess to having taken a sharp kitchen knife with which to whittle. Co-workers often disbelieved us staff children. We were indeed naughty, but I, at least, rarely told a lie. My mother had explained that with every untruth, my heart would gain a black spot. As I did not like this thought, I took care to tell the truth as much as I could.

I began to worry that I would never see her again. Many of my friends lived with one or no parent. Divorce happened in Camphill as much as anywhere else, and some staff children had to live in dormitories because their parents could not care for them, or they lived between two parents, not knowing where was home. With the end of Heathcot, was this going to happen to me too? Would I end my days sharing a room with Erika? I told no one of my fears, just dreamt horrible dreams and woke up in the dark, the tears wetting my pillow, to lie uncomfortably in my wet sheets and wait for the morning and another lonely, dreary day.

Living in Camphill House meant that to go anywhere I either had to brave Pitangulley's Brae with its historic and invisible but all too vivid gallows and limepit, or go down the front drive to the bottom where my father had had his accident. I was afraid of that spot, terrified that another lorry might come and run me over too. The lane wound its way up a steep hill to the North Deeside road, running under the railway bridge. We used to walk there with my father when I was very small and still living in Camphill Lodge, and I remember that we believed that when passing under it, if you uttered a sound, it might fall on your head! This superstition particularly terrified my sister Leezy, who was mortally afraid that my father, being unaware of this fact, might start talking! I too, was deathly afraid that it might really and truly fall down. I suppose the idea came from the fact that one's voice echoes under bridges. These two serious hurdles haunted me all the time that I lived in Camphill House.

And then my mother came to collect me. I don't know where I had been but I came down the little slope of the drive towards Camphill House and there stood a large vehicle. It could have been a taxi, it could have been the Dormobile, but I remember it as a coach. Out of this stepped a very small woman, her stiff leg protruding through the door, uncomfortably feeling for the ground. I saw the laced up brown sensible shoe on its foot. I was instantly amazed at her smallness, her fair hair in a bun and her tweed pinafore dress just as I had remembered it. But I had not known how small she actually was.

As I began to run to her with huge anticipation, as if in a dream of fulfilment, I heard the sound of my mother's footsteps as she used to skip down the stairs beside our nursery in Heathcot, *da–de–da*, *da–de–da*, *da–de–da*, to answer the telephone at the bottom. I saw the telephone exchange in the treatment room, the black covers over the white disks with numbers on them falling down in rhythm like blinking eyelids to the ring of the bell. I flew faster and landed in her arms. The great hard lump in my throat finally dissolved into a mighty sob and I howled out my joy and relief. Over my head loomed the severe, scraped-back hair of Erika, asking me if this was how I saw fit to welcome my mother. I cried all the more. My mother told her to leave me, they were only tears of joy. Oh, the relief and light that filled me. Now I knew I was once more where I was meant to be, safe in my mother's embrace, embedded in the certainty of her voice and body.

How could I explain all this to Erika, who had truly tried her best to care for me? I knew she could not be expected to understand. After all, she had no children of her own. The best part of me forgave her instantly. What was there to hold against her, now that my mother had come? Everything would be quite all right from now on, and I could well afford to like Erika just a little bit.

I showed my mother the room that I had slept in, the swing, the classroom, the dormitories and tried to talk as fast as possible in order to fit everything in. I was terribly excited and quite hysterical. She took me for a walk to the river to calm me down. I did not tell her about the dentist and the black dog. Even though she was my mother, some things had to be kept secret.

We left Camphill and Scotland by train and travelled down to England, to our new home. I watched for the changing colour of the cows and houses and tried to look forward, rather than regret my leaving the country of my birth. I did not want to remember it, it was so mixed up with colour, light, festivities and pain, and so I allowed myself to forget a huge amount of it.

Top: My father. Student at Berlin University, 1933.
Bottom: My mother. In Vienna, still called Sali, 1938.

Top: My maternal grandmother and my mother's brother, Moritz at Pilgramshain, 1930.
Bottom: Hertha Sielmann and my father in Berlin.

Top: Dr Karl König.
Bottom: Murtle House.

Top: At my christening on Heathcot steps. Elizabeth, my mother, Agnes and baby Veronika.
Bottom: Pauly Bould.

Top: A summer pageant in Heathcot.
Three little girls with flowers in their hair: Leezy, Agi and Gony.
Bottom: Maypole dancing, Heathcot House, 1 May.

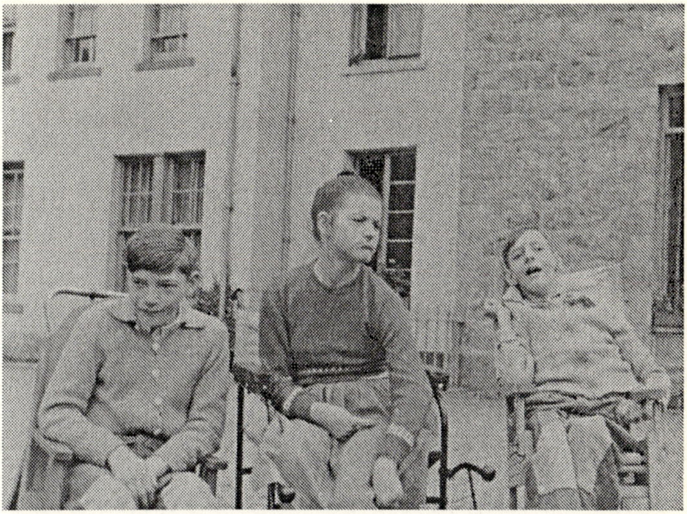

Top: Three of the Green Nursery children.
Bottom: The other half of the Green Nursery children.

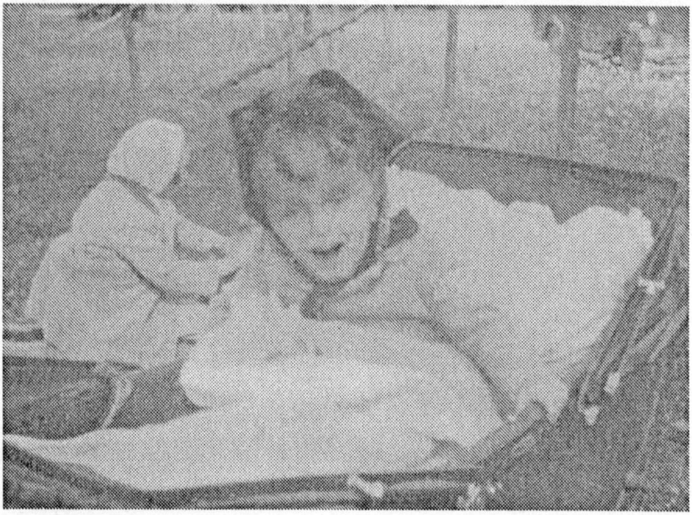

Top: James Embleton.
Bottom: Marisha and Vanessa.

Top: Planting trees at Candlemas. My father talking to Bob (with the flatcap) in the background. Me in the foreground.
Bottom: My family outside Heathcot. Spring 1957, the year we were to leave Heathcot.

Top: Me, aged ten years, at Danby Village School.
Bottom: Thornbury Park.

Top: My father in the Thornbury garden with the castle in the background.
Bottom: Me in Thornbury with Polly, the fertile ginger cat.

Top: Glencraig House.
Bottom: Johannes and I on an outing.

Top: Henry, milking a Jersey cow.
Bottom: Rehearsing a Michaelmas pageant, Glencraig.

Top: Rob with a child from his dormitory, just prior to our wedding.
Bottom: Children's picnic on Glencraig Beach.

Top: Helen Barbara.
Bottom: The wedding. *Front row:* Me, my mother and Rob.
Second row: Miriam, Rob's mother, Huib and Agnes.
Back right: Rob's father. Very back: Sundry villagers and co-workers.

Chapter VI
ENGLAND

My first impression of Botton Hall was from the top of the ridge as we motored in an unspecified ancient rattletrap of a vehicle from Middlesbrough to the village. I looked out of the window over the vast stretch of the moors, the heather purple and brown in the winter mist, the peat bogs dark and deep. It was impressive and threatening, sheep peacefully grazing in that vast loneliness. I remembered *The Secret Garden* and felt very akin to Mary, wanting to fuss and stamp my feet and declare that Scotland held everything dear to me, whilst Yorkshire could only offer dreariness and coldness. These moors were so unlike the Highland ferns, brownish bracken and purple hills. I felt the lump in my throat faintly thickening, but the feel of my mother's hand in mine sent it away into the depths of my consciousness.

The road wound on and ran along the edge of the ridge. Down below was a tiny house with lots of chimneys and some trees around it. In the distance of the dale, I could see farms lying and fields green in the moisture of the air. There, said my mother, pointing to the house with the chimneys, was Botton Hall, my new home.

The car took a fierce turn and rolled at breakneck speed down a very narrow bendy road, past a chapel, that later I learned was a Wesleyan house of prayer, and down to the crossroads that forked at a big tree. We turned in at the gates of an even narrower track and pulled up in front of a huge imposing house with a great front door. What had looked so tiny from the lip of the dale was in fact a great country mansion that had been given to Camphill by the ever-generous Macmillan family. Unlike what I had been used to, there were no pillars, but the squareness of the edifice was regularly broken up by tall windows.

My memory of Botton Hall is of coldness, dampness, long

corridors and that distinctive ancient smell of old English country residences. This special aroma consists of heather, bog, damp, drains, peat smoke, sheep's wool, pine logs, beer, coal, dogs, cats, horses and all mounted on the background of a faint smell of overcooked cabbage. Our bedroom, no longer called the nursery, was halfway up the main staircase. To get to the toilet, you had to walk down some steps and then onto a landing. The door handle on the door was smooth and very, very cold. Inside, the lavatory stood on stone tiles, and if I went without my slippers, I thought my feet would freeze fast to them. The window was small and high up and it was so cold that I debated for ages before daring to pull down my knickers.

The weather, in my memory of Yorkshire, was always cold, cloudy and often rainy. There never seemed to be any sun and I did not want to go barefoot at all. Botton Hall was huge and cold and our bedroom seemed the only warm place. In it were three beds, each with their own bed cover over them, and each with our own special picture hanging above it. From now on, every time we moved (which we continued to do frequently, if not from centre to centre, then from house to house), I knew I was home when I saw that bed cover and picture. Sometimes we even moved rooms within houses, according to the available accommodation. The bed covers were woven in blueish purple, handmade, so that each had its particular variation on the theme. The picture my sister Leezy had I cannot remember, oddly enough. Agi's picture was of Mary in a garden of flowers with a crown on her head, painted by an Italian master. My picture was of Mary with the Jesus child and the little bird, painted by Raphael, I think. My memory becomes hazy as to particulars, but I loved to lie in bed and look at the serenity of her face and the fatness of her child. Also hanging in our room was a picture of the Angel Gabriel by one of the Italian masters. Was this Leezy's picture?

Looking out of the window, we had a view spreading over the high hedge and the gravelled front drive. Over to the left was a cluster of buildings around a cobbled courtyard that had been the stables and the coach house. This became my playground for that one year in which we lived in Botton village. Leaving the Hall, you entered a vast sea of mud and grass and overgrown rhododendron shrubs. Everyone wore wellington boots. The back entrance to the Hall was a sea of boots at supper time, and smelled of wet rubber and cheesy feet. Clothes sometimes lay on the ground, damp and muddy and mildewed. The boot room was not a nice place to be.

Botton Hall was a very big house by any standard. It had extensions of passages all over the place and I never quite got to grips with the layout of them. I could get lost, right up until the time we left, and was always a bit anxious as to where I might find a door that would lead to a familiar part of the house. The passages were bare floorboards, uncarpeted and often dusty. My sister Leezy, whom we had now upgraded to 'Lizzy', perhaps in honour of living well and truly in England, used to get one of her sneezing attacks when walking down them. The dust may have been due to the fact that here in Botton we lived with adults with special needs. Lived *with* was really the correct way to describe this community attempt. As the ill children grew up, the wonderful community existence of full acceptance would come to an end. Parents were anxious that this should not happen. They had learned from Camphill that people with disabilities could be useful, well-adjusted citizens of the world, and they wanted this attitude to extend beyond schooling.

Dr König took up the challenge. By the time we arrived in 1957, the Reverend Peter Roth, and Kate, his wife, had become the practical applicators of the first village community. The emphasis was to be on living and working together with people with special needs in a village setting where school, church and shops, workshops and farms would develop around this new impulse for social change. So we all lived as equals and cared for the fabric of the community, each person carrying out their tasks to the best of their ability. Some were better at housework than others. Some kitchens were clean, some were pretty ghastly, with the smell of compost reeking out from behind the cupboard doors under the sink. Sometimes the plates and cutlery from which we ate were cleaner than at others, depending on who did the washing-up. Some passages had gobs of dust on them, others shone with polish. What was really remarkable was that no one commented on these disparities of hygiene. The effort to leave education behind went very far indeed! Sometimes I found it hard to accept the dirt and dust, but my mother told me to be still. I was to learn to accept people's goodwill, she said.

My mother went out to work every day. She worked in Falcon Farm, one of those that I had seen from the ridge above. She ran the laundry for the community. Every morning, she would put on her boots and trudge up the side of the dale to the farm. The laundry was very old fashioned. A huge copper stood above a fireplace that had to be stoked and kept burning so that the water in it could boil up the sheets and other bedlinen. When it boiled, it smelled of Sunlight soap and dirty laundry. Being so small, my mother would mount some steps and, taking hold of the huge wooden paddle, she stirred and twisted the boiling cloth, her face red and shining with exertion.

I suppose she rinsed the linen in the wooden tubs along the wall, which did at least have cold running water in the taps. Then the laundry was put through the mangle to wring out most of the water. Heaving wet sheets about must have been a terrible burden to her small frame. Finally, having rendered the linen clean, white and beautiful, she carried the wicker baskets out to the line to hang the sheets in the damp Yorkshire air, in the hope that they would dry. I remember one frosty morning, how she carefully unpegged the stiffly frozen sheets and carried them in to lean against the wall so that they would defrost without cracking. I suppose she might have had to mend them otherwise. As always, we were very poor and bedlinen had to be cared for. During that year, my mother's hands were raw and red.

She must have had some villagers to help her in the laundry. The disabled adults were a force very much to be reckoned with in Botton village. The atmosphere was different from what I had been used to in Scotland. Everyone was a grown-up and worked as a grown-up did, their tasks being a part of the day, and their interests feeding the evening activities. The whole place was filled with work. Everyone had their jobs and went about their daily tasks with devotion and involvement. Indeed, some people needed a bit of help and had to be shown what to do, but most people carried their responsibilities well, and seriously. Meeting someone on the path from one farm to another, meant that they were going about their work, and they would not, or could not always stop for a chat. I had to tag along whilst chattering away about what interested me, or asking them what they were doing. I also had to ask whether I could go with them, as often they did not have time for me. Some of the grown-ups had peculiar habits, and some spoke with foreign accents, and some worked more than others, and some smelled cleaner than others; but otherwise, every adult was an adult and received the same respect as any adult would expect from their fellow human beings.

I do not remember individuals amongst this working group. Perhaps I lived in Botton for too short a time. This may be the reason, but I think a better one is that I was too busy finding out about the place to pay enough attention to each person. So I do not remember who worked with my mother in the laundry.

My father worked in the garden. He too had villagers helping him and I remember a thin, sandy-haired man who dug rows of the soil in wonderful straight lines and worked ceaselessly at the job. His movements were staccato but regular, and each sod that he turned was equal and measured. I loved the regularity of his movements.

For some strange reason, I remember little about my father from that year in Botton. He was just there, but settling me in the evenings was no longer his role. I could read very well and so stories were less in demand. I loved those evening hours, lying snug in bed with the 'little light' on, a book comfortably resting on my pillow, and reading as though I was gobbling up the pages. My mother would come in to say prayers with me, and what an agony it was to put the book away and sit up as requested, to recite the evening prayer:

From my head to my feet,
I am the image of God.
From my heart to my hands,
His own breath do I feel.
When I speak with my mouth,
I shall follow God's will.
When I see and know God,
In my father and mother,
In all loving people;

In flowers and trees,
In birds beasts and stones,
Then no fear shall I feel;
Only love then will fill me,
For all that is around me.
Amen.

I had recited this for as many years as I could remember. It was both reassuring and comforting. It was the ground of my home. In Camphill House, I had had to say it by myself. Here in Botton, my mother said it with me, but not my sisters. Lizzy was still in Newtondee, and Agi was at Wynstones, so I was on my own during term time. The other two beds in the room were empty, waiting for the holidays, to be filled by my sisters. Then bedtime was thrilling. I didn't need to read because as soon as the three 'little lights' went off, we began to chatter. I listened to stories about my old home with longing and pleasure, about the friends that Lizzy still had and that I had left behind. I listened to exciting boarding-school stories, wondering how it would be when my turn came to leave home for school in Gloucestershire.

But now I was on my own, and the villagers were my companions for a large part of the time. In particular, there was Michael Hogg. He lived in Botton Hall and his voice, when he spoke, was rich and precise. He wore very thick glasses behind which his near-sighted eyes glowed with enthusiasm for life. He had a remarkable gift. He could play the piano. He listened to records on his wind-up record player, and then reproduced what he had heard on the piano. I used to go to his room, perch on his bed and listen to his plummy voice telling me about each piece of music that he was going to play, who had composed it, what date and year and what it would tell me if I listened quietly. Then he would vigorously wind up the machine, cock his head to one side and gently place the needle on the first groove of the record and wonderful sounds would come forth from the horn. We would sit and listen, concentrating fiercely on Wagner, Beethoven or Mozart.

At other times, I would go into the room where the piano was. I cannot remember its decor, only the piano. And Michael sitting, his head weaving round and round, a tic he had which fascinated me, his hands lustily banging out the music on the piano. In retrospect, I don't think he had much feeling for the piece that he was playing, because he crashed it out at speed and volume. But it was a masterpiece of learning from listening. He played the *Trumpet Voluntary* and the *Turkish March* most loudly and spectacularly and I loved them best, always asking for a repeat. Sometimes, Kate would walk in and tell him to tone it down as it was disturbing Peter's concentration.

We shared the Hall with Kate and Peter Roth. Kate was short and square of build and walked around the house confidently and with emphasis. One always knew where she was because of her great presence. She had a sharp and precise way of speaking, saying her words with clarity and precision. I liked her but did not feel drawn to her. She was not a cuddly sort of person. Peter, on the other hand, had a warmth in his voice and a slur in his speech. He used an atrocious English, heavily accented and very Austrian in inflection. He limped because of a bout of polio that left him with a problem of balance and a crooked mouth. I loved looking at his lips as he spoke. They were finely cut and his face shone with a hidden smile behind his eyes. He had black hair, combed severely back from his forehead, rather like my father, though his hair was curly and needed a wet comb to keep it down and in place.

Peter had a wonderful habit of saying something clumsy, then giving a great gust of laughter that went on and on, uncontrolled and all embracing. One had to join in. Kate would tell him not to be so silly and look severe, but he ignored her primness, and laughed the harder. He sometimes stumbled as he walked and sat down on the nearest available seat rather abruptly as though about to fall down. Then he would exclaim, 'Oo–la–la!' which sent me off into gales of laughter. I would try to do the same, almost falling down, catching my balance again and saying, 'Oo–la–la!' as he did, but I could never quite find the same humour in it as when he did it. I loved him very much.

They were both as busy as my parents, busy at daily ordinary tasks, as well as busy at community building. They were always in meetings. Peter was, at other times, in his study, reading and working at his sermons, I supposed, because he was a priest of the Christian Community, the first to live and work in Camphill. I thought he must be very holy, but could not see where his holiness was, because he was so very nice, funny and kind. He did not hold himself aloof as I thought priests should, but welcomed his fellow human beings as friends and companions, even me, who was a rather naughty girl.

Peter and Kate had a son, Simon, whom they both adored. His grandmother, Mrs Elderton, a sharp-voiced, rather proper elderly lady, cared for him. She followed Simon around wherever he went, calling him by his name all the time. I found this exceedingly irritating and could quite understand why he never seemed to listen to her. He just did exactly as he liked. I thought he was very spoiled and wondered why Kate did not look after him herself as my mother looked after me. Mrs Elderton even settled him and gave him all his meals. When I saw Kate with him, it always surprised me. But he listened to his mother when she spoke, though he often whined at her requests. She seemed to adore him, and yet be inept at handling him, responding to his demands always with agreement. Peter was not a proper father in my eyes. He talked to Simon, but he did not read him stories. Sometimes, I wanted to read to Simon, or tried to play with him, but he was much younger than me and did not have the same interests at all. He just wanted to own my toys, or books, but not to play with them. And like many spoilt children, he could not share his with me.

However, in the flat above the weavery, which was situated in the coach yard, lived Ann Trier. Her husband had died and she had come to Botton with her youngest son, Christopher, and with her horses, to run the workshop below. Charles and Sally, her other two children were at Wynstones. So Chrissy and I played together. Though he was younger than me, we got on very well. He was independent and quick on the uptake and had some good ideas of fun, but he was never quite able to replace Pauly, whom I missed very badly. I felt lonely in my soul and frightened of the world, but Chrissy helped to fill the gap a little.

The weavery was a lovely place to be. It was warm and light and full of quiet work. There were looms of all sizes and shapes and I found it peaceful and fulfilling to walk around and watch the villagers at their work. They wove cloths of many colours using soft woollen threads. It was like magic to see Ann prepare a loom. She used long carefully selected threads and pulled them through the wire loops with a hook, something like a crochet hook. The warp looked like soldiers ready for battle. Then it was wound around the wooden pole at the back and fixed to the wooden pole in the front and the bobbin was wound with its special colour and the work could begin. The process is not very clear to me any more, but the atmosphere is very vivid, as is the smell of the wool and the sound of the clack of the looms.

Men and women worked here and no one minded if I squeezed up on the narrow bench beside them to watch and chatter. I most clearly remember a lovely kind of blueish-mauve cloth being prepared, which later on became bed covers and tablecloths. It reminded me of the Scottish hills in the distance on a sunny day. All the cloth woven in the workshop was used, and made into something that visitors could buy. Later on, these items could be bought in the big shops in London, bringing in a steady income which Botton badly needed. There was only a small payment for those with special needs; it was no longer fees for education, as had been the case in the schools. Now people had to earn their living and so everything had to be of marketable value, or food to feed the village.

I loved the tea breaks. Then everyone downed tools and sat around, in good weather in the courtyard, in bad weather in the workshop, and we chattered about everything and anything. Once again, I cannot remember specific people, but the smell of their bodies and the warmth and humour of the villagers is as bright in my mind as when I was with them. They always told tales about other people, gossip being food and drink for them. They were interested in everything that went on in Botton. This was *their* village, *their* home and they lived here with *their* friends.

So much so, that couples formed as in every normal village. On Sundays and on Saturday afternoons, when work stopped, the villagers bathed and got dressed in their finery and went visiting, or sometimes courting. Couples walked sedately hand in hand, or arm in arm, along the paths around Botton village. They sat in each other's sitting rooms and drank tea. It was genteel and safe and real. Mary and Jim were always together. I heard the grown-ups talking about them, because they wanted to get married. To my childish mind, this seemed very strange. I had been used to ill children needing care and being less able than I was. Now I was living with these same kind of people and they were far more able than I was, but still not quite normal.

I was, at last, realising that there was such a thing as 'normal' and 'handicapped', as we called people with special needs in those days. So the idea that two handicapped people wanted to marry seemed very strange to me. But apparently, this was not so strange to the grown-ups. Mary, who worked in the weavery, told me that she had had talks with Peter and that he had said they should wait a bit and see how their love would grow. When they were really sure, then she and Jim should talk to him again. She was very happy with this solution, and to see her and Jim on Sundays, their faces glowing with love, melted my newfound scepticism.

Above the weavery and running round its three sides was a high wall. As in Heathcot, Chrissy and I loved to sit on this wall. In the hot summer, when the sun shone and the moors were drowsy and hazy, we lay on our tummies in the heat, each of us with a jam jar in which was a little red jam and a great deal of water. In our hands we held a piece of plywood. We lay, quiet as hunters, waiting for wasps. They came in hoards, buzzing lazily and unsuspectingly, alighting on the jammy edges of our traps, only to be triumphantly whacked into the water to drown as our plywood lids descended on top of them. I derived a great deal of guilty pleasure from watching them struggle, but I could not hold out for as long as Chrissy. There was always that cut-off point when the pleasure turned into a slight sickness, and I had to lift the plywood and dunk the victim so that it drowned more quickly. At the end of such a session, we would count the corpses to see who had caught the most and then display our prizes to the cook in the Hall. We thought we were doing a really good deed, to rid the world of wasps.

Sometimes Chrissy and I went riding over the moors with Ann. This was wonderful and gave me a sense of freedom and adventure. I loved the feel of the warm horse between my knees and never wanted to learn to ride with a saddle. But Ann said that I must and so I did, watching impatiently whilst she tried to teach me how to tighten the girths so that I would be safe. But I never learned to rise to the trot. I enjoyed sitting and being bounced around, not minding the inelegance of it. I had become quite fat during my stay in Camphill estate.

The moors were lovely. You had to climb up and up at the back of the dale, through scrub and heather and bracken, and then you were up, walking in heather amongst the sheep. We picked blueberries in the summer, bringing them home to eat with caster sugar and milk. I loved the way the milk turned blueish purple in the bowl, and was willing to break my back to pick the berries only because of this thrilling end. Usually, I tried as hard as possible to leave any work to others, skipping away at washing-up time, and being too busy playing outside to help my mother clean our room on Saturdays.

The ritual cleaning and preparing for Sunday continued in Botton, just as it had done in Scotland. So did the festivals, though I cannot remember any special event except Carnival, or *Fasching*, as we called it in Camphill. We had pancakes for supper and then the dressing up began. The villagers appeared, gloriously and extravagantly attired in costumes that Kate designed for them, men as women, women as babies, animals, kings and beggars. Then the dancing began, with folk dances from Scotland, England and Ireland, and the catchy tunes spun round in my head. I loved the rhythm and the excitement, joining in and dancing with the best. The smell in the room became hot and fierce, sweat dripping from people's heads and underarms, but we danced and laughed and had a great time. The villagers had such a capacity for fun and enjoyment that it carried us all along and when I went to bed, later than I could ever remember the tunes, and the fun stayed with me. I felt as if I had been in a peasants' feast in Russia, or some other faraway fairy-tale country.

In Botton Hall lived Alistair. He spoke a beautiful kind of English and walked with a mincing step. He had an ugly yet imposing face and a slight hunch on his back. His voice was pitched high and his manners were exceptional. He also had what I thought to be a very funny side to his character. He loved to dress up as a woman. To me this was hilarious, but I could see that to the grown-ups it was rather horrid. They would hurriedly send him to his room to change when he appeared in a dress. He used to wait eagerly for the post and glow with suppressed joy when a plain brown paper parcel arrived for him, which it quite often did. Then he would snatch it up and cradle it all the way to his room, which he reached on those days by way of the backstairs and the long servants' passage. I would follow him, eagerly asking him what was in the parcel and he would shush me up, glancing furtively over his shoulder to see if any one was listening.

It was mean of me to ask him, because I knew what was inside the wrapping paper. It was probably a corset, laced and boned, or a bra with frills, or a pair of long Victorian lady's knickers, all of which he would don in the privacy of his room and then preen in front of a mirror. I knew all this because the door to his room did not quite fit the frame and Chrissy and I could peer in as he played out his obsession, taking turns to look and turns to giggle. I am fairly sure that Alistair knew we were there, because we were unable to be really quiet, but he did not seem to mind. Sometimes he dressed himself in his male working outfit wearing the lady's underwear underneath. On these days, he would be particularly jocular and talkative until Kate would sigh and send him to his room to dress properly. How did she know when he was wearing his transvestite costume? You could never see it, he hid it so well. It always amazed me that she could know, and I gained a huge respect for her.

Along the same passage as Alistair lived was the room of a former teacher. Because of his profession, he warranted a great deal of respect from me. I used to visit him in his room. But I was always disappointed in him. He was large and fat and smelled atrociously of stale sweat and cigarette smoke. He was never without the little white-papered tobacco rolls, and used to light a fresh one with the butt of the old, grinding it out in an ashtray that was overloaded and foul. With hindsight, I now know that he had had a breakdown and stopped teaching because of this. He was in Botton to find a new direction for his life. But at the time, I simply found his repulsiveness fascinating and found myself, against my will, knocking at his door to visit. He rarely talked to me, just let me sit there, until I could bear the bachelor fug no longer and I left with a polite 'thank you' for the visit.

The Christmas holidays were ending and I was to go to school down in the village of Danby. I had been for an interview in the schoolhouse on the corner of our road that turned into the main village street. It was a bare room, with bare dusty floorboards and rows of high wooden desks with the benches attached to them. Only half the long room was used, the other half behind the blackboard being empty. At the far end were props from a stage show. The classroom clearly doubled up as the village hall and social space. It was painted a prison green, pale and watery with bits peeling off. There were no decorations, no show of colour and no plants in the window. My old Camphill classroom at St John's School was very, very different. I was used to a beautiful room in which to do my lessons, with paintings hanging on the walls, flowers in a vase on the teacher's desk, the floor clean and smelling of floor polish. It had been a second home to me, lending its warmth and colour to my already rich life. I felt alienated and cold in the unaesthetic atmosphere of the village school.

Danby was really a small hamlet with a few council houses and some very old cottages, and the children who attended the school came from all the outlying farms around the dale. Botton was situated at the end of the dale, with Dale Head as the last and highest farmstead, so I did not know the children with whom I would be sharing the classroom.

The teacher, a tall thin man with a bright toothy smile, scared me. There was no reason that I could voice for this feeling because he was extremely friendly and polite to me and my mother when we came for the interview. He showed us round and asked me some questions, which I could answer easily. He smiled and smiled. Then we left and I felt a strange shiver that never left me all the time I went to that school.

When the day came, I got up trembling and feeling slightly sick. I could not eat my breakfast. My father took me by the hand and we walked down the drive to the big tree where Chrissy was already waiting, looking around hopefully for conkers that might still be there, though autumn had long gone. A car arrived and the driver opened the back door and we got in – that is, Chrissy and I got in with some other boys, whom I have quite forgotten now.

My father stood under the tree as we drove away. On the car radio, 'Music While You Work' was being played. That tune haunts me to this day and when I hear it, the sick feeling in my stomach returns with a little flutter.

I entered the classroom to a huge din of boys and girls shrieking and squealing and greeting each other with boisterous slaps and thumps, their voices heavy with the Yorkshire dialect. I could not understand one word that they spoke that first day. I was in a panic of fear and retreated inside myself. I knew that they were speaking English, because we were in England, but my ears had been tuned to Scottish sounds, or foreign-accented English, and I could not tune in to this flat, long-vowelled language at all. Moreover, the noise level was shocking. In Camphill, we entered the classroom quietly and in good order, seating ourselves one at a time as our teacher showed us where in the rows of desks our own particular place was to be for the term. Now everyone was milling around and seemed to know where to put their books.

Chrissy deserted me. He had been to school already and knew everyone and could speak in their peculiar manner. I stood still and waited, there did not seem anything else that I could do. The teacher came in. He stood next to me, put his hand on my shoulder and snarled something foreign and evil over my head, whilst his face and lips smiled. Instantly there was a hush and the big boys scrambled as quickly and quietly as they could to the seats in the front row, the girls took their seats on one side and the little boys sat behind the big boys. Though this was not a segregated school, we sat safely with pupils of our own sex.

I thought I would die of embarrassment and fear, but he looked down at me and led me gently to my seat in the front row with the girls. I did not stay there. The front row was for the clever children. You got sent progressively further back in rows according to your academic ability. Day by day, my seat went further back until I was safely and inconspicuously sitting in the far back left of the room. Here I stayed for the rest of the year.

Lessons began. There was no morning verse to start the day, as we had done in St John's School, standing piously behind our desks and reciting a verse in praise of the earth, the stars, the heavens and God, praying to become truly human. Now, the teacher stood in front of us and barked out the title of a book and the page to which we were to turn. I watched my neighbours on that first day. They took their books out of their school bags and opened them. They were readers, and turn-by-turn, each was asked to read a passage out loud. I had no book and so could not read. As the days passed and I moved back, I saw that some people pulled their books out from under their desk. Carefully, and as unobtrusively as possible, I felt under my desk and found that I too had a book from which to read. I pulled it out. Then my turn came to read. I looked at the page, the letters swum and no sound came out of my mouth. There was a horrible hush. Everyone stared. I could not even cry! Mercifully, my guardian angel must have whispered in the teacher's ear, because he said I should leave it and pointed to the next child beside me. The humiliation was awful. I *could* read, fluently, but fear had got me by the throat.

When reading was over, we had to get out the next book and turn to the designated page. This was number work. There were sums laid out on the page with the answer blank and a note at the bottom of the page to say where the answers could be found. I stared at this book in bewilderment. What was I supposed to do with it? Where was I meant to write the answer, which I instantly knew, since arithmetic had always been easy for me? Was I supposed to write it in the little space in the printed book at the end of the sum? Was I meant to work it out, or to look for the answer at the end of the book as the postscript seemed to suggest? On that first day, I watched my neighbours scribbling in their copybooks, but I had no arithmetic book from which to copy. The problem of what to do only arrived when I was seated rather far back and so the teacher could not see what I was doing.

Some days passed before he finally arrived at my desk, on one of his prowls round the room whilst everyone was supposed to be working. He stopped and looked at me, then asked why I had no copybook. I sat dumb. He sighed and went to his desk and gave me a copybook with little squares in it. Now I was faced with a new problem. What did I do with this squared paper? Did I write in the squares? What would happen if I did not fit the numbers in precisely? So I wrote nothing at all, and spent the arithmetic hour staring at the printed sums and doing them in my head.

Break time came. Everyone raced out to the little tarred yard and started shouting and racing aimlessly around, eating their sweets and sandwiches and generally making a huge din. I stood hovering in the doorway, terrified of the racket and wanting desperately to cry. But I would not. Chrissy was still out of sight with the boys and so I stood and watched, inching my way round the edges of the yard. Some girls were playing hopscotch and some were skipping and others playing ball. I had never been good at these precision games, perhaps because of my undiagnosed short-sightedness. I could not catch a ball, and invariably missed the rope as it swung passed and hit me on the shins or calves, or sometimes my head, so I did not like this game at all. Hopscotch too, was a bit tricky, because I was never sure what square my puck landed in.

I spent that first day in the village school of Danby in a state of silent and paralysing panic.

After break, we were told to sit in a semicircle in front of a square box. I thought it might be a wireless, and it was. The teacher handed out books with words and notes in them, which I had no problem in reading. Moreover, I already knew most of the songs as they were popular folk songs sung in every school, also in St John's School. Now a lady's voice came on and asked us if we were ready. I nearly answered her, so happy to hear a feminine English accent that I could finally understand. She told us, this disembodied friendly woman, to turn to a certain page. Then she said, 'Are you ready? One, two, three…' and she started singing. Everyone sang along, and this time I found my voice and sang with great gusto. Then she said, 'Good. That was lovely!' and told us to turn to another page.

Here was another complete mystery. How did she know if we had sung along? And how did she know whether it was correct, good, or maybe even bad? How did she know whether we knew the tune? Where was she? I was so mystified and once again afraid that I did not sing anymore, except silently inside my head.

The teacher was always very kind to me. No matter how stupid I must have appeared to him, he treated me kindly and gently. But he was less kind to the boys. The girls were all spoken to in a quiet voice and the older girls he even joked with, and sometimes stroked their heads as he passed them by on his walkabout. Sometimes he touched my head too, and on one occasion as the year rolled on, he took me on his knee, to my huge embarrassment and fear. This was because he had heard me playing the recorder.

By this time, I had found a way to understand the children's speech and had found a few girls who also did not want to play loudly and lustily. We spent break times together, exchanging stories, each one more outrageous than the other. Somehow or other, maybe to save face because I realised that I must appear very stupid and dull to them, I boasted that I could play the recorder. And so I brought it in to school and played for them behind the toilets in the yard. The teacher heard and was entranced. Maybe he too thought that finally I was showing some kind of ability. He made me play for the whole school. Needless to say, I could not squeeze out one single note and was as close to tears as ever was. So he took me on his knee and told the children that I really could play, that he had heard me, but that I was too overawed to manage in public. This was very kind of him, but gave me the name of teacher's pet!

He treated the boys much less kindly. I could rarely see what the reason was, but he seemed able to find a few culprits every day. He would send a boy behind the blackboard which stood on an easel. Then he would go behind that board too. I could see both pairs of legs. And I could hear the thwack of the cane as it fell on the poor victim's bottom. I could hear the stifled moans, and see the clenched fingers of the boy, bent double to receive this punishment. I lived in fear of these moments, wanting to cry, to scream, to protest, being too frightened to do anything. A part of me suffered from being a dirty coward who did nothing to protect the boys, and a part of me said I should leave well alone in case I became the beaten one.

No one ever reacted whilst these little trips behind the blackboard went on. Everyone just went on working, as though it were nothing. And so I told no one about it, assuming that once again I did not understand what everyone else obviously did comprehend.

To see why being in the village school was so difficult for me, one would have to visit a Waldorf school. I had been used to the teacher teaching the lessons. Nowhere had I yet come across the method of learning from a book, or a machine. I went into the classroom and the teacher told the most wonderful stories. There would be a picture on the blackboard relating to the story and this picture would change and grow as the story unfolded. Then we would recount to the teacher what we had heard, everyone chipping in with their own special memory, and then we would write it down, making our own books from which we could read the story back to ourselves, having written it in our own words. If someone could not write, then they could copy it from the blackboard after having told the teacher what to write. Those children who could not write drew a picture about the story, and those children who could not even do that had a special picture drawn for them by the teacher in their own book. In this way, week after week, subjects were brought into my awareness. Learning was an artistic experience, not an intellectual one.

Every lesson was taught in this way. For geography, we went out and looked at the landscape. For history, we invented kings and queens, battles and victories, by using drama as the medium, as well as stories. We sang together, learning the notes and only then writing them down. We learned the recorder by ear, and only then related the fingering to the notes on the blackboard. Everything was practical and visible and artistically human.

Sitting in a classroom where the teacher acted as a monitor and disciplinarian was like being on another planet. Moreover, our teachers had taught us with love and understanding for each individual. Now I experienced a necessity to conform to the norm and did not even really know what the norm was! No wonder I was bewildered and paralysed and afraid. To top it all, I did not know how to tell my mother. I still suffered from the small child's inability to say things clearly. All I could do was be sick every morning before school, in the hope that she would find me too ill to go that day. This sometimes worked, but not always. I am sure she knew that I was unhappy, but she probably hoped that I would settle down and get used to the new situation. I did, of course, gradually acclimatise, but my school report for that half-year says that though I did not appear to be handicapped, I was certainly incapable of learning!

Finding friends was not easy either, when I must have given off an air of stupidity and snobbery. I stood back from involvement because I could not understand the other children's attitude. And though I learned to understand their speech, I could not share in their life experience. Mine was of a community with strange and interesting people living in it. Theirs was of farming or shopkeeping. Their Christmases included Santa Claus, mine did not. They did not know what a *Wichtl* was, and I did not know who Mickey Mouse was. We had almost no ground on which to meet, not even our national heritage, because my parents were so obviously not English; and I only knew a few Scottish traditions and my classmates were from Yorkshire.

In the last term I found a bridge. It was not a nice one, but it worked, and for a time I was a little happier. I discovered that I knew an awful lot of dirty jokes, having learned them from the Newtondee boys and Cairnlee girls. I became very, very popular all of a sudden, especially with the boys. We would huddle in corners in the break times, whilst I regaled them with yet another rude and filthy story. I hated it, but loved the attention, and allowed myself to think that I finally had some friends. But when the year came to a close, I plucked up the courage, being now ten years old, and declared to my mother one afternoon under the washing line, whilst she was bringing in the sheets, that I wanted to go to boarding school with my sisters. I would no longer go to Danby village school, and if she did not send me to Wynstones, I would not go to school any more. To my great relief and gratitude, she listened.

Outside of the misery of school, I was very happy in Botton. I could roam about freely and come home to my mother and father. The dale was long and exciting and there were four farms to visit. Botton Farm was up the hill at the mouth of Botton estate. Up the one side at the end was Falcon Farm, and up the other side towards the dale's end were High Farm and Dale Head.

Each farm was very different. High Farm was square and imposing, with concrete outbuildings, very clean and efficient. Botton Farm was small and cosy, the little farmhouse filled with children and the good smell of cooking. Hendy farmed it, often with a child up on the tractor. I envied those children, and wished that my father was a farmer and not a gardener. Kitty was at home and looked after the other children. I used to visit with my mother, because I was too shy to go up on my own and the children were much younger than me. Kitty had a baby that winter in Botton, and that was very exciting because my mother helped with the delivery and the midwife arrived in a helicopter because of the snow. I tried to imagine what it was like to give birth, but could not really envision it.

Falcon Farm was very muddy, messy and the nearest to the Hall. Because my mother worked there I was often up and around, but I do not remember who ran it. Dale Head was a fair walk away and I think that Hubert Zipperlin farmed it, though he may have been actually the farmer at High Farm. For some reason or other, my memory is very imprecise at to who was, and who was not a part of my life in Botton. By now, I must have met hundreds of people from all nations and walks of life and they rolled themselves into one vast sea of vague faces and voices. Individuals stick out because I had something directly to do with them. Others sink down into the sea of humanity.

Dale Head had a lovely old farmhouse, which I imagined to be a place where scenes in the stories that I avidly read could actually happen. It was tiny and perfect. The housemother there kept it immaculate. One had to take off one's shoes on entering because it was so highly polished. Though it was beautiful, I never felt comfortable in all its shining neatness. But I suppose it may have been a reaction on the part of many women to the mud that was everywhere in Botton. Trying to keep clean was so very difficult, and being a wild child, I slightly resented the demand that the housemother put on me. Nothing was paved; every path was a dirt track and tractors churned up the ruts that passed for roads. How could one keep clean when one was having such a good time playing? The whole dale was a wilderness and a great nature park.

When I first came to my new home, it rained everyday, but my mother baked Christmas stars, and made the stollen as always at this time of the year. It was a fragrant introduction to Botton Hall, and did much to counterbalance the damp. The big kitchen in the

Hall smelled of cinnamon and cloves and the biscuit stars shone golden brown with egg yolk painted over them. Some of them had white icing sugar on them, making a frosted sugary pattern and an explosion of pleasure in the mouth. Some she covered in chocolate. It was so very reassuring to have all the old traditions happen even in a new home environment.

I learned about the English Christmas cake. I had seen pictures of it in cookery books, and seen it in shops, but now I learned how it was actually made. Such a lot of dried fruit went into it, and pouring the forbidden alcohol over the mixture was fascinating. People in Camphill did not drink. I did hear (as we staff children always heard everything) that Thomas Weihs had wine sometimes. I even heard that he always took a bottle of wine with him on the long journey from Aberdeen to London, when he drove Dr König to clinics in Harley Street. Apparently he said it helped his driving! Sometimes, when we were on holiday, my father would want a pint of beer, and my mother would frown and they would have a German argument that often ended in my father having a pint and my mother not talking to him! But alcohol never appeared in the Camphill of my childhood. Yet here in Botton village, we were all grown-ups and we were to live a normal village life. Kate said that the Christmas cake was no Christmas cake without the brandy, so that was that. When I finally came to eat it, it tasted just like the gas that I had had at the dentist and I hated it, bitterly disappointed that a dish that took so long to prepare and mature should taste so awful. Likewise the Christmas pudding; I truly detested it.

That season, I heard the *A Christmas Carol* by Dickens for the first time. Every evening we gathered and read about Scrooge, about the poor children and the timid clerk, and about the ghosts of Christmas who came to haunt the wicked miser. I loved the mood that these stories created and watched the faces of the villagers as they listened to these classic tales of Christmas in bygone times. It was cosy in a new kind of way. I was living with grown ups and was a child amongst them. The pressures of having to set a good example were lifted during the time we lived in Botton. I could be simply a child.

Botton was a real village, with many houses and farms,

outlying sheds, sheep and people of all sorts. There were, however, no shops in this village. We had to go to Middlesbrough for our major stores and of course for our clothes and shoes. Middlesbrough was a market town, not very nice but very practical.

We could also have gone to Whitby, but the shops there stocked mostly souvenirs and curios. It was a lovely seaside town of the Fifties, empty in winter, and full of candyfloss and toffee apples in the summer. We so rarely went there. I also remember the fishing boats and the smell of the fish and the rough sound of the fishermen as they threw their boxes of catch out onto the quays. Other men sat there, mending the nets. It was very different from the Aberdeen fish market that we had visited with our class, shortly before my move to Botton. That had been a huge kind of factory, with big bits of ice lying about on which one could slip if not very careful. And I learned the true meaning of 'fishwife' on that visit. The women, their hair beneath handkerchiefs tied like the proverbial charwomen's turbans, and enveloped in nylon overalls, shrieked and swore just like the flocks of hungry seagulls that swarmed outside the fishing sheds. The noise was tremendous and sucked me into its coarse cheer.

As well as Whitby and Middlesbrough, we sometimes went to York. This was the most beautiful of the local towns, with its minster dominating the skyline as we approached by train, or in the rattling car that was Botton's transport system. The houses were old and tilted over the streets, and the shops were just like those Charles Dickens described in his books. It was here that I first came across Robin Hood. Someone gave me a book with a few stories, and one played in York city. I was enchanted. The hero of the Middle Ages had come alive in my mind. I could picture him with his merry men, striding boldly through York to market and to the priory, which I imagined must have looked like the minster, only with monks in brown habits sleeping in it, and eating their sumptuous repasts. I wondered what God thought about eating in church; but then I knew that the monks were not really men of God, but greedy envious humans, so I thought God probably would punish them in good time.

Middlesbrough, however, was where Botton shopped. I did

not always go on these trips, but I loved to receive the returning travellers. My personal mode of leaving the dale was on foot, by taxi to school, on horseback, or with a pony and trap. Sometimes, Ann harnessed up the pony to an old yet serviceable cart and we were off, up the steep winding road, passed the Wesleyan chapel and on to the main road to Middlesbrough. This road took you wherever you wanted to go. It was a passport out of Botton, and sometimes I longed to just walk and walk, away from the closed dale, over the moors and to join Robin Hood. You could also go to Guisborough from this road, but the stories of Guy of Guisborough made me dread visiting that town. It seemed like a place of treason and betrayal.

Because leaving Botton was always a journey, the snow, when it came, created havoc. It fell out of the grey sky in great big soft flakes and simply did not stop. To my great joy and relief, we could not go to school. We were snowed in! For us children, this was a pleasure and a thrill. For the grown-ups, at first, it was also exciting. It meant heaping up the fires, and stoking the boiler. It meant wellington boots, but this was not really anything new. It meant shovelling snow away from the doors so that people could get to work. It meant putting ash on the paths so that no one would slip.

After the first week of snow, everyone expected that the thaw would come. But not only did it not melt, it snowed again. Every time we thought, now the snow will be gone, it snowed again. Great drifts built up against the stonewalls and hedges, against barns and outbuildings. The farmers had to go on foot to check the sheep that could be heard plaintively bleating, away on the moor. The cattle were inside, but feeding them became quite a process, because the tractors could not breach the heaped-up windswept hills of snow.

Every day, someone faithfully set out with a home-made snowplough on the front of the tractor to clear the road, and usually it got stuck and had to be towed out by another tractor. Going from house to house meant ploughing through waist-high drifts.

Then it froze up fast. Out came the sledges. This was much better fun for us. No longer did I risk being buried in snow, now

I could slide on its surface and the sides of the dale became our playground. Moreover, this hard-packed snow was my greatest friend. We could not go to school; the road to Danby was quite impassable except on foot, on skis or by sledge. Even the horses could not make it. Ann harnessed them to sledges so that we could go out to get food from the village shop, but the horses were so heavy they sunk in the soft whiteness and had to be coaxed back home to their warm comfortable straw.

Roger Livesey, I think it was, together with a co-worker dressed up like Santa Claus, went out pulling sledges and made it to the village. …and back. It took them all day, but they returned with some basic provisions. I wondered if we were going to starve our way till spring.

The snow lasted for six heavenly exciting weeks. And then it thawed. The mess was tremendous, the mud horrific. The houses were decorated with muddy footprints and no one dared set foot in Dale Head for fear of retribution. It was impossible to keep clean and dry. And I had to go to school again.

The end of the school year featured the summer fête. This festival was quite unlike any festival I had ever attended. The classroom was cleared to become the Village Hall. Canvas chairs were brought in from one of the outhouses, faintly smelling of mildew. The stage was set with a backdrop that the older boys and girls had apparently made one weekend. It was a collage depicting a pop idol, whose name I have quite forgotten. Many acts were performed that night by various groups of school children. The parents sat in rows, watching and applauding what to me were incomprehensible jokes and sketches. The highlight of the event was a mime to a record by a pop singer with slicked-back hair, the performer making weird gyrations and noises.

Most of it went past me, because I was so busy looking at everyone's clothes. People from the ordinary world dressed quite differently from us in Botton. The women had their hair cut short, brushed neatly down in a fringe, or swept back to one side with a dressy sort of grip over one ear. The men had no beards, were clean-shaven and had their hair cut short at the back and sides. This was similar to the men I knew, only *their* hair was often windswept and ragged at the edges.

The women wore smart straight skirts with twinsets and pearls. Some had large brooches pinned to the lapels of their smart tweed coats. The collars sometimes had what appeared to be an animal fur on them. Some collars were trimmed with velvet. They carried handbags in their hands and wore bright red lipstick. On their feet were smart, highly polished shoes, or patent leather high-heeled pumps. The women I saw daily often wore sack-like skirts in drab tartans or grey. They wore blouses with collars, and V-necked cardigans, often ill fitting and of bright colours. Their stockings were Lisle, with the seams crooked and wrinkled at the ankles. Some of the women loved jewellery and wore brightly coloured glass beads, often clashing with the colours of the cardigans.

The men at that summer festival were dressed uncomfortably in suits and ties which they tugged at as the evening wore on and the hall got hotter. Their brown brogue shoes were highly polished, and clumped as they walked to their seats. They would clearly have been more comfortable in corduroys, with thick socks hidden in their wellington boots. The men I saw daily wore just the latter outfit, but the trousers often hung loosely and the boots were always muddy. At mealtimes, you could smell the socks, which probably had one or two holes in them.

I became painfully aware that we Camphillers were not dressed fashionably at all! We wore clothes that worked for our very countrified lifestyle and we did not go shopping very often. The villagers' clothes were often cast-offs, because we were so dependent upon charity. And with their questionable hygiene, they suddenly appeared to me like beggars. For the first time I felt inadequate and ashamed of Camphill. I felt that we too should be caring about what we wore and how we looked.

Sometimes important people came to visit, to see this newfangled idea of a community actually at work in daily life. They walked through the village and 'oohed' and 'aahed'. They admired the woven cloth, the baked bread and the living garden and farms, and they looked at the people with surprise. They never seemed to know who was, and who was not, handicapped. Now I realised why they could not tell the difference. It was our universal badly dressed ragged appearance. Until now, I had been proud of being poor. I had looked at the posh clothes of the visitors and had laughed at their 'townies' dress. Now it seemed all wrong and shameful.

No wonder the villagers loved Saturday afternoons and Sundays. They wore their best clothes and felt smart and beautiful. Now, I too wanted a dress, a posh one, with frills, a wide skirt and a touch of petticoat lace showing beneath the hem. I wanted patent leather shoes. I wanted my mother to wear a twinset and pearls. I wanted her in high-heeled shoes, though with her stiff leg, I knew she couldn't wear them. My father, at least, was wearing the right clothes; his Sunday suit was as smart as any of the other children's fathers.

Chapter VII
BOARDING SCHOOL

In September, what I imagined was going to be the biggest adventure of my life, began. My sister Lizzy and I were to start boarding school. From reading the books by Enid Blyton, I thought that I was going to meet exciting times in a large hostel with lots of naughty and interesting boys and girls. In fact, boarding school turned out to be rather boring as far as adventures were concerned. Apart from one year in a hostel run by people whom I knew from Heathcot, I lived with families of whom I was very fond, and never had the fun and games that hostel life apparently afforded the children in Erid Blyton's books. Adventure for me meant Camphill. At home (and as the years passed our home changed a few times), all the light and drama awaited me. Though I loved school, my real life seemed to happen at home in Camphill.

We went to Elmfield School, in Stourbridge. Reg and Mollie Bould were the hostel parents and this was the reason my parents chose to send us there and not to Wynstones. As Agi was well settled at her school, she did not need a change; but Lizzy and I were starting our boarding school career, and my parents thought that as I was so young, it was better to send me to someone that they knew. Sending Lizzy with me was probably because they knew that she was desperately shy and that I had always been a good ice-breaker, with my noisier and more confident temperament. Besides, apart from the usual sibling squabbles, we were actually very close, and very good friends. I needed her gentleness, her smartness and her humour and was very glad that she was with me.

So we packed our trunk, a big brown cardboard affair with a shelf in it. At the bottom went our underwear, shoes and books, etc. In the shelf went the blouses and dresses and the blazers. Our uniform was cherry red and grey; red pullovers, white shirts, and cherry blazers, very smart. My mother packed with care. The shoes had to be polished, the clothes neatly folded and tissue paper between the woollies. I sat on the bed and watched her, feeling sick with nerves and excitement. It was such a big adventure. I could not imagine how it would be. The biggest worry was: who would do my hair? I had not yet learned to comb and plait it, and Lizzy had declared with determination that she was not going to do it for me. I should learn to do it myself. My mother said that Mollie would help me, and I sincerely hoped that she would. Whenever I tried to tackle it, I seemed only to make the tangles worse. After the first term ended, during the holidays, I had it cut. We went to the hairdresser and after checking with my mother that my hair was really to be cut short, she took the scissors and chopped off each plait, like an executioner. I was thrilled and horrified and kept them for a long time, tied off at each end with an elastic band.

The trunk was taken off to the train to be sent as luggage in advance. A few days later we rattled to Middlesbrough and caught the train to Birmingham. I cannot remember who took us, or whether we went by ourselves, escorted by Agi, a seasoned traveller. I also cannot remember who met us and how we got to the hostel. But get there we did.

The hostel was situated right by a busy road, but a wall safely separated us from the traffic. Turning down the quiet lane on one side, we entered its grounds. It was a large red-brick house with many rooms, stairs and passages. Outside, along one side of the original house was a small attached cottage with its own front door. Here was my room, part of the Bould's family quarters. It had a sloping ceiling and two beds. I think I must have shared this room with my sister, but everything about Elmfield hostel is very vague in my memory. The grounds and the playing fields behind the house are much more vivid. I suppose I spent a lot of time out of doors, as had always been my habit.

At last I was reunited with Pauly! I had looked forward to it so much. And of course it proved to be a bit of a disappointment. He had become a boy, and I was suddenly conscious of being a girl. We did, of course, greet each other ecstatically, and we did play together, actually quite a lot, but Pauly had other friends – boys – and they did not always accept me, although I was a tomboy enough to please them most of the time. But it wasn't the same.

And the homesickness was back in full bloom. The lump in my throat settled in again, so much so, that I got very ill and could not stop crying. I could not eat because I could not swallow anything. This was somewhere in the middle of the first term. Mollie was very kind. She cooked special things and Reg came to read me stories, but I just wanted my mother. So Reg phoned her and she came to see me. She stayed for the weekend and my sickness passed. After she left, something had changed in me. I felt harder and more able to cope, but I also realised that I was actually unhappy.

I accepted that this would be my life from now on: the pleasure and wonder of Camphill in the holidays, and the challenge of loneliness at school during term time. I had to make a go of it, however, because the alternative was a state school, and this was completely out of the question. I had tried that and could not learn. I *wanted* to learn, wanted the main lessons, the history, the language lessons, the music and the art. If I could only get them by living away from home, then I would have to manage.

Elmfield School, like all the Waldorf schools in England, was run like any public school. We had Monday morning assembly where we sang and listened to a short tale, heard the announcements for the week and ended the half-hour with a piece of music. Sometimes we saw some eurythmy, or a short play, especially at festive times of the year.

Then we trouped in crocodile formation to our classrooms. I was in class five, having missed class four whilst attending Danby village school. I expected to be completely behind the rest of my class, but to my amazement, I found myself well ahead of them, all but in French, which I had never heard before. I had also missed some of the Norse mythology and some of the Greek. But my avid hunger for books was a huge help. I went to the school library and got out the stories that I had not had and read them, enjoying them enormously. As to French, I just listened and found that gradually I could understand something, but I could not speak it.

Other subjects that were entirely new to me were gymnastics and sports. In St John's School, we had never played cricket, let alone lacrosse or tennis. At Elmfield we played all three, plus hockey. And I had never climbed a rope or run a race and I did not know what 'cross-country' meant. At Elmfield, sports was a big thing. We had to go to the changing rooms in the girls' toilets and put on shorts and gym shirts and gym shoes. This was all right in the summer, but freezing cold in the winter. And I had also grown rather fat. I seriously hated those days of exercise! The shorts would not stay up unless the elastic was tight, too tight for my chubby waist. And the smell of the toilets was horrendous. They smelled of drains, old dried blood and damp, over-ridden by disinfectant. The seats on the toilets were wooden, screwed-down strips that cut into the thighs as one sat. I began a lifelong habit of not emptying my bladder from nine o'clock in the morning until four o'clock in the afternoon. A stomach ache was preferable to using those lavatories.

The school was an old manor house on a hill. What must have been ornamental gardens below had been turned into tennis courts and here I had my first game. I could not understand it at all. A small ball was hit by the racket in a most peculiar way and flew towards me. I was supposed to hit it back, over the net, with a swing of my arm that did not come naturally at all. And I could not see the ball coming. It always appeared in my vision too late for me to aim the heavy racket at it. Besides, I could not see the point of all this. Why should the ball not bounce? And why should it sometimes bounce? And what was a score? When did I hit it and when should I leave it? And why should the ball be thrown up into the air before hitting it in the first place?

Lacrosse was worse. We had to jog in line, in our shorts, to the playing fields behind the hostel. Often, another school was passing by, jogging in the opposite direction for their cross-country run. We used to shout abuse at each other as we passed, and they always won these word games by calling us 'backies', their obnoxious name for someone with special needs, more politely known as 'backward'. As I knew at first hand what a 'backie' was, I felt vastly insulted and wanted to hit these rude children. Once we reached the field, we had to be chosen by the captain in order to join the team. I was always chosen last, with a groan of resignation. Needless to say, I was as bad at this game as I was at tennis, again because I never saw the ball till it hit me or passed me by.

Hockey was another nightmare. Now the ball could be very painful if it hit you and so could the hockey sticks. Both lacrosse and hockey meant running, aimlessly on my part, because I could not see where the ball was and so could not guess where it might arrive next!

Gym was a bit more fun. At least I could see the ropes, and do the exercises that were known as Bothmer gymnastics. We had to stand straight, raise our arms to shoulder height, then over our heads, back to shoulder height and then down, and jumping all the while to a rhythm or a count, in an orderly way that satisfied my tidy soul. Perhaps these movements were a forerunner of the weird gestures that aerobics developed. I liked them, feeling fit after a gym lesson. But the running and jumping was harder to tolerate and excel in. The boys were always much better than the girls.

Our class teacher, Mr Gough, had a strange disfigurement. He had a deep hole behind his left ear. It fascinated me, and I wondered if it affected him at all. But he could tell wonderful stories, and was a gentle kind man. So I enjoyed the lessons. I cannot remember particular classes, only that on the whole I was happy to be learning and to be able to understand the system and the relationship that teacher and pupil had. Our class remains a vague blur, only Pauly and one other individual sticking out as memorable. Her name was Katie.

Life at the hostel was similar to the community life that I had known for ten years. We had grace before meals, and the food was the same. There was, however, more to chew, and fewer mashed-up soups, which I enjoyed. I was settled to sleep with a story and prayers and a candle. Perhaps I received this treatment because I actually lived within the Bould family. Chris and Lizzy Bould lived in the hostel part of the house, sharing a dorm with other boarders. I loved going into the house and being with the older children. They did exciting things like listening to records, great black plastic platters that they put on the old wind-up gramophone.

The little needles that scratched out the music used to lie in a box on the mantlepiece above the old fireplace in the playroom. I liked sorting out the sharp ones from the blunt ones and then playing the records with both sorts, so that I could laugh at the different sounds they produced. I suspect I ruined several of the plates!

This was my first real introduction to pop music. I listened to Paul Anka, Lonnie Donnegan, and Frank Sinatra. I loved the music, the beat and the wail of the voices. It was strange, American and foreign. It was also forbidden. I knew that my mother would frown at such ugly sounds and this made it especially thrilling. At home we did not even possess a gramophone. We listened to live music, played or sung by co-workers. Here at Elmfield, I watched the older children jiving and bopping about to the music and this too was very funny and smacked of forbidden fruit. I did not recognise their movements as sexual, but part of my body responded to the mood and I became excited and nervous at the feelings that this dancing aroused.

I also became aware of 'being in love'. Some of the boys and girls were going out together and this stirred my body too. They seemed to need to keep it secret and so I assumed that they were up to something wrong. I would never have told on any of these couples. But one day there was big trouble for Chris. He was in love with a girl and apparently, as I heard afterwards from Pauly, he had gone to her room in the night, and they had both climbed out of the window and been out together! I knew about it the next day because there was a stupendous row and Chris did not appear till lunchtime and then he had very red eyes. Reg was in a towering rage and we all felt it best to steer clear of him.

The grounds around the hostel had the usual shrubberies and bushes. We played there, inventing jungles and forests. I always wanted to play with Pauly and the boys, which *he* did not mind, but which the other boys did. One Saturday, I followed them, wanting to join in, and to my surprise, they seemed to want me to. With great enthusiasm, I ran behind them only to find the ground fall away under my feet. I landed with a huge bump and an explosion of pain at the back of my head. They all ran away, screaming with laughter. I had fallen into their elephant trap that they had dug for me. I could not get out easily and sat at the muddy bottom, crying. Eventually, Reg came and hauled me out. The blood ran down my neck and I felt furious and humiliated. How could my friend Pauly let something like this happen?

Reg, with great kindness and gentleness, treated my cut head (the scar is still there), and tried to get me to say what had happened. But my loyalty to Pauly and fear of Reg's temper kept me silent. Besides, now that the shock and pain were fading, it made me an interesting person to know! And my silence paid dividends. The boys let me play along with them at last because I wasn't a snitch.

So we got up to quite a few naughty things. We went roaming on Saturdays, looking for things to destroy and break. The worst thing we did was to smash the cricket club windows. At the end of the playing fields was a white wooden hut that the cricket team used in the summer. We went down one rainy afternoon and threw stones through every window. The sound of the breaking glass was frightening and thrilling, both at the same time. That Monday morning, in school assembly, we were all addressed as to the evils of meaningless destruction. We sat quietly and said nothing, and no one found us out. But it preyed on my conscience. I wondered what my mother would say if she knew how naughty I was becoming...

At school I went from strength to strength. Not only was I good at the lessons, but I began to get ahead of the rest of my class, and I wanted more. Mr Gough, though I liked him well enough, was too kind, and I began to be naughty, also in the lessons. I began first by contradicting him when he got something wrong, and then I started reading under the desk during his lessons. I was often sent out and had to sit outside in the passageway. The smell of cooked cabbage tormented me, and my boredom increased.

I no longer wanted to play with the boys as the year rolled on. They did silly things and I wanted, at last, a girlfriend. But the girls did not like me, perhaps because I always had to be right and was indeed quite clever, and they resented me: all except Katie.

Katie had brown curly hair, a sharp face and was as thin as I was becoming fat. She loved singing and giggled easily. She lived in Sunfield Homes, a curative home for children with special needs, the place my father lived in after Gerrards Cross. It was not a part of Camphill but had many similar features. They too lived in community with the ill children. So we had a lot in common. I loved going to visit her, because I felt at home with all these strange 'backward' children. We played very silly games, however. With hindsight, I think she must have been a rather neglected child because her mother was unable to control her. Katie spoke to her rudely and nastily, which shocked me to the core. I would never have dared to tell my mother to shut up. In fact, this phrase was banned at my home. But Katie said what she liked to her mother.

We used to raid the larder when we arrived from school and then go out to sit on an embankment by the road and watch the cars go by. There were not that many. Katie would wait until a man drove past and then she would decide whether she was in love with him or not. She talked about 'fucking', and described it in detail. I listened and giggled. I found her both repulsive and fascinating. Sometimes she would stand waiting for a car, her knickers down and her dress held up so that she could display her parts to the shocked drivers as they passed. She would then dive back into the bushes, giggling hysterically at their reactions. This too, I found disturbing, but was equally enraptured by her daring. She tried to get me to do the same, but I was too afraid of what might happen if my mother found out.

Living with the Newtondee boys should have given me a bit more experience of the facts of life, but I had always taken their words as jokes, not believing that grown-ups would do the disgusting things that they talked and laughed about. But here was Katie, a little girl and my friend, telling me the same things and what's more, telling me that my mother and father did it too! This was really too much for me, so I dropped her, gradually, because I did not want to hurt her feelings.

However, something was spoiled for me in the adoration that I had for my parents. If they were doing such things, (heaven forbid that it was true!), then might not even Dr König be doing it too? This was such heresy that I expunged it from my mind.

The homesickness that I continually felt played its part. It rose and fell according to how happy I was on that particular day.

When it came to the festivals, I missed Camphill sorely. We saw the same Austrian Nativity and Shepherd's Play as I had seen year after year at home, but the voices of the characters were English, not German, and the names of the shepherds had been anglicised too. This did not ring true to me and I longed to go home and see the *real* Christmas Play.

At some point in the year, our family moved to the community in Thornbury, Gloucestershire. My parents packed up and settled there whilst we were still at school. So we returned to a new home. I had made no real roots in Botton. Though I liked it well enough, it had never really become a part of my being and I did not regret the move at all. The butterflies in my stomach as we travelled by train to Bristol were pleasurable. I was beginning to enjoy the thought of being somewhere new again. I knew my mother would make it a home for us and only longed to see her, and my father again, and to have the family all together. Moreover, living in Thornbury meant that the nearest school would be Wynstones, and I had always wanted to go there, like my big sister. Maybe I would get to live in the hostel with her. That was a thought that warmed me. I had no regrets either for leaving Elmfield. My friendship with Pauly seemed to have dribbled away, and I had no one whom I would miss there at all. I had lost respect for Mr Gough, and wanted a teacher who would neither send me out, nor give in to my teasing, but who would actually teach me something, the way I had been taught in St John's School. I wanted to learn, not pass the time with uninteresting and easy stuff.

My faith in my mother's homemaking skills was not unfounded. And I loved Thornbury Park on sight. Wynstones too, turned out to be all that I had hoped for. However, I did not live in the hostel with my sister, Agi. Instead, my mother decided that termly boarding was too much for us, and she placed Agi with a teacher's family by the name of Wood, and Lizzy and I went to live with the Syeds. Now we could come home every weekend.

Mrs Syed was a gentle woman whom I liked very much and who always treated us like paying guests. We were not allowed to help her at all, something to which I did not object, but which sometimes made us feel stiff and ill at ease, because all we could do was sit in the sitting room and be polite. She had been married to an Indian and, most romantically, had also lived in India. But they were divorced now and she lived in a council house in Brookthorpe, a little village between Stroud and Gloucester. Agi lived just across the road in the lodge of Wynstones School hostel. It was a very small old-fashioned building with an outside toilet. It smelled damp and was not always clean. But Mr and Mrs Wood were lovely people and she was quite happy with them.

I saw very little of her. She was still the big sister, who had no time for her little sister; she had her own friends, even a boyfriend, and lived her own life. This was at school. At home at the weekends, she was part of the family and community life and did have time for me. She kept school and home severely apart and we learnt to do the same, hardly speaking to her when we met in break times, because anyway she would have answered in a very condescending way.

Lizzy and I lived in the council house with all its attendant miseries. There was no heating and in the winter the ice formed not only on the window, but also on the walls of our bedroom, thus necessitating the use of a hot-water bottle, and so I developed chilblains for the first time in my life. They stayed as a background itch all through my boarding school years.

In order to fit us both in, Mrs Syed's old mother slept in the tiny boxroom, Mrs Syed and her daughter Lila in the big front bedroom, and my sister Lizzy and I in the other upstairs bedroom. The older son, Jon, occupied the sitting room. Mrs Syed and her mother lived in the kitchen and the rest of us used the sitting room as our living room. This meant that Jon, who went to technical college, had to study whilst Liz and I sat huddled by the fire, reading. The coals blazed and heated the water, what there was of it. There must have been a very small tank for the hot water, because when it was my bath night, I sat in two inches of tepid water in order to try to get clean. The rest of my body froze up. On most evenings, washing meant taking a kettle of boiling water to the bathroom. By the time I had steeled myself to take off my clothes to wash, the water in the sink had become as tepid as my weekly bath. Needless to say, I began to skimp on ablutions, and at the weekend at home, luxuriated in a steamy hot bath filled with water.

Perhaps it was the cold and damp, perhaps it was my usual homesickness, but I got ill again, this time with such a severe sore throat that they suspected diphtheria, a disease that was supposed to have died out. Whatever it was that I had, I was so ill that I could hardly breathe and could certainly not eat or drink. My mother, once more, came to fetch me, this time by car, and took me home. On the journey, something burst and I swallowed foul-tasting slime. By the time we reached my familiar and cosy bed, my temperature had gone and I was on the mend. The warmth of Camphill enfolded me for two lovely weeks. I lazed about and read books, and ate the food to which I was used and was thoroughly spoiled. Then back to school and the Syed's cold house.

Actually, I quite liked living in an ordinary council house, just like so many other ordinary people did. I was becoming very conscious of the fact that my home was very different from that of most of my classmates. I liked listening to the radio, walking to school in a uniform, having school dinners and not saying prayers at night. I was growing up and beginning to want to be like other children in their nuclear family homes. I started to feel a bit ashamed of being part of a community, living with backward children and amongst so many foreigners. I did not like it when my parents visited the school. They seemed so foreign and a bit mad, in their shabby clothes and with their foreign accents. I wanted to be English and ordinary.

During the year that we lived with the Syeds, I discovered the public library and cowboy books! Jon read them and I borrowed them from him. I went through one a day, loving the predictability of the baddies and the goodies, and especially enjoying the romantic bits. That kiss on the last page filled me with immense satisfaction and untold longing. My favourite author was Zane Grey. I was half in love with Jon, in the way that the lovely ladies were in love with their cowboy heroes, and wanted him to see me as the love of his life! The fantasy filled me with satisfaction. In reality, I was a bit afraid of him and hardly ever spoke to him. It was true romantic idealism!

Apart from falling in love for the first time, if one could call this adoration love, I also began menstruating. This was a complete surprise to me. What I knew of the facts of life came from the Newtondee boys and from my friend, Katie, and neither of these sources ever said anything about monthly bleeding, sperm or ovaries. My mother had told me nothing, either. Now I found dried brown stuff in my knickers. I thought that I must be very sick, that I had a new kind of illness, and was very scared indeed. I debated telling my sister, Agi, but as I so rarely saw her, this was not an option. So I would have to tell my sister, Lizzy, with whom I shared a room, and who lately had also decided to ignore her younger sister. It must have been a Wynstones tradition of the day that children only noticed a younger sibling if they needed defending!

So I plucked up courage and showed her my knickers. She laughed! This was truly appalling. I was probably dying from some obscure disease and Lizzy was laughing. But she explained in short terms that this was blood, that girls needed to bleed once a month in order to have babies. I understood nothing, was only shocked to think that God had made such discomfort necessary. Why didn't boys have to go through all this? Lizzy could not explain that at all, but she gave me some sanitary towels and showed me what to do with them. She said that she had been getting her period for two years already and that it was quite normal.

I felt reassured and glad that I was not dying, but hugely resentful of the information that this would happen every four weeks. It did have its spin-off however, because she also said that I could not go swimming when menstruating. I hated swimming. On one occasion during the Elmfield days, I had visited the swimming pool with friends and whilst they were messing about in the water, I sat by the side, watching. I was wearing a heavy winter coat and boots. Some boys passed by and pushed me in. I remember sinking down and drawing in water as I tried to shout for help. The water closed over me like a tunnel and I rose up to try shouting again, only to inhale more water. I sank to the bottom and sat there quietly and then I remember being roughly thumped to get the water out and I was violently sick beside the pool. It was a humiliating experience and did nothing to make me like deep water.

The lessons in Gloucester pool were torture. I could not bring myself to tell my teacher that I was afraid, but every time that I was told to duck under and come up on the other side of the pole that the instructor held over the surface of the water, I was grateful that my face was wet anyway and that my classmates would not see that in the drops of water were tears. I had to hold my breath to prevent myself from vomiting.

Now I had a wonderful excuse. I loved my periods and invented more than one to get out of those dreaded lessons. Eventually I plucked up the courage to tell my teacher, Miss Jacobs, that I was terrified of swimming, and she was very understanding and did not make me swim any more.

A new experience was weekly pocket money. We both got a shilling every Friday. I spent mine on sweets and comics, loving the forbidden feeling of doing something that my parents did not approve of at all. I liked *Jackie* best, enjoying the silly stories. In fact, being away at boarding school seriously affected my reading habits. I adored books and would have read anything. If there were printed words, I read them. Even whilst sitting on the toilet I would read the instructions on the Harpic bottles. Now I read unsupervised and gobbled up a great deal of rubbish interspersed by a few good books that my parents gave me at home.

We stayed two years at the Syeds' and then we moved to Rose Cottage, a lovely house nearer to the school. I had made friends with a girl in my class called Jenny and we went to live with her family. This was to be my second home until I left school aged eighteen, with three A levels and four O levels and absolutely no wish to study at all. I was going to learn to look after small children and babies. I wanted to be a nursery nurse.

The Hayn family were wonderful people, English, well bred and warm. Mrs Hayn took it on herself to teach us good English manners and customs, and I appreciate them still, having passed many of them on to my children. The room we lived in had flowery curtains, was painted a pale yellow, and had a plain red wool carpet and comfortable warm beds with sheets and blankets. This took some getting used to and reminded me of the train journey that we had taken on the 'Steener' Train a long time ago. It was much more difficult to roll up in blankets than in an eiderdown. But the house was centrally heated, not damp; and the food, though vegetarian, was very good and plentiful.

Mrs Hayn not only let us help in the house but encouraged us to do the dishes, cook, babysit (there were five children in the family, besides Lizzy and myself), and generally made us feel entirely at home. Sometimes, when we could not go home to Thornbury for the weekend, Mr Hayn would take us out in his Morris and we would go and eat Chinese food. This was a novelty and very exciting. Camphillers of those days never went to restaurants. Perhaps this too was part of the education that the Hayns gave me, namely the ability to manage public eating and entertaining.

We used to go for long walks in the Cotswolds and visit the cinema. My pocket money increased and I began smoking. By now I was thirteen and a very stroppy teenager. I had many friends at school, and though I liked the girls, I still preferred to be with the boys. As most of them smoked secretly behind the toilets, this seemed to be a necessary evil. I tried a cigarette one weekend at home. It made me dreadfully sick and dizzy. I lay in bed and told my mother that I was too ill to go to school! But the next day I was better.

Having to smoke in secret disturbed me. I had never told my parents any lies and I trusted them. My father smoked a pipe and many co-workers smoked cigarettes. So one day I boldly announced to my mother that I was going to smoke. I was fairly certain that she would look very, very sad and make me feel that I had hurt her terribly. This was her usual mode of controlling my wilder and nastier side. To my surprise she said I could. This was all the wind taken out of my sails, but unfortunately it did not stop me. It did, however, mean that I never smoked at school. It was against the rules and you could be expelled if you were caught more than three times. As I was allowed to smoke at home, I did not need to break school rules, and I could not see the point of flouting authority for no good reason. So I smoked at home and at the Hayns', but never in school.

Though I loved the Hayns and was very happy at school, I was always homesick. I wanted my family to be all together, and I wanted this to be in Camphill, where so many interesting and exciting things happened all the time. I still loved community life and lived from weekend to weekend, knowing that when we got home on Friday night, something would be happening that was worth being at home for. Perhaps this was why, when I turned fourteen, I developed a sickness that made me ill on Sunday and better on Friday. I would always have a temperature by four o'clock on Sunday afternoon and would need all week to recover. Sometimes the fever stayed down, and then I had to go to school, but it would rise during the week and I would have to go home again.

Truthfully, I did not invent this strange weakness. When I wanted to become a nursery nurse I had to have all sorts of inoculations, one of them against tuberculosis, and then it proved that I already had an immunity. The doctor asked me if I had ever had unexplained fevers, and so I discovered that these rises in temperature must have been TB. What a relief to realise that I had not been inventing it! Some part of me worried that I might be cheating myself and that I had fabricated an illness so completely that it had become real. Now I knew that this had not been the case.

My mother was, as always, wonderful during that time. She never accused me of skiving, but always cared for me and made me feel that I would be all right. Though my sisters snarled and called me a liar, she always believed me. She let me be, and so I read good books, comics being banned at home, and went for walks, enjoyed the safety of the community and felt at peace until my sisters came home at the weekend to tease and pester me again.

Apart from Jenny Hayn, I made another friend at Wynstones. This was Peter Oram, a boy in my class who reminded me of Pauly. He was round faced, just like Pauly, and he had freckles all over him. He had an infectious and cheeky grin and was enormously clever. He could do everything that we learned in school and with an ease that was breathtaking. Needless to say, he must have been a bit bored and so he was up to a great deal of mischief. But despite this, he was popular with teachers and pupils alike, because there was not an ounce of malice in him, and he had an appetite for learning that made the lessons swing along because of the questions that he asked.

Peter became a sort of mentor to me in my insatiable appetite for books. He introduced me to the detective novel through writers such as Agatha Christie, Dorothy L Sayers, Peter Cheyney and G K Chesterton. Funnily enough I never took to Sherlock Holmes, though Peter loved him. Perhaps it was because I always enjoyed a bit of lust and romance in the books that I read! I found Sherlock too dry and passionless. Peter also showed me the thrill and enjoyment that science fiction could offer. To me these were the fairy tales of the future and I gobbled them up. Fantasy fiction too, became a passion for a time, and *The Lord of the Rings* by Tolkien was a kind of Bible. I loved the poetry and the wonderful literacy of Tolkien's work, as well as the battles between darkness and light.

My relationship with my father returned through literature. My father too was an avid reader, and he read the books that I read and so we shared our findings, enjoying heated and often hilarious discussions about their contents. I sometimes wished that I had the nerve to invite Peter home because I knew that he would have got on very well with my father. But, as I entered fully into my teens, I was becoming more and more ashamed of Camphill and its strangeness, and at the same time more and more homesick for it. It was like a love-hate relationship. I could not bear to talk about my home, or invite people in, but I wanted to be in it all the time, always missing the warmth when away from the community.

During my years at school, I contracted measles and was very ill indeed. As a result, my eyes were tested at last, because it was well known that measles affected the vision, and of course I could not tolerate lying in a darkened room and not being able to read. So as soon as my mother left the room, I opened the curtains and read! Once I was well again, she took me to an optician and at last it was discovered that I was extremely short-sighted and needed glasses. Oh, the shame of it! They would call me 'four-eyes' and all sorts of names. But glasses I got – dark rimmed and square National Health spectacles.

The first time I put them on, I screamed and ducked, much to everyone's dismay. I ripped them off, panting and gasping, and gazed, mystified, at the tree that was outside the window. As soon as the glasses had touched my nose, the tree had leapt out at me. Cautiously, I put them on again. This time the tree stayed where it was, but I saw every tiny leaf and twig on it. How amazing that was! Until now, I had thought that only artistic licence allowed the great painters to depict such details. No one, I imagined, could actually *see* individual leaves from a distance. But now I saw them too! This was wonderful and resigned me to my spectacles, at least for reading and writing and distance viewing.

Whilst I was still at Wynstones, Dr König died. The news was brought to us by Dr Lissau, a teacher whom I greatly admired and who had known my mother in Vienna. He had an egg-shaped bald head and spoke with the familiar Austrian accent and he seemed to me to know everything. He taught us Latin, making the grammar and logic interesting and challenging. Though I was never any good at it, I loved his lessons and sat O level Latin only because I loved it so much, and got a U, for unmarked, as the result. But those Latin lessons gave me a love of language and its origin that I have not lost, and Dr Lissau was the purveyor of this knowledge, so I admired him very much.

Now, during Monday morning assembly, he gravely announced that Dr König, the founder of Camphill and a great visionary, had died of a heart attack. I burst into hysterical tears. I felt as if my world had shattered. Why had my parents not told me this? Why did I have to hear such earth-shaking news in public? Did no one realise, as I instantly did, that this was the end of Camphill, and that now I would never have the home that I so loved ever again? How could Camphill continue without the great influence of this short fat man whom I feared and loved?

I asked permission to go home, but neither the school, nor my mother would agree to this. My mother assured me that Camphill would continue, that Dr König had already long ago passed on much of the organisation and administration to groups of people, including her, and that my future was as safe as ever, as was my home. I did not entirely believe her, but as time passed I became more secure and less afraid of what might happen now that he was dead. My mother was rather subdued and quiet for some months after his death and I dimly realised that she had loved him very, very much, as a dear friend and companion, as confidant and as mentor.

Chapter VIII
THE PARK

By the age of eleven I really understood the joke that my father had made about Camphill being a movement. Thornbury Park was the sixth house that I could call my home. It was, as were all the Camphill centres, a very large and imposing building, once again a country house and this time of Georgian origin.

It sat amidst rolling fields, with parkland around it, and looked out over the River Severn in the distance. The most memorable aspect were the trees around the house which most probably gave it the name of The Park. They were all tall, individual and carefully laid out, and all were rare specimens. Beautiful oaks, beeches, firs and horse chestnuts, the latter bearing pink or white candles in the early summer and yielding great crops of conkers in the autumn. I had begun to leave the tomboy phase behind me, and so the shining brown nuts only tempted me a little. The gardens around the house were laid out well and the roses were magnificent. At the back of the house ran a beautiful sloping lawn in the centre of which stood an ancient mulberry tree. Here we picnicked in the glorious summer sun.

Hot summers were a new experience for me, coming from Scotland via North Yorkshire. Here in Gloucestershire, with its mild inland climate, I discovered the joy of sunbathing and wearing flimsy skirts or shorts in the long summer holidays. I missed the sea, but only marginally, because the weather was so wonderful. The winters were cold and sometimes the hoar frost on the trees at Christmas made me feel as if I was living inside a Christmas card.

Thornbury village itself had a fairy-tale feeling to it. The Plain in the centre was surrounded by little shops with bow-fronted windows. One of them held sweets in glass jars and you entered it by stepping down into the sugar-smelling interior where two old ladies in aprons served you with barley sugars, humbugs and lollipops. The butcher had a predictable red face and the watchmaker, an old woman, wore a screwed-in eyeglass to examine the broken bits that one might bring in to her. She would put the fragments into a triangular bit of paper and then into a drawer for her son to look at and fix when he would come in. Her shop also repaired jewellery. She handled the gems with loving old fingers, admiring the cut and setting of my mother's precious necklaces and brooches.

I loved the fact that I could walk into the village to shop. It was just like real life! I began to feel more normal, though the local children were never my playmates. Because of going to boarding school, I could not get to know them and sometimes I regretted this, especially when the Girl Guides were camping in the field beside The Park. I could hear them giggling and having fun and in my envy I made myself despise them and their silly ways. But secretly I would have loved to join them and have the sort of fun that Enid Blyton wrote about.

The Park itself was a lovely house, and though big, it felt homely and cosy to me. My mother, being the matron, made it safe and warm. Our room was small, and looked out over the side entrance onto a big beech tree that spread its branches right up to the window. The birds in the springtime were so loud that they used to wake me up. I heard a cuckoo for the first time, and loved to lie in bed at four in the morning, around midsummer, and listen to its endless calling to its mate, whose cries would return from far distances.

Next door to us was Thornbury Castle and the parish church. The estates were separated only by a wall, which we loved to climb and explore the overgrown neglected castle grounds. It was said that the owner of the castle was mad and this made our little forays very exciting because we were terrified of meeting him. Walking from The Park up to the village, you had to pass the water pump where a ghost lived. No one had actually seen him but everyone knew he was there and coming home late at night could be quite scary. Past the church the road took a sharp bend and then you were at Thornbury House, another big building which was part of the community. Next door to it was The

Hatch, a very old house with sloping floors and low timbered ceilings and little lattice windows that let in light in small doses only. This was my favourite house and I spent a great deal of time in it.

The Park itself was home, however, and when the holidays came I was so happy to unpack my trunk and settle down to enjoy the community once more. I would always have to roam about for the first few days, familiarising myself with the children and with the co-workers, who might have changed during the term whilst I was away. I was now of an age when they began to interest me more that the children, who were mostly spastic and in wheelchairs and not very mobile. I started to notice that the co-workers also had a life and were real people whom one could spend time with and even perhaps make one's friends. Formerly co-workers had been virtually strangers to me, my parents and friends being far more important. Now that I was approaching my teens, the co-workers, all young volunteers, seemed less distant.

I began to want to help in the dormitories, more because of the contact with the volunteers than because of any real wish to look after the children. I particularly liked the small boys' group because their dormitory father was a very likeable young man called Andrew, which we shortened to Andy. He had a great sense of humour and loved playing with words. He would let me put his children to bed, keeping, no doubt, a close eye on me from behind whatever book he was reading. His dormitory was next door to our bedroom, and later, when we moved across the passage, directly opposite to it. It was a lovely room and he made it into a home for those little boys. I cannot remember their names, but I remember the bath times when they would flood the bathroom, and Andy would stand by and let them. My mother used to tell him off and he would laugh at her in the friendliest of ways. I thought him very brave indeed!

Downstairs there was a very different group of children, older and more physically disabled, and amongst them a boy called Danny, whom I already knew from our Heathcot days. He spent his life in a wheelchair but there was absolutely nothing wrong with his mind. Children reach each other even without words and we had a friendship that lasted until he left The Park. We used to play together, chatting and laughing, and the best part of this relationship were the books that I read to him. It was through Danny that I entered the world of Arthur Ransome. *Swallows and Amazons*, and all the others that followed on, became real to us. We didn't just read those books, we lived them. For me, growing up in such a different way, those books gave me access to another way of life. For Danny they must have been a way of living normally too, because of his extreme physical disability. We talked and laughed, though I don't think anyone else understood the weird noises that he made, as being speech; but I did.

I became his personal mealtime helper. The nausea that I had suffered until now when eating with the ill children vanished, and interest took over. I loved sitting next to him and making sure that the portions that were on the spoon were palatable and manageable for him. We sometimes made such a noise at the table that my mother would threaten to send me out and Danny would howl his annoyance and so she let me stay. Some of the feeling of being useful and needed was returning to me, but now I felt that a little respect could also be offered. Some co-workers gave this naturally, others still treated me like a nuisance, but I was learning to ignore them rather than antagonise them for their stupidity. Besides, Danny had a way of laughing at them which helped me enormously; and there were more co-workers who enjoyed my company than those that did not.

My father ran the huge and beautifully laid out walled-in garden. It was situated beside the house and quartered by box hedges that smelled leathery and tart in the summer sun. Beside the garden was an apple orchard with rare fruit trees and a variety of apples that I had not known existed. My favourite was the American Mother, a golden sweet-sour variety that lasted all the winter in the apple shed. This shed was a wonderful place to visit. In the summer it was empty and cool and smelled of cider. In the winter it was full of different shapes and sizes of apples that smelled as fresh as the summer sun. I used to go there and help myself, taking my spoils up to my room to munch whilst reading, a pastime that grew into an obsession in those Thornbury years.

In the orchard were the beehives. My father cared for these as part of his gardening duties. Smoking his pipe and wearing no protective clothing, he would gather the honey and feed the bees, placid and unafraid. He made me stand at a distance whilst busy with them and I would watch his quiet movements and see the little creatures crawl over him without ever stinging. He would hum softly as he worked and they would settle back after he was done in a very short period of time. He always said that as long as you told them the day before, and treated them with proper respect and thanked them afterwards, they would not sting. Later on, a man came to work in the garden with my father, and he too took care of the bees. But with him they became angry and fierce, buzzing madly around him, and he had to wear appropriate clothes to manage the honey.

He was brisk and German in his ways. He treated my father like a handicapped person, condescending and superior in manner and he was the first person I really disliked, not because he did anything to me (in fact, I think he liked us all very much) but because of the way he went about life itself. To give him his due, he was very new to Camphill, and had never lived with people the way that we tried to do, which may have been why I was so offended by him. I found his attitude intolerable. He treated everyone in this stiff fashion, but it was nevertheless horrid to see my father dealt with in such a way. I complained loudly to my mother and she said that in community one has to learn to live with everyone, even those one may not like so much, and that I would learn to love him.

Serenity reigned in the Thornbury years, at least for me, though I believe my parents were not so happy there. They often quarrelled, something that I had not noticed before. My mother's room was down the corridor from my father's little cupboard of a room, and sometimes I could hear his voice, loud and angry, coming from her bedroom. The next day she was silent and he was red-faced and tense. Perhaps the discord came from our not having our own quarters, because until we came to Thornbury we had always had our rooms together and were able to have a family meal once a week. Here we all slept in different areas, still close, but not next door to each other, and the rooms were so small that family meals had to be eaten in the kitchen, which was prone to interruption by other people. I missed the family closeness, but enjoyed the branching out into the wider house community.

Dr Lotte Sahlmann lived with us, and Elsbeth and Marga. These three ladies entertained me enormously. I loved them but was also just the tiniest bit afraid of them, each for very different reasons. Lotte was round and loud and warm, but she found it no problem to tell me off in no uncertain terms, if she felt that I needed it. Marga often criticised and laughed at me, which I found very offensive; and Elsbeth could so easily be annoyed and would not hesitate in telling on me to my mother if she wanted to. I tried hard to be good when they were about. They were rather strict though always fair, with the ill children, which I also found hard. I wanted everyone to be happy and did not always enjoy the educational atmosphere that filled the house.

Dr Lotte's greatest delight in life was driving. She had a little car, which she drove with more vim and vigour than skill. Heaven help the other drivers on the roads when Lotte was out! She crashed and ground the gears and revved the engine till it screamed with pain. She moved that car with will power and somehow or other she never had any accidents. We used to get up on the verge rather smartly when we heard her coming, which we recognised from a distance because of the protesting noises that the engine made.

Lotte had a cat called Richard the Lionheart, because he was a ginger Persian. She loved this creature very much, but very few other people did. Richard was father to a ginger female, quite unheard of in veterinary circles, and she was most fertile, producing endless litters of multicoloured kittens. Her name was Polly and she used to yowl a lot. When she was happy, she would lie on top of you and knead with her paws, drooling mercilessly all over you. In the summer, lying on a blanket sunbathing under the mulberry tree, this cat was a constant companion of mine. I loved her, amused that a cat had the silly name of a parrot. Her mother, wife to Richard, was a tortoiseshell beauty and rejoiced in the name of Jemima.

Beside the apple store in the garden was the tool shed on the one side and the garden shed on the other. Here my father had his tea breaks, and here too were fed the Thornbury Park cats. Every morning, my father would take the leftover porridge out to the shed with a jug of milk. Behind him in an orderly row walked the three cats, tails up at periscope stiffness and purring loudly. He would set down the porridge and milk on the wooden table and tell the cats to sit down. They did so, in a row, watching him closely as only cats can do, their heads turning and their tails twitching. Then he would wash out the dishes, one for porridge, one for milk and set them on the floor. The cats would twitch and he would tell them firmly to wait. Then he filled one bowl with porridge and one with milk, stepped back and said, 'Now you may start.'

Elegantly, and as if they had never really cared, they would get up, stretch and put their little tongues into the food, drinking quietly only once they had eaten. They ate out of the one dish, all three together in true community fashion. I loved watching this daily ritual; there was something comfortably predictable and safe about the ceremony and the confidence with which the cats waited for the meal that was certain to be given.

Along the outside of the garden wall on the south side was another of Lotte's pets, a large and fertile fig tree. It bore luscious purple fruit, and it was a close-run thing who would get to them first, Lotte or I. She could get very cross indeed if I beat her to it, but I loved the sweetness of the flesh and got up earlier in the morning than she did! Lotte, however, could be generous and she could also laugh at herself and was never cross for long. Besides, I always left a few for her, because too many made me sick.

Whilst we were in Thornbury, my Aunt Jeanette came to visit us. This was a watershed in my life, because during her stay she told me about my father's relationship to Hertha Sielmann, now called Helen. This was not something a twelve-year-old girl could easily understand about a father whom she loved. She also told me that my father's accident had made him handicapped. This was a body blow. Suddenly I had a father who had loved another woman, and still did, according to my aunt, and that he was also handicapped, just like the villagers in Botton. I looked at my father with unveiled eyes and wept. How could I talk to him now? Was this why the German man who worked with him treated him so arrogantly? Was my father stupid? Was this why my mother quarrelled with him and so often told him to stop talking?

I withdrew into myself whenever I was with him, and watched him as he gently spoke to the bees, the cats and the trees, and answered everyone, including the insolent co-worker, with warmth and humour and humility, and a huge admiration grew inside me for this man who had had to suffer so much and could still laugh at life. He is still the only person I have ever met who treated every human being he met exactly alike, and with the same warmth and wit. I never heard my father say he hated any one or anything. I decided that if this was what it meant to be handicapped, then it was a blessing that there were handicapped people at all, and I loved him the more for it.

I also took stock of my mother in the light of these revelations. I found her to be honest and true, and also faithful. Where Helen stood in my soul remained confused and unclear. I quite liked her; I saw that my mother did not, and that my father usually returned from his visits to her looking relaxed and refreshed. I decided that their friendship had to have some reason and some goodness and didn't try to work it all out. But I was growing up.

It was during that period of doubt and uncertainty surrounding my parents that I got the measles. Never had I felt so ill and afraid. The spots seemed to be everywhere, inside and outside, and I thought that I might die. Lotte came to see me and prescribed medicines, and her bracing yet tender manner reassured me. I screamed a lot those first three days, everything frightening me, because everything had become so uncertain and I did not trust the future or life at all. But eventually I began to enjoy the fuss that people made over me because I was indeed very ill and people were concerned. The recuperation time was lovely. Many people came to visit me and brought me books and fruit and I felt like a queen. My sister, Lizzy, complained and said that I was spoiled, but even she was kinder than usual, on the whole.

I recovered just in time for Christmas. I had a new grey dress and red tights and descended our backstairs feeling very posh and grown-up. Because of my illness I had lost weight. At the foot of the stairs stood Lotte, who burst into gales of rude laughter. She found my red tights predictably me, because, she said, they showed my true fiery temperament. As always when with Lotte, I would find myself giving a rude answer, and she invariable teased me more. But this time, she was sorry when she saw my face going probably as red as I felt. I often found it difficult to take the ragging that people seemed to feel my strong little soul required. That day I was more vulnerable than usual and it showed.

I had always been a great chatterbox and I still loved to dish out what I considered to be good advice to everyone, particularly the new young co-workers. After all, I had been born in Camphill and thus felt quite justified in giving unsought pearls of wisdom and experience. Lotte never failed to tease me about this little sin of mine, and I would invariably lose my temper at her and shout. Now I felt mortified and very, very offended. But I was growing up and would have to learn to hide my feelings, and when she said that she was sorry, I tried to laugh with her.

I went to look at the Advent calendar on the window high above the front stairs. It was a special calendar with a window for every day and was very beautiful and colourful. The tissue-paper pictures glowed in the weak winter sunlight. Only the Christmas picture remained to be opened. I knew that I would not be chosen for such a holy task. By now I could accept that the ill children would always come first. But the light of the candles held by the angels as they descended the broad red carpeted staircase was as warm as I remembered from earlier days, and the window, when it was finally opened, as bright as any other year. The only difference was that I felt outside the celebrations, and seemed to watch them like a spectator, not wanting to involve myself as wholeheartedly as I had always done before.

Altogether, the festivals in Thornbury lived up to any of my early childhood memories, but now I was older and could be a part of their preparation, and even perhaps contribute something towards them. Amongst the co-workers was a beautiful and gracious Englishwoman. She had long brown hair with golden glints in it and she always wore long dresses like the ladies of the middle ages, laced up tight to accentuate her beautiful breasts. They looked like two round soft cushions above the tight bodice. I thought, since I had just discovered King Arthur and his Knights of the Round Table, that she would have fitted well into his court at Camelot. And she could dance. Perhaps that was why she tended to wear little black pumps that looked like ballet dancers' shoes. She walked with her toes slightly turned out and a spring in her step. She wore her long hair piled up on top of her head in a knot that miraculously never fell down, though I could never make out the hairgrips that she must have used. She taught us many and varied folk dances, and I loved the light summer evenings when we danced until late. We used to go out onto the lawn at the side of the house, under the spreading copper beech that in the spring sheltered a carpet of colourful crocuses, and dance and dance and dance. The scent of the wisteria that grew up the walls of the house and shone mauve in the summer evenings was heavy in my nostrils.

At midsummer, we performed these dances for the whole community and then lit the St John's bonfire and danced around its embers. Late at night, when the stars came out, we chose partners and leapt over the embers into the future, and I fell in love, every year, with a new young male co-worker! Not that I ever let on to this little weakness, mainly because I fell out of love again the next morning when, grumpy and tired, the new day had lost the sheen of that magic night.

We used to get blankets and sleep out the solstice around the glowing fire under the stars, and I remember those nights as being clear and bright with never a raindrop or cloud in the sky. The field beside The Park was always cut for hay, and on the days before the St John's festival we would all go out to rake and stack the fragrant dried grass. We worked in rows, with big wooden rakes, handicapped and co-workers, children and adults, and laughed and sang. I found the rakes heavy, but the work was fun and we drank Ribena and ate biscuits in the breaks. The smell was intoxicating and I still get a buzz from the scent of dry hot grass.

Carnival was another occasion of dancing and fun. Jens was a star on these evenings. Together with John, an English gentleman in the best sense of the word, they would act out village country scenes in a broad Gloucestershire dialect that had us rolling in our seats. On one occasion they performed *You are old, Father William* by Lewis Carroll. Jens took the poem to excruciating heights of fantasy and caricature, playing a Gloucestershire yokel to the hilt.

John, on the other hand, was as British public school as only a true Englishman can achieve. These festivals took place in the hall that had once been the outbuildings. Here too, we saw eurythmy performances and many, many plays. Jens was a good actor and got together groups of co-workers to perform all kinds of theatricals. I loved the possibility that my age now afforded me of joining the evening adult activities.

To my horror and amazement, the Englishwoman of dancing fame, whom I so admired, fell in love with the German co-worker whom I so detested. How could she do this? It was my first serious contact with the blindness of love, and it appalled me. I complained bitterly to my father who said that destiny never worked as one wanted it to, and also that it was none of my business. He said, 'Who knows but perhaps they were meant for each other.'

I thought about this terrible fate and hoped that, as she was so lovely, she might make her German lover a bit kinder. I watched them walk arm in arm, she in her soft dark green velvet dress, and he looking military in his dark trousers and conservative pullover, and wondered about God's will.

I had been lonely for the first year in Thornbury, but then a Dutch family came to stay in Thornbury House. The mother, called Ans, a name which I first thought was a misspelling, was elegant, tall and white-haired, with a gravelly voice rather like some jazz singer, Louis Armstrong, perhaps. But she could not really sing at all, she simply spoke a very broken English in her rough yet warm tones. She had three children: Peter, Winny and Inger. Her eldest son had grown up and no longer lived with her. I thought, Winny, only two years younger than me, might become a friend who could match my abilities, and so I began to court them.

I visited every day during that long summer holiday, unable to communicate at first because they spoke Dutch and I spoke English. But I could be patient when I wanted something badly enough and so I used to sit and listen to them talking whilst waiting for them to learn English. To my surprise, I realised that I could understand what they were saying. They were not learning English, but I was learning Dutch! So I added another language to my repertoire of German and French, which I was picking up very fast in school. Not that I could speak any of these languages, but I found that as long as I didn't try to understand and listened in a casual way, I seemed to know what people were saying.

Eventually, Winny began to try out her English and from them on we were friends. It was quite a novelty for me to have a girlfriend. Apart from Katie, I had always gravitated to boys. But I was becoming a teenager, and with this physical change, I was also becoming very self-conscious. Winny, a slim and pretty girl with a dancers' walk and grace, was mightily attractive to me, with my low self-esteem. Being seen with her filled my heart with pleasure. I loved watching her dancing. She would take a record from her collection and go to the eurythmy room with her portable record player. Dressed in black tights and a body suit, also black and sensuous, she would place the record on the machine and begin to dance, on her toes of course, as did all real ballet dancers. The grace of it stunned me. I wished that I had had the chance to learn this form of movement rather than the flowing veil-covered mystery of eurythmy. Walking to a rhythm, moving in fixed ways to music and waving my arms about in set patterns to the sounds of vowels spoken alarmingly in a false theatrical voice by the eurythmy teacher, was not nearly as free and gracefully compelling as the controlled swings of legs and arms that ballet taught. But I was too old and stiff to be able to master this graceful art, and though Winny did try to teach me something, I always fell over, and that was that.

Inger was a little girl of five years old and not really a companion, but I loved looking after her for Ans, whose favour I would have died for. Peter was a blond god in the distance, and at first I felt not only shy but also a little afraid of him. He was very clever and went to the local grammar school. Winny attended the local secondary school, and so I could only see them at weekends and during the holiday times.

Being older now, I did not have to go to bed so early and I used to spend my evenings with the Dutch family, listening to records or the radio. Winny had a little transistor and we used to tune in to folk music. This opened up a new interest for me. I learned to play the guitar. The van der Stok family came to live in

The Hatch for a while and Rosy, deeply interested in African American music, taught me how to sing calypso. This was an enormous incentive to guitar playing, and so I practised endlessly, to my sisters' annoyance. They banished me to the garden shed because they said they couldn't stand the noise. But I learned to play well, and soon they joined me by singing. I had learned a wonderful social skill. It was something I had that Winny did not have. And the young co-workers who came to Thornbury encouraged me to sing and play for them. This was a lovely way to make new friends and so take yet another step towards adulthood.

In the second summer, I fell deeply and helplessly in love with Peter, of course at the midsummer bonfire. And to my humble amazement he seemed to fall in love with me. Now my evenings stretched into nights. Sometimes I only came home at one o'clock, creeping upstairs as quietly as I could so as not to wake my mother. This never worked. Though she said nothing, her light was always burning and I could see it go out from the crack under the door. It was a leash of the kind to keep me somewhat in check and it was, moreover, very tactful and trusting of her that she said nothing in words.

The love affair lasted about a year, but because I was away at boarding school, we could only see each other intermittently. I was much more besotted than Peter ever was, and needless to say, the love of my life eventually found a much more attractive proposition in his own school than I could ever be. The betrayal was hurtful and I carried the scar for many years, believing that a girl from Camphill could never seek to compete with a girl from the normal world outside. Besides, my curly brown hair and buxom figure could not measure up to straight blond hair and slim hips. The days of the Sixties had arrived, and pale features and skinny figures that could wear clothes of any kind were coming into fashion.

During my years of being in love, I haunted The Hatch. Ans became a second mother to me, a mature friend and confidante who seemed to appreciate my help and involvement. She put me usefully to work, letting me help out with practical and also caring tasks. The Hatch was the adolescent house. Most of the young people were disadvantaged, rather than handicapped, and they could do many things that needed to be done in life. But their behaviour was obstreperous and rude. I used to go there after their school was over and join them in supper making, or tasks on the small farm that had cows, a donkey and pony.

I learned to prepare a meal and clean a house, something that I had avoided like the plague at home. Whenever there was a job to be done, I was not to be found. My sisters did all the washing, ironing and cleaning for my mother, except during the holidays when the children were away. Then our job was to do the dishes after the meals and for once I joined in, taking my fair share of the work. This was because it was a grand opportunity to sing all the songs we knew in rounds and parts. We still loved singing together as much as we had done in the back seat of the Strachan buses on our way to the Highlands. However, in The Hatch I worked, as did all the co-workers, washing up after meals and accompanying the young people to their evening activities, supervising and assisting them. It was enormous fun, and I did not feel superior, I just enjoyed the responsibility.

The years from thirteen to sixteen all blend together. Somewhere in that time span, my eldest sister met a Dutchman called Huib. He appeared one summer as a co-worker on a short stay to help out in the garden and with the maintenance that every summer holiday required. This was the time to repair and renew the houses before the new school year began. Huib arrived, and my sister took one look at him and fell in love. I was furious! This was not how things should be done, I thought. And I was also jealous. But gradually I got over my distaste because not only could he dance like a dream, but he could also play the piano. I loved listening to him rolling out sonatas and preludes by the great composers.

We went on holiday to Austria, the summer of Huib, and my sister moped the whole time, convinced that when we returned home he would have gone. But he was still there when we got back and the affair deepened and blossomed. When Agi left school, she went to Holland and later married Huib. Some part of me had foreseen this outcome on their first meeting and this was what disturbed me so much. I had lost sight of my sister, Agi, when she went off to boarding school at the age of ten, and we had never had the time to find each other properly again. She figured more as the wise counsellor, the big sister with knowledge and sense, and I wanted her to stay around forever, so that I could get to know her, now that we were together every weekend. But I had to see her go to Holland and settle there. I wished that only English co-workers would come to Camphill, and then we wouldn't have to face such a wide separation.

Another holiday we took during those English years was a trip back to Scotland. I looked forward to it with deep anticipation, certain that I would feel instantly at home. But Camphill had changed, it had grown bigger and I did not know everybody who lived there now. The families that I had grown up with had moved on. We spent those three weeks in a cottage beside the army huts of St John's School, where Thomas and Anke Weihs lived. Here I experienced my first Bible Evening. My parents wanted to celebrate it with the Weihses and they expected us to come too, as the Weihs children often did.

I had discovered some wonderful books on the shelves above the bed where I slept and one of them was *Lady Chatterley's Lover*, by D H Lawrence. I buried myself in this masterpiece of human knowledge and discovered that everything that I had experienced so far with regard to love and sex paled in comparison with what these characters achieved. I lusted after such love and passion, but knew that my mother would be horrified to find her little girl reading this book. On the night of the Bible Evening, I was so deeply engrossed that I forgot the time and my father found me lying on the bed, still reading. I am very sure I must have been as red and guilty as if I had committed a crime. But he only said that I should hurry and that I should not let the book keep me away from my obligations.

I was amazed. Not only did he not tell my mother, but he took me for a walk and discussed the contents of it with me, praising its literary merits, and somehow he managed to do this without grilling me about the sex in it! A wonderful man was my father. So the magic of this first encounter with real sex, albeit through literature, was not destroyed, and could live on unsullied by judgements or disapproval. Needless to say, I remember little of the Bible Evening, though it should have been as great an event as it was a great compliment. One was not usually invited to join a grown-ups' festival at such a young age.

Having lost the love of Peter the following summer, I was lonelier than ever. Thornbury Park had a library and I began to browse through it, wanting to read away the misery. I decided to take it on as a challenge and made up my mind to read every book it contained. I began to the left by the door, with fairy tales and fables, children's books and travel books, and moved on through philosophy and history to science fiction and biographies until I reached the anthroposophy section – what there was of it in English, much of it being German. But here I stopped. I could not absorb the lecture cycles of Rudolf Steiner. And I could no longer share this gift of literature with Danny because he had left Camphill.

Whilst we were away at school, the decision had been taken to discontinue work with seriously physically disabled children. Living on the job, as it were, meant long and arduous hours, and with the low income we had as a charity, we did not have the physical aids for lifting and carrying that many other places were beginning to install. I came back for the summer holidays to find them all gone, all my friends and extended family. No one had thought to include the staff children in the decision, an oversight that I felt very bitter about.

I felt particularly bad because during the long Whitsun weekend, something had happened between Danny and me that made me feel sick to remember. The community had decided to take a walk with a picnic down to the River Severn, for a day's outing. Because of the many wheelchairs, I naturally got to push Danny. It was great fun, and downhill all the way. We raced along, giggling and squealing and had a lovely day out together. Then came the return journey, uphill all the way! Now it was hard work, and it was also a hot day. I didn't giggle so much but puffed and pushed, having to put my head down to make the effort. Danny sat and did the giggling. I chatted a bit and then, getting really tired, I said, 'Aren't you lucky that you can just sit there!'

After a shocked silence, in which I listened to my words as

though someone else had said them, Danny howled with rage and fury, and I burst into tears of grief and remorse. Of course we hugged and tried to make it up, and co-workers came to see what the fuss was about, but something was spoiled and ruined. The guilt of my all-embracing tactlessness has never quite left me, and that summer a part of me felt that I had caused Danny's departure. So I tackled my self-imposed task of reading through the library out of loneliness and also as a protest that my friends had gone. Probably, I would have grown out of them, but the sudden wrench was nevertheless very hard to take.

Of all the authors I came across in that library, Eleanor Farjeon and Joan Grant have stayed with me down all the years, the one for her magic of fantasy and poetry, the other for her fascinating depictions of history, which comes alive in the pages of her work. I lived those far memories with Joan, and created a world of fun, goodness and culture with Eleanor. They became friends and soothed my soul. But Rudolf Steiner was too much for me, so dry and didactic was his approach to the mystery of the spirit. I tried one or two, but gave up. The library had done its job; I was due back at school and my head and heart were filled with knowledge and interest once again. I had my friendship with Winny and we were moving to live in The Lodge. We were to experience real family life for the first time, because the house was so small that it only fitted our family. My sister, Agi, had to sleep in the sitting room on a bed that doubled as sofa during the day.

My mother had been granted a sabbatical year and so we could have this precious time together. It seemed strange to me at first, not to be living with ill children, but I didn't mind too much because I wanted to pretend that I was a normal person. I had stopped talking about Camphill at school, not because people weren't interested, but because I had become ashamed of such a strange upbringing and I wanted to fit into the real outside world as much as I could. Now we were going to be a real family and I looked forward to it enormously. The year out was especially wonderful because I did not need to miss out on any of the community events. We were still living in a Camphill community! I felt that I was getting the best of both worlds and looked forward to the coming year. I would not have to be quiet all the time, I would not have to set a good example all the time, I would not have to do enormous washing-ups after the meals, and I would not have to be polite to co-workers whom I did not like. It seemed to me that it was going to be a bit of heaven. And best of all, I would have breakfast, lunch and supper with my mother and father and sisters, without other people, so I could talk as much as I had always wanted to!

We got a record player when we moved to The Lodge. This was a huge development in modernisation. Previously all machines that recorded were considered to be a bad thing and only live entertainment was appreciated. But times changed, even in Camphill, and as we grew older we demanded more and more worldly things. So the gramophone was purchased and I got to listen to the great composers on record. I began to borrow folk music, and this my mother found seriously objectionable. It was not cultured enough for her conservative taste. But I persisted and so Joan Baez came into my life. Her voice was so pure that even my mother accepted her as a real artist and I could enjoy the songs without guilt. We never ever progressed to pop music, though I did try to persuade her that Simon and Garfunkel, the Beatles and other good groups were really worth the bother. Within the community itself, however, records were still frowned upon and we were once again labelled as spoilt brats by the co-workers. I was becoming more and more aware that my mother was seriously unhappy and unappreciated in Thornbury.

The last summer that we spent in England was very hot. The garden behind The Lodge was sheltered by a high hedge and I loved to lie there and sunbathe. In the evenings, I put on my roller skates and went over to The Hatch. Roller skates were a passion for me. The road was smooth and used only lightly by cars and I could get from home to The Hatch in one minute instead of five. It gave me pleasure and freedom. The other great passion was to walk barefooted, much to the disgust of the village people. I walked between the dog's messes on the road and enjoyed the feeling of freedom. I was always looking for ways to be different, partly because my upbringing had made me feel odd, and partly because I felt that this oddness should be put to good use. Moreover, the Sixties was a time of rebellion and pushing out of frontiers, and even a staff child of Camphill felt the moves at work in the world around. Teddy boys, mods and rockers were all around me, and the village of Thornbury had its own fair share of fads, fashions and trends.

Winny and I used to go up to the fish and chip shop beyond the Plain and hang about looking at the boys. We did not join in the little groups that formed amongst the other teenagers who gathered there, but hung in the background, watching and for my part, secretly envying their normality. I wanted to wear make-up, tight trousers and V-necked pullovers too. So I tried it, but only when away from The Lodge. Coming home, I scrubbed off the lipstick, and put on a blouse under my pullover. I wished I had the figure for very short miniskirts but knew that this was going too far, not only for my mother, but perhaps also for the rest of the world!

Winny, Peter and I began a project to renovate a pony cart. It had high wheels with spokes and a leather bench seat. We scraped off all the cracked paint and decorated it primrose yellow and black. This took us most of the summer. It was to be repaired for the chestnut pony that The Hatch owned, predictably called Chestnut. He was fat and neglected and in no fit state to pull a cart full of children. As I was hopeless with tools, it was my job to rehabilitate him. I rode him faithfully every day, groomed him and took him to the blacksmith whose shop was just beyond the chip shop. I loved the looks that people gave me as I walked him up the streets. To own a pony meant status and this was something I seriously craved. Another small step towards normality.

The blacksmith was fat and wheezed as he spoke, but he certainly knew his job. These visits reminded me of the days in Heathcot and I found myself at war with my need to be accepted by the world and my great love of Camphill. Without it I would not have had a pony to work with, I would not appreciate and love music, I would not have access to a library that filled my life with dreams and culture. I would not have known so many people from so many distant lands. I would, without Camphill have been very poor and uneducated, I thought. But I would have been ordinary, have spoken with a Gloucestershire accent, or perhaps a Scottish accent, and I would not have had to go to boarding school and be forever homesick. I would perhaps have been allowed to wear lipstick and tight clothes. I might perhaps have had a boyfriend and been allowed to go to the pictures more than once a month. I would have been allowed to read comics and maybe have had a television.

But again, my other self argued, I would not have had such rich Christmases or Easters and I would not have known about St John's fires. I would not have been in so many plays and I might never have learned folk dancing. So the discussion raged inside me.

To gain some peace I used to visit the graveyard. It lay just up the side road from The Hatch. It had a low wall around it and comforting dark yew trees at its porch entrance. Inside lay the rows of graves, amongst them that of James Embleton, who had travelled to Thornbury when Heathcot was given up and had died aged ten years. Someone had placed a very simple headstone on his little patch of ground and sometimes I weeded around it. I loved to walk down the rows and read the inscriptions. I imagined that here lay the bodies of those who had ceased to have a war inside them. They were at peace with God and man, they knew who was who, and who had what was irrelevant to them. Sometimes I took a picnic of juice and biscuits and sat in the peace of the hot sun, just being and not thinking. Sometimes my sister, Liz, came with me on my visits and she, too, would fall into a companionable silence and simply enjoy the solitude of the place.

The project of the pony cart led to my first encounter with fear in connection with the handicapped. When I was a little girl, the ill children had been my friends, then in my early teens they became my companions. But now they were becoming my charges. In The Hatch I was becoming as useful as a co-worker. Being of the same age as the young people in residence meant that they could compare themselves to me and become a little more active and positive about their lives. I loved the mealtimes with them, the chat and the bustle and especially the closing of the day, because after supper, we would clear the table and get out songbooks. We sang rounds, canons, and catches, learnt four-part songs and had a good choir going. Everyone loved this half-hour.

Except for Arnold. He was a boy of perhaps seventeen years, with sandy hair, a red face and very thick lips. His eyes were blue and sometimes they shone with a sort of malice that threatened. He used to stare at me a great deal and made me a little uncomfortable. He suffered from moods and sometimes outburst of violence that meant someone removing him to his room till he had gained control of himself. There seemed no apparent reason for these outbursts.

Arnold took a liking to me. When I was around, he was much more amenable and cooperative and would participate more willingly in the work and the social life. Because of this, the co-workers used me to help him. I didn't mind this at all, feeling not a little flattered by my power. Sometimes he would refuse to do things unless I did them too. We therefore made supper together, and I enjoyed this very much.

I was still living with the hope that Peter might notice me again, and hung around when the others were gone, waiting for the impossible. Once or twice he was kinder than usual and I would feel a golden glow as I held the yellow paint can for him, or passed him tools as he worked on the pony cart. On one or two occasions I felt as if we were being spied on and saw Arnold, from the corner of my eye, disappearing into the house. But I thought nothing of it.

Then, one evening Peter went just that little further and kissed me. I heard an in-drawn breath, and peered out from behind the door where we had been standing. But no one was there. I told Peter that I thought it might have been Arnold and he only laughed. But the next day as I began to make the supper as usual, Arnold arrived. He did not, however, begin to help me. He just stood there, watching me, refusing to speak and refusing to help. I told him, rather impatiently, to slice the bread. He picked up the bread knife and announced conversationally that he was going to kill me. In a strange way, as though it were a matter of fact, I saw that he really meant it. There was no one in the house at this time of the afternoon, which was not uncommon, as it was my job to do the supper with him.

He came at me with the knife and I stepped back, unfortunately into a recess between the dresser and the wall. Now I was trapped.

His eyes glittered and he smiled an ancient, weary sort of smile. I stood quite still. Some part of me knew that to move would be wrong. I looked him in the eye and waited, quietly. He did nothing, but his breathing was very loud and I thought it sounded like thunder. I was not, at the time that all this was happening, in the slightest bit afraid. It seemed a very normal sort of thing to happen, and so I waited patiently for whatever might come next.

The fear rushed into my blood only when a co-worker called to him from the doorway and broke the spell. Arild, a Norwegian man, kind, quiet and confident, spoke to Arnold in a peacefully humorous tone. He told Arnold to put down the knife, which he did, and then he took him gently by the arm and led him out. I went on making the supper, wondering whether I had dreamt this scene, the shaking of my hands and knees the only thing that made me realise that it was real. But I was very afraid after this and did not like being left alone with The Hatch boys any more. Something was spoilt for me. Something of my freedom was curtailed and I hated the ill children for what they had done to me. I did not tell my mother, my father or my sisters. I was ashamed, and felt guilty. I thought it must have been my fault and that I was to blame for making Arnold behave so strangely. A part of me knew that it had something to do with my kissing Peter.

Eventually the cart was finished and we took it for its first run down to the River Severn, past the graveyard and down through the Gloucestershire lanes in the heat of the summer's glow. It was huge fun! We were barefooted and dirty, Peter, Winny, Inger and I, and we laughed and yelled at Chestnut to get on, trotting happily down to the water's edge. On the way home we went more sedately up the hill, Winny and I walking in deference to the pony's age and strength. Round the corner came an open-topped car driven by American tourists. We recognised them immediately by their clothes and cameras. They stopped and cooed over these picturesque gypsy children and we did not enlighten them. Somewhere in America are photographs of us in the black-and-primrose cart pulled by a chestnut pony, entitled *The English Gypsies*, no doubt.

Then again, my mother came back from the Movement Council and brought the news that we were to move to Ireland.

This was really the end of all ends. Where was Ireland? In our history and geography lessons Ireland only figured as the Irish question that no king or queen ever solved. It was beyond the moon on some other planet. Once again I was to be separated from my friends and my home, from Winny and Peter, and I would have to go back to termly boarding again. I cried a great deal, shouted and roared, but the decision had been made.

My sister Agi had gone to Holland. She had been to the technical college in Bristol to get some more A levels and was now living near Huib in a bedsit and had enrolled to do a social worker's training in Amsterdam. My sister Liz and I would move with our parents to Glencraig in Ireland. This bad news bonded us both, and for the first time since leaving Botton, we began to spend time together. We went to the graveyard a lot and walked the lanes and fields, saying goodbye to the beautiful southern English countryside and wondering whether we would ever feel at home anywhere.

Coming back from one of these walks, barefooted and dispirited, we found ourselves surrounded by a group of Teddy boys wearing sharp polished winkle-pickers and tight, tight jeans. They began to taunt us. I was so angry that I told them to fuck off and pushed my way through the menacing circle that they had made around us, dragging my sister behind me. Then we ran like mad to The Lodge, giggling hysterically. When we got in, my ever-loving sister said that she was going to tell my mother that I had sworn. I felt this to be so unfair, considering that the shock it gave to the boys was the reason they had freed us from their threatening shoes, which they wanted to use to stamp on our bare feet. So I told her myself.

My mother innocently said, 'Oh, how ghastly!' – clearly not knowing what the word meant! We both laughed so much that I forgot my anger. This scene is the last of my memories of Thornbury. What those boys taunted us with was being 'backies' because we lived in Camphill.

Chapter IX
IRELAND

We arrived at the Belfast docks by the Liverpool boat at seven o'clock in the morning. I remember this time so perfectly because I had to do the same journey to and from Wynstones three times a year for the next four years. The boat had docked beside a huge warehouse and we walked down the gangplank onto the concrete quay, suitcases bumping on our legs and I, for one, feeling weak from seasickness. The smell of seaweed, tar and sulphur stank in my nostrils. I knew I was going to hate this town and this country. I felt fiercely resentful of belonging to a community that sent families all over the place without consulting the children about their wishes, hopes and fears. I wanted simultaneously to cling to my mother, and hit her for her willingness to oblige a force greater than her family. The conflict inside me was mounting rapidly. My father seemed quite happy. He loved the sea and had spent all night awake and outside, 'meditating on the state of the universe'. My sister, Liz, was as grumpy as I was.

Down on the quay stood Christof König, sturdy and bearded, beside a ramshackle Land Rover. We piled in and rattled off, along the harbour factories of Harland and Wolff and Shorts Brothers, along the Sydenham bypass, past the gas tanks that filled the air with sulphurous fumes. My eyes stung and watered and I wanted to cry and howl. This hell of Ireland was simply getting worse by the minute.

I wanted to be back in the West Country, where the birds sang, the air was mild and clear and my friends were getting up to face a warm summer's day. Here it was cold and blustery and the clouds hung over the Belfast Lough. The Land Rover rattled on, through Holywood and out again, past hedges and houses, and despite my determination to hate it all, the view opened up onto the lough that revealed a very definite beauty. The Antrim coast on the other side appeared in a misty blueish grey. Eventually we turned off the main road at the Devil's Elbow, as Christof informed us, and down a narrow drive into the woods. The little lodge at the entrance sat sweetly amongst the uncut grass, and over the railway bridge the trees began. I felt something melting inside me. The hardness that I had tried to rebuild was thawing. The woods were so very messy and although the road went downhill, it was so reminiscent of Heathcot's homely tangled summer green that I could not resist it. Round the curve and then once more a straight stretch of narrow drive and at last we came to a halt in a car park edged by a high stone garden wall. In this car park stood a crowd of people and, as the engine stilled, we heard them singing a summer song in a round, lustily and merrily. Clearly this was the welcome committee, and it consisted of most of the co-workers in Glencraig!

I could not believe it! But I learned as time passed that this was always the way to greet newcomers, and when people left everyone went to the car park to wave them off again. Warmth and generosity were the hallmark of this extraordinary place on the shores of the Belfast Lough between Bangor and Holywood.

We got out, each in our various clumsy ways, and hands were shaken. We were urged to come and have breakfast. My hand too was shaken and formal introductions made as though I were a real grown-up! It was unnerving, and again my hatred faltered, but I shored it up with memories of Winny and Peter, The Hatch and the graveyard which I had been forced to leave behind. We went down a pathway towards the courtyard that separated the main buildings, Glencraig House to the left, the Bangor Wing to the right, and the Causeway at the back. We walked through large gates that carriages must have driven through in the olden days, and entered the Causeway for breakfast.

Manfred ushered us up the stairs to a dark wood-panelled dining room where the table was set beautifully, and just for us. We went down a narrow corridor overlooking the courtyard, ugly and concreted, and into what was to be my parents' rooms. The view was staggering. A meadow stretched down to the beach where rocks were clearly visible, well out into the sea. I saw the colony of seals and we were told that this was what 'Craigavad' meant, the rock of the seals, and that they had been there forever. We were told at breakfast that if we sang to them they would come right up, and that co-workers had been accompanied by one or the other when out swimming in the dusk or early morning. My heart lifted again. I could walk straight down to the beach, any time I wanted to, in this beautiful place.

Manfred offered me a cigarette. I was stunned! I did smoke, of course, having started this awful habit out of defiance and because it was the only way in which I could feel really a part of the Sixties culture, not having straight long blond hair, or a figure like an ironing board. I looked at him and at my parents and accepted the proffered smoke. Somehow this gesture made me feel adult at last. Here was someone who did not know me, and therefore did not know that I was a naughty girl. He treated me as someone of fifteen years of age and gave me the respect to which I was quite unaccustomed. The melting ice thawed a bit more.

My sister and I did not sleep in the Causeway. Our family was supposed to live in the newly renovated Bangor Wing, later renamed Ceridwen, but it wasn't yet ready for us, and so we were to sleep in Colm Cottage. Here was another wonder. A tiny house that had once been Carlo Pietzner's garage had been converted into bedrooms. It was set down almost at the water's edge, beside the first purpose-built house called Columbanus, that volunteers from Shorts Brothers and Harland and Wolff had erected at evenings and weekends. Our bedroom looked out over the sea. It was a short walk past Miss Hasting's cottage next door, and we were on the beach with only the seals for company, or some dormitories of children out for a walk. I could go there in my swimming costume with a towel, and come back for a shower without needing to take bags and picnics. The ice melted a bit more.

In Columbanus lived Saralies and her little son, Johannes, who was five years old and the liveliest little imp I had ever met. Saralies was a Dutchwoman, with black hair that had silver threads in it. She wore long skirts that swished as she strode from school to home and back. She was an excellent teacher, had the right level of authority in her voice, and was certainly someone with whom to reckon. No one would ever disobey Saralies! She had the Dutch hearty and brash manner and called a spade a spade. Johannes, her son, had his hair cut like Christopher Robin, as though a pudding basin had been tipped over his head and the scissors had cut round it. It was of a warm chestnut colour and his grin, which he usually wore, stretched his wide mouth even wider, so that one feared it might split his face in half. He wore this look particularly when his eager cheeky mind was planning some devilry. We took to each other on sight, a kindred spirit of rebellion and naughtiness instantly recognised by both of us. Here was Pauly, much younger than me, but just as inventive. Saralies too, became a good friend. She was the most unstuffy co-worker I had yet met, who treated me like a friend and ally and let me look after her son with faith and trust in my good sense. This was a very new experience for me. I had been the naughty staff child for fifteen years, and now suddenly I was a fellow co-worker, perhaps a bit young and in need of guidance, but a person whose goodwill might be of benefit to the whole community.

Glencraig estate was beautiful, flowing up over the hill to the railway and the road, and running down to the seashore, whose beach was ours. It was private, and walkers were only allowed to pass through it on their way to Bangor or Holywood. The Craigowen estate that bounded on the golf course, and Rockport School on the other, protected us on either side. A belt of mature trees separated us from these two country parks. Who would have thought that the narrow entrance at the road would open into so vast and lovely a spot! I fell in love, and to this day am still in love with this little patch of the great big planet Earth.

But it was all too much for my soul and heart. I went to bed and almost literally slept for a month. I seemed not to be able to wake-up. Sometimes Saralies would come in and shake me out of bed at eleven in the morning, but by one o'clock I was fast asleep again. I did eat, however. I remember lunches in the Causeway with my parents and lots of loud handicapped children whom I hardly knew, and I remember swimming in the lough, but much of those first four weeks are a blur of withdrawal. I had so much to come to terms with.

Johannes got me up and out of bed. He seemed to need someone to play with and I became his companion. We went for walks, played on the swing in the playground between the wild rose bushes and unclipped hedges; we swam in the sea and rode the ponies. He had an imagination that filled his days, and in the evenings, after bathing him, I read fairy tales to him until Saralies said it was time to sleep.

Perhaps it was the easy way in which I found it possible to fill his day that gave some people the idea that I might like to run a kindergarten for the little children. This was a mixed group of handicapped and staff children and I was to take them for three hours every morning. The children were difficult. Some were severely withdrawn and autistic, some were lively and emotionally trying. The staff children too were not easy. They were undisciplined and haughty, not given to doing as they were asked. The three little Mentzel girls, with their hair in plaits and round, pink cheeks, reminded me of my own siblings, and their high shrill voices plagued me at times. But they were so cheerful and good-hearted that I loved them all. I played ring games, sang nursery rhymes with my guitar, told them fairy tales and took them out to the playground on the swings. This last was not a great success. I could not keep the six of them together, and the staff children took over, bossing and yelling. So I kept them indoors all the time. But on the whole we had fun and I could not get over my amazement that I was trusted with such a great responsibility – except on Thursdays.

Thursday was a special day, as it had been in Heathcot. The children had a rest morning and the co-workers cleaned and polished the lovely wooden parquet floors that were laid in all the houses. The walls of many of the dormitories were panelled in plywood and the warmth of all this wood added to the cosy feeling of Glencraig. It was almost tangible. The dining room tables were strangely shaped so that no matter where you sat, you could communicate with your neighbour, except for at one spot on each table. Here you found yourself sitting at an angle. This little place was great for autistic children, who dislike direct contact.

I did not want to remain in Colm Cottage, eating my meals in Columbanus, and so I moved up to the Main House, because I wanted to be nearer to my parents who were still lodging in the

Causeway. I slept in a tiny room over the backstairs, and it was the hottest room I ever lived in. The bed was built up over the stairwell because that was the only space available. Otherwise, it was just a passage with a door. The window opened a mere crack for very necessary ventilation – or else the sleeper might have suffocated! I was there a month and then went back to school.

I could hardly bear to leave. No more weekend refresher visits at home in Thornbury, because it was no longer my home. Of course, I had arranged to visit, and as often as possible, and I knew that I would always be welcome in The Hatch, but it would not be the same. I feared the lump of homesickness, and fought it as it began to rise in my throat well before we even began to arrange the journey to Gloucester. We packed the brown trunk and sent it, luggage in advance, a week before travelling ourselves. That week put me into a state of mourning. I went for walks over the fields, up the little overgrown farm tracks flanked by flowering gorse, and gazed over the lough, feeling a longing to return before I had even left Ireland. The Celtic soul had enchanted me. England seemed cold and distant, though the thought of seeing the Hayn family, and Winny, did engender a flicker of warmth.

But go we must, and at eight o'clock on a Saturday evening at the end of September we departed on the Liverpool boat. I lay in my narrow bunk bed and felt sick all night. Liverpool docks at six on Sunday morning were miserable and damp, and the smell of coal and sulphur stung our throats. We took a taxi to the station and then spent the rest of the day chugging slowly down the railway tracks in the way only Sunday trains in England can achieve, eating our brown bread sandwiches and hard-boiled eggs on Birmingham New Street Station whilst waiting interminably for the next connection to Bristol.

We spent Sunday night in Thornbury and went to school on Monday afternoon. This journey repeated itself for the rest of my time at school. It always seemed to rain when we left Ireland, and the same rain welcomed us when we returned. The smell of cold wet sea and coal reminds me to this day of the sinking sensation of homesickness that emptied my belly, a horrible feeling that now accompanied the lump in my throat and pervaded the next four years. Ireland had me in its grip and I never liked to leave it, finding England boring after the brightness of the air and the changes of the Irish sky. Its blue seemed more blue than anywhere else in the world.

Returning home for our first Christmas in Glencraig, we found ourselves living in Ceridwen at last. Our room had our bed covers and pictures in it, but not our chairs. Where were they? My mother had left them in Thornbury! This betrayal of family identity went very deep. I felt a shiver of insecurity, and with it came the realisation that I would not always be a part of the familiar family warmth.

I was finding my feet more and more with the co-workers of the community. Glencraig embraced me as a useful person. I could help out in workshops, like the laundry. I could run the kindergarten. I could look after Johannes. I could make the suppers and I could take on to teach a very new little boy to eat at table. He only ate chocolate pudding at first. So to persuade him to diversify, we covered everything with chocolate pudding, gradually leaving the odd potato uncovered, then a bit of carrot, then a trace of meat, until by the end of the holidays he was eating a small plate of food without the chocolate sauce, provided it stood ready in a bowl for him to gobble up after his plate had been emptied. What a feeling of achievement this was!

In the summer evenings, when the sun went down at midnight and the skies were a clear soft blue, the co-workers would go down to the beach, light a fire and sing folk songs till all hours of the morning. We were an innocent lot; no alcohol and no drugs. Caring for the handicapped was taken seriously and trying to build a meditative life was taken just as seriously. We were told that narcotics and alcohol would not help us to achieve full spiritual control. We were not so innocent that we did not know that they would certainly hamper any physical discipline. So we had lovely times together and my guitar became very popular. Liz and I sang together and sometimes held little impromptu concerts in the dining room when the weather was dreary.

It was an odd feature of the Glencraig houses that they had no sitting rooms. One lived in the kitchen or the dining room and the children played in the big dormitories where they slept together in groups of eight. Unlike the other communities in which I had so far lived, there were many houses in Glencraig, and all of them were cosier than Heathcot, Botton Hall or The Park in Thornbury. They were more like The Hatch and had a family atmosphere. I loved to visit all of them, feeling welcomed and at home wherever I went. I particularly loved the tiny farmer's cottage, Pestalozzi, a house named after the Swiss social reformer who created homes for homeless children. The attraction here, apart from the fact that this house *did* have a sitting room, with a beautiful stone fireplace, was Christof and Annemarie König. Christof was so different from the other co-workers. He was more like a staff child, which of course he had been, but had now, as an adult, decided to join Camphill as a co-worker. I had not known him when Camphill started in Scotland because by the time I reached an age of consciousness, they had moved to England with Mrs König, and no longer shared their home with their father. However, growing up in Camphill is a bond that works subliminally. Staff children recognise each other and know each other because of their common background. Camphill ethics are universal within Camphill communities.

The Königs lived with four adult villagers in the wooden ceilinged old-fashioned little house. The Aga was warm and the food delicious. It became a second home for me. When Annemarie, a warm and pretty woman who always wore jeans (an unusual type of dress for the women who worked in Camphill!), had her first two children, I loved helping her by babysitting or childminding, because it was the nearest thing to a real family home. Christof taught me to play chess, and in the evenings when the cows were milked and the farm put to bed, we sat and competed very unfairly because I could never grasp the rules. Sometimes I went to Pestalozzi just to sit and read, because this little house, with its tiny sitting room and spluttering fire embraced me. I felt free enough to use it when the mood took.

Christof, however, could be very strict, and he expected that everyone would do something for their living, so I often made supper or cleaned the house by way of earning my keep. It was a good foundation for housekeeping and rearing children later on when I grew up.

The farm itself, which Christof ran, was attached to one side of the courtyard next to Ceridwen and Causeway, and one reached it by taking the passage between these two houses. We had a herd of pretty Jersey cows, and the rich creamy unpasteurised milk was a holiday treat. Any other milk tasted weak and boiled in comparison. Needless to say, I got fatter than ever, but I didn't care. The milk was far too good to resist. The villagers who worked the farm with Christof were friendly people and did the milking more or less on their own. In those days they milked by hand and so even disabled people could learn how to do it. Sometimes, Christof had to finish off for them, because such a degree of thoroughness was not always within their capability.

I loved watching Henry bring in the cows. He had been to school in Glencraig and, once grown up, had declared his wish to become a farmer. He was Christof's right-hand man. Christof always said that he could never have managed without Henry, a short, squat and rugged figure, whose mouth was his dominating feature, large and crooked and sometimes a bit wet. He trudged with heavy steps ahead of the herd, calling them in a special way as he trod. They followed, trustingly, with Derek, a tall and gangly villager who never stopped talking, bringing up the rear. To see these pretty animals in the meadows around the estate that were fenced with planks still covered in bark, was like a fairy tale. With a bit of imagination, one might have thought they were deer.

Sometimes, in the early morning, the fox came by over the hill, his coughing bark sounding wild and disappointed. Obviously our chickens were too well fenced for him to get at them. There were also badgers, living upstream in the woods along the drive. One year Christof hopefully nurtured a flock of geese, supposed to be for our Christmas dinner, in a dammed-up bit of the stream. The badgers, however, got every one of them, biting off their heads and sucking out the blood. Christof was furious. He lay in wait for them with his gun, but in the end could not bring himself to shoot them after all, they were so beautiful and free in their wilderness of woodland that bordered the drive to the road. Organic as our farm was, the wildlife belonged as part of the natural ecology.

When we first came to Glencraig the main meal of the day was prepared in the central kitchen in the Main House on a huge coal-fired Aga. Various middle-aged women came and went, each producing the same revolting boarding-school menus. Overcooked cabbage and devilled bacon, with sausages that swam in grease and potatoes watery from over boiling, was our daily fare. Villagers worked here peeling and scrubbing vegetables, and in the afternoons, they baked bread for the community. The wholemeal bread, unlike the dinners, was delicious. Lunches were transported in buckets to the houses, pulled by wooden carts. Each house had only a tea kitchen, so small and unpractical that only breakfasts and suppers could be prepared there.

My mother began trying to persuade the community that lunches too could be cooked at home. She said that a house was not a real home without someone who cooked. But the kitchens were too small, and the co-workers were all working in the classrooms, or in therapies, so it took a while until cooking at home could become the norm. With the purchase of Craigowen estate, which was to become the heart of the village, whilst the Main House, now called Comgall, remained as the heart of the school, the central kitchen at last vanished. But it took a few years to raise enough money to make the individual kitchens big enough and properly equipped for hot meals to be produced in them. Cooking in the tiny tea kitchens must have been a nightmare.

Craigowen House, when it became ours, was a delight of dark little passages and stairwells leading to hidden rooms. Though the windows were large and gave a breathtaking view of the lough, the house itself was Victorian and painted in browns and bottle greens, with a bit of olive grey-green, just for the sake of variety. It was filthy, the old man who owned it having kept chickens in the kitchen. But eventually it made a beautiful home for the village that was growing bigger with each year as children grew up and yet wanted to stay in the community. Attached to Craigowen was a billiard room, connected to the house by an overhead passage which boasted a bowling alley. This beautiful parquet-floored and wood-panelled room became the Village Hall and service room, until the Seventies, when a charming pentagonal little chapel was purpose built between the two estates. A break in the hedge that had divided them was created by a group of young people from the International Voluntary Service, who camped one summer and took this on as a project, and so Glencraig estate grew bigger. Still later on, the fields behind Rockport School were purchased. This benefited the farm enormously. The fields, when we bought them, were nearly dead, starved of nutrition because they had been forced to grow barley every year without organic fertilisation. It took seven years of careful husbandry to bring them back to life again.

The workshops too, were growing, as was the school. Carlo Pietzner, who had started this Camphill community in 1953, and had then moved on to the USA to start a Camphill community in Pennsylvania, came to visit. He was very impressed with all the developments that Dr Hans Heinrich Engel had created. He took over from Carlo. The memory of our first encounter in Heathcot House at the bottom of our stairs never ever left me. I remained a tiny bit in awe of him, and could never quite build up a firm friendship because of it. He was always kind, direct and fair, but hardly as approachable as I would have wanted. His health was often poor, and this made him sometimes rather inaccessible and remote. But he gave wonderful lectures on Irish history and mythology, was a very good doctor, and could be relied on to help if one was ever in trouble. I deeply respected him. Under his guidance and through his great vision for development, Brendan and Comenius, two houses suitable for adults, were built to augment the needs of the village, and later, Colman and Ciaran, houses especially for the adolescents, were constructed. He saw that young people need time to prepare for adulthood, and started the first training college for adolescents with special needs.

However, this great pioneer did not include in his plans a sitting room or adequate kitchens. Most of the newly built houses that were erected before, or shortly after we arrived, had only a small kitchen-cum-dining room. This was only one of the things that caused some disagreement between my mother and Hans Heinrich. They did not always see eye to eye. He lived in Comgall with his wife, Turid, and later on, their little son. The rest of the house had become a cultural space with a hall and service room. A music room and other therapy rooms filled the rest of the spacious building, as well as a treatment room for surgery, and the offices.

Turid used to sweep round the houses telling everyone what to do and then return to her place in the treatment room. She was an excellent nurse, and when one was ill there was no one nicer than Turid to care for one. At other times she held court, keeping everyone in their proper place and protecting Hans Heinrich, who was so busy lecturing, doing his medical work and developing the community that he probably needed a guardian. My mother was a housemother, the days of the matron having gone and more emphasis being placed on the home. She struggled to bring about the change from institution to home life and sometimes quarrelled fiercely with the Engels, though at no time did I ever detect disrespect or dislike between them. They worked well together, all of them outspoken and honest, serving the good of Glencraig seriously and warmly.

All in all, the quarrelling was productive, not a fundamental problem that could interfere or damage their very true and trusted friendship. Community life, I was beginning to notice, required an all-inclusive energy that bound the social life, permitted discussion, encouraged contemplation, could cope with disagreement and finally reached for a consensus that sometimes left aside one's personal wishes and wants. I admired these people very much for their earnest attempts to overcome differences. They strove for the remarkable level of allowing argument that nevertheless valued the individual as a human being.

In my second year of living in Glencraig, a German girl came to help the Mentzel family. Manfred and Margaret, both working as teachers and houseparents, also had four little girls of their own. Renate came to be their nanny, aged seventeen. Being only one year older than I was, we naturally became good friends. She was very attractive and had a sparkling smile. Moreover, she was extremely gifted artistically and had a way with children that entered their little hearts instantly. Renate and I enjoyed being the teenagers that we were, because sometimes the adult responsibility of having to behave like a co-worker was too much, and I just wanted to play. We went to the pubs in Bangor and discovered the great singing bands and their folk music. They seemed to start up casually in one corner of the smoke-filled stuffy atmosphere and instantly raised the tone from serious drinking to cultural splendour, filling the pub with song and laughter. I gained a vast new repertoire from these 'singing pubs' and sometimes brought my guitar to join them. But I never touched alcohol, being afraid of what my mother might say to me.

Margaret's youngest daughter died when still a small baby and this changed her life. She took on her own children and became less of an absentee mother, and Renate left to work in Holland in a Camphill Community. My mother greatly applauded and supported these new developments within the families, encouraging parents to bring up their own children. She said that one does not give birth to babies merely to have someone else bring them up. It was one's own responsibility. Times were changing, and the staff children now growing up in Camphill should not only be left to the community but should be able to identify closely with their families. I watched this next generation of staff children and was glad that my mother was bringing them into a clear concept. More children would now have the chance to be recognised as having needs, not for special education but for sound family values. Only Johannes did not seem to be able to take advantage of this new approach. Although without doubt Saralies loved him very much, she was a single parent and could not always manage to give the time and discipline that her lively son craved.

When he was seven, she sent him to board with a family who lived in Botton. He would come home for the holidays very unhappy and wanting to stay at home. But send him off again she did, term after term. He took to spending a great deal of his holidays with me and I tried to mother him as much as a big sister could, not yet really understanding what motherhood really was. He became my little brother and I looked forward to the holidays, as much to be at home with my family in Glencraig as to see him again.

Sometimes we went on outings together, because during the holidays Saralies made special time for her son, doing the things that he loved. She could drive, very badly and energetically, but we always got there eventually. We took the VW Beetle, her pride and joy, and drove all over the Northern Irish countryside, exploring the roads and walking the hills and woods. We went to the Giant's Causeway, a very long trip in those days, and spent most of the time trying to prevent Johannes from drowning as he climbed the honeycomb rocks and walked the cliff path, a dangerous venture in those days of unprotected coastlines.

On another trip, we visited the Struel Wells, said to be blessed by St Patrick. The water was renowned for healing eye diseases. In great secret hope, I bathed my face, paying special attention to my eyes, and offering up a fervent prayer that my sight would improve and that I would no longer need to wear glasses. I did not use them all the time, though I was supposed to, and only wore them for reading. But I resented them, wanting to see properly without these aids. Unfortunately, the saint must have been busy elsewhere, and did not appear to have heard my prayers.

Other types of outings began to happen now that I was older. I got a bit more pocket money and so began to explore the cinema, a form of culture that delighted and amazed me. I began to learn more about the world and to feel less of an outcast. My father took me to see *West Side Story*, the only time he took me out on my own. This was because it was an 'A' film and I was not yet twenty-one. I loved it, crying bitterly at the tragic end and loving my father for taking me to such a grown-up film, despite the fact that my mother had tried to dissuade him. I tried to tell her about it, but she considered the cinema uncultured and vulgar and she showed no interest. However, I was hooked on this medium, and craved the pleasure and the definite culture that could be found in films. Moreover, I was a teenager and wanted to discover more about the wonderful world of love! I started reading romances, books being a form of culture that everyone around me encouraged. They did not always enquire as to the contents! I wanted to find 'true love' everywhere and began to drop my standard of literature, as Mills and Boon entered my life.

Alongside this sad state of literary affairs, Georgette Heyer fortunately came to my notice, introduced to me by Birgit Engel, the daughter of Hans Heinrich. She was a couple of years older than me, but the childish separation that differences in age creates was gradually diminishing. She was friendly and available, living at home whilst studying physiotherapy in Belfast at Queen's University. I devoured Georgette Heyer's novels, learning the

English language all over again with great enjoyment. I also learnt a great deal of history. I shall be forever grateful to this great novelist because my sister, Liz, also began to read her books, and this formed a new bridge between us. Somewhere, during the move from England to Ireland, we had begun to grow apart again. She was doing her A levels and had little time for me. She was worried about her future and did not know what she would do after school. She was considering studying but did not know if this would suit her at all. She was still rather timid in public, and disliked meeting strangers.

After leaving school, she took a dormitory whilst marking time. She worked with a group of girls who slept in Colm Cottage but belonged to Columbanus. She enjoyed the children and was an excellent dormitory mother. I loved hearing the stories she could tell about life as a co-worker in Glencraig. The adventures were often amusing, as on the occasion of an official visit by doctors and social workers. These visits were quite common and usually very friendly. Strangers were always inquisitive, and often impressed, finding our way of life odd, challenging, yet wonderfully rich. It was important to make a good impression because such professionals were able to send more children or adults to join our community.

On this particular occasion, Liz was busy with one of the girls, tying her shoelaces, when the visitors arrived. They were delighted with what they saw, remarking that we were obviously true to our word about being a community that disregarded differences between the normal and the handicapped. Here was proof that even the children helped each other! We found this terribly funny, but were also secretly quite proud of Camphill. What was even funnier was that on another such visitation, my mother had been sitting on a bed in one of the dormitories, keeping a sick child comfortable and happy, and was kindly asked, very slowly and clearly, whether she too, was sick!

If it was hard to detect differences between the children and their carers, it was possibly even harder to see any difference between the co-workers and the villagers. Nobody dressed very smartly in Glencraig, just as it had been in Botton. We were, as always, poor, and got our clothes from handouts and charities, always gratefully received. The furniture in the houses was also second hand, but unlike the clothes that we suffered, the houses were furnished with beautiful antiques for which we paid nothing. Davenports, walnut dressing tables, chests of drawers made from oak darkened with age, roll-top beech desks and heavy wardrobes with discoloured mirrors graced the rooms.

Mr Laing, a round, bald middle-aged man, repaired and refurbished these beautiful handcrafted pieces in a tiny workshop tucked away in the passage between Ceridwen and Causeway. He was an artist at his work, but too grumpy for me to sit and watch, as I had done with Bill in Heathcot. But nobody could make our clothes look good. It depended on how clean they were and on the body that wore them. And the villagers, who either slouched or walked in a jerky way, could not make these shapeless and often discoloured garments look anything but appallingly shabby.

Rosy Chambers always wore a pinafore apron over the checked tweed tube of a skirt that she liked best. With a drab felted cardigan, she looked the archetypal Mrs Mop, and was often to be seen with a broom as her job was in the housekeeping. She had frizzy short hair and a jutting chin. She needed people to say, 'Hallo, Rosy,' whenever she encountered someone, and on one occasion, neglecting to say it yet again as I was carrying trays to and from the central kitchen, she hefted that broom and hit me over the head with it. Needless to say, I did not forget to greet her again! But usually Rosy was sweet and kind, did her work very well and sang like an angel. Her voice, a pure soprano, rang above everyone as we sang together at festivals, or just for the fun of it at adult social evenings. She also loved folk dancing and could do it very well indeed, but with a rather stiff gait.

Living in Ceridwen, which looked out onto the courtyard, meant that everyone passed by sooner or later – to the office, out to the car park (or 'parking place' as it was commonly called), or through the side door of Comgall for medicines, or to see the doctor in the treatment room. Timothy Ballam loved to hang out and watch the passers by. The walled in garden on the other side of Ceridwen was where he should have been working, but as work was not something that he did very well, Peter, the gardener, let him roam. Timothy was not a pretty sight; he had a swollen cheek and he dribbled, and spoke – if at all – with a very unclear diction. But he was extremely social and very well loved. He would lean in the little kitchen window and blubber out things to which one did not have to give very concentrated answers. His coat, a drab brown duffle, always hung half off his shoulders. But he made a lovely undemanding companion whilst one worked.

Peter and Susanne lived in Comenius house, and Peter ran the garden whilst Susanne ran everything else. He had a round face, a very German accent and ground his teeth when angry which happened at very regular intervals. He was a man with little patience. My father worked with him for a time, but after his first heart attack, he was advised to do something different and less strenuous. So he began to work in the office, keeping the books. Because he was also advised to take a daily walk for the sake of his constitution, he began the job of delivering the letters that arrived in the office twice daily. The whole community had only one address, that of Glencraig.

My father loved this job, setting out with his hat at a jaunty angle, his pipe puffing merrily in his mouth and his eyes on the envelopes that he carried. He liked guessing who the letters might be from, and learnt people's handwriting so that he could annoyingly tell you who your letters were from. He read the backs of postcards, declaring that if they didn't want them read, they should put them in an envelope! He also delivered the newspapers. He would arrive and say that paragraph six on page four was the only news worth reading, and quite often he was right. People loved his daily visits and would stop to talk to him as he passed by, each one feeling a little better, or brightened by his warmth and good cheer.

My father loved Susanne, and had a lot of time for Peter, whose ungoverned moods often put him in the wrong, not so much because he was actually at fault but because of the way he delivered his thoughts. My father too was used to being unheard, and had sympathy with this awkward yet kindly young man.

Peter grew wonderful vegetables but had a problem letting us eat them! By the time he allowed them to be harvested they were usually past their best and no one wanted them any more. One year he had so many cabbages that he decided to turn them into sauerkraut. Poor Susanne, with the help of Rosy Chambers, got the job of cutting them up. Peter then laced them with salt and, taking off his shoes and socks, stepped into the vat and began to trample the pottage. As he was at that moment in a raging fury, he trampled mightily and the juice flew everywhere all over him. Intermittently, he let out a scream or a yell. I could not take my eyes off him, wanting to laugh and yet not daring to pass by on my way to Columbanus to get Johannes, who wanted to play. The stench of the raw cabbage and the thought of Peter's dirty feet all over the potential food had its effect, and has made the eating of sauerkraut a difficult thing for me to face.

Glencraig was no different from all the other communities in which I had lived, in that so many people came and went that I can remember only a few, and not really in their right order at all. The children too did not always stay. Some were able to be happy in Glencraig only for a time and some were too difficult to do anything for in such an open and family-like setting as our community provided. But some, despite their problems, managed for a time – like Jane, who could recite every TV advertisement for the last ten years. She sang them just as they were sung on TV, accents and voices in perfect mimicry. She could also be very violent and self-destructive at times, and quite calm and placid at other times. Eventually, her unpredictable nature became too much for her, and for us, and she had to leave for a closed institution. We missed her very much because during her time with us she had become a dear friend.

Many of the children in Ceridwen were very disturbed and ill. John Henry, a Downs boy, sat most of the time, grinding his teeth and swinging his eyes loosely in his head in an unnerving manner. He could scream as well, but he was such a darling that we all loved to take care of him, as we did of John Francis, though he was often wild and liked to run away. He was blond and beautiful and was the boy who loved chocolate pudding.

Karen was perhaps the most challenging of all the children in those early years. She used to injure herself and was quite violent towards others, though when one knew her she could be very sweet. She took all the new co-workers for a ride, refusing to cooperate with any instructions. It always amused me to see a new girl trying to take Karen for a walk. She would sit down, refuse to budge and finally even lie down. However, she would behave quite differently with those whom she knew. If any of us passed by and told her to get up, she would rise with a grimace, making the poor new girl feel very foolish. She would do as she was told, even when it was only me at home on my holiday from school. The new co-workers would complain to my mother and she would say, 'The children are our teachers.' And indeed they were.

Johnny was the first child to be admitted to Glencraig. He came with Carlo and his family from Camphill in Aberdeen to help to start Glencraig. He was thin and pale, with a very large head, small body and a severe hunchback. He had a glorious laugh, wily and loud, and would roar it out whenever anybody hurt themselves or made a fool of themselves. This could be very humiliating, but one got used to it and learned never to be too proud. It was said that Johnny knew before an accident could occur. On one occasion, a builder up a ladder heard Johnny laugh with glee seconds before the ladder slipped and he fell to the ground!

We all loved Johnny very, very much. His wheelchair attended every occasion. He could walk a little, but only with help and not for long distances, and it caused him some pain. But he loved being upright and rarely fussed about it. Sometimes the pain was greater than at others, and then he would cry, big tears rolling down his cheeks, refusing to eat and vomiting up any food that one might try to give him. He was a young man now and sat in the variety workshop, a place that produced goods as its name described, or in the laundry, where he occasionally folded a flannel or two. Work was not his strong point. It was his sociable nature that made him a great contributor to the community.

Eventually my mother gave up being a housemother in a children's house and we moved to Brendan, situated along the road between the farm and Columbanus. It looked out over the fairy ring, an old rath overgrown with tall beeches and ash trees. Hawthorns too grew inside the circle. We shared this small village house with six adults and Beattie, an Englishwoman of uncertain age. She had iron-grey hair scraped back in the inevitable bun, and glinting eyes that filled with humour and laughter. She and my mother shared the responsibility of the house.

I began to involve myself less and less in the work of the community. I wanted to get out into the outside world. I was doing exams and trying not to be scared of moving on into adulthood. Beattie had no time for this. She expected us all to contribute, even though we were staff children. She loved my sister, Agi, who always helped out when she was at home, and was now married to the Dutch co-worker she had met in Thornbury. They had had their civil wedding in Amsterdam, a month prior to coming home for the religious ceremony. Nevertheless, my mother, an old-fashioned lady with Victorian morals, did not consider them really married, and so she prepared two single rooms for their arrival at the end of July.

A community wedding in Glencraig was almost better than it had been in Heathcot. Comgall Hall was prepared with flowers and an arch was created around the door outside. The whole community prepared for this great day. People bought clothes for the occasion and attended the ceremony bathed and polished, with shining faces. No one was left out; children and adults all came to celebrate. The priest who usually officiated at all the sacraments came from Edinburgh, which was our nearest centre of the Christian Community; but on this occasion the Reverend Peter Roth, who was Agi's godfather, performed the ceremony, and travelled all the way from Botton to tie the knot. Huib's family came too, feeling shy to be in so odd a place, but liking it nevertheless. I, of course, fell temporarily in love with Huib's brother, but it only lasted about five minutes. Agi's friends came for the festival and we had a hugely decorated and lovely meal as a wedding breakfast. Everyone wore their best clothes, Huib's mother having splashed out into a silk suit, which in those days would have cost a great deal of money. During the photographs, I brushed against her with a lighted cigarette in my hand and burnt a hole in it, right at the front. I wished that I could have died, but she was very nice about it, though she never let me forget it!

In the evening we had a social gathering and danced the folk dances that we had learned in Thornbury as a tribute to the place where they had first met. These dances were, in point of fact, standard in Camphill and were the source of our social material. I sang and played my guitar and people had a great time. Social occasions were common in Glencraig, and we used any excuse to have a bash. We would create skits about people we all knew, acting out all the funny, silly, tragic events that occurred throughout the year. A wedding was a wonderful chance to clown, and we took full advantage of it, enjoying ourselves, laughing, talking, singing and dancing, the villagers blending us all together in their innocent enjoyment of the fun.

For their honeymoon, Huib and Agi said they would go for a camping holiday round Ireland. In fact, they pitched their tent up at the top of St John's field, (all the field's had names in Glencraig) overlooking the lough and out of sight of the houses. Here they stayed happily for ten days. Liz and I visited them in the evenings to sit round their campfire and chat. Only mother and father did not know that they were so close by. We kept it quiet and enjoyed their company! They too, like the rest of our family, though they never actually lived in Glencraig, had fallen in love with its beauty, which, despite all the building in recent years, still remains to this day.

That summer, Liz passed her A levels, and we decided to go on a hitch-hiking holiday to the west coast, travelling up through Larne, Derry, Donegal and down to Galway. It was our first independent holiday without parents or grown-ups. We felt quite safe because Ireland was a generous country and no one would ever come to any harm. It was quite common to walk up the drive and hitch-hike into Belfast, or wherever one wanted to go. Pocket money was scarce and the train had no halt near to us, though the line ran right through the top of our property. Cars stopped readily but odd questions were asked, as happened once when I got a lift into Belfast and the driver quizzed me about our 'commune'. He asked if we really believed in love, and when I innocently said that we did, he asked coyly whether we all slept in one bed.

We set off without a qualm, my mother and father having given us £20 each, I think, and trusting that we would be fine. And it rained. Sometimes we were so wet no one would pick us up. Sometimes we could not get into the youth hostels and had to beg for a corner till the warden gave in and made space for us. I hated it, not enjoying the uncertainty, and not wanting to carry the heavy rucksack. I had imagined that the freedom would be thrilling, but the hard work it turned out to be was far less enjoyable than the thought had been when we planned the trip. Though the countryside was superb, green and grey in the mist and the rain, and though everyone who picked us up was as kind as they could be, I felt homesick once more. It seemed as if I could never feel well away from Camphill and my family.

One of the cars that stopped for us was driven by a stocky man who Bible-bashed at us all the way to Larne. His wife sat mute and petrified next to him, whilst I got into my stride and argued about what might have happened to St Paul at Damascus, and whether everything that was written in the Bible should be taken literally. The man shouted and harangued us and my sister kept nudging me to shut up and just let him talk but I could not listen to the rubbish that poured from his thick lips. I wished that my father were there because he would have been able to quote chapter and verse back at him. Years later, I saw the same man on the news on TV. It was the Reverend Ian Paisley himself, and I laughed, though I remembered his wife's scared face with not a little pity.

On that same trip I lost the watch that had accompanied us on all our outings from early childhood. My mother gave me her gunmetal timepiece when I turned fourteen and I loved it dearly. But somewhere between Sligo and Galway it fell off my wrist and was never seen again. A big chunk of my childhood went with it.

All too soon it was my turn to worry about leaving school and what I might do with my life. I had absolutely no idea, except that I wanted to get right away from Camphill and anthroposophy and as far away as was at all possible. Together with my friend, Annette, we decided that working with children was the best thing to do. I did not want to study, and she did not feel that she could. Though a very bright girl with red hair and a lively expressive face, she was dyslexic. She had become a close friend of mine at Wynstones, joining our class when we lived in Thornbury.

Though Winny was still my very best friend, Jenny and

Annette were my friends in the class. At first, Annette challenged me, a bit too much for comfort sometimes, but I liked her very much nevertheless. She came from a very, very English home, with horses and Cheltenham Ladies' College as a background. My Camphill upbringing made me feel a little insecure when visiting her home, but because I liked her so much, I braved the possible gaffes I might make and went anyway. Gradually, as I became more comfortable with her, our friendship also stood on a firmer footing, unemotional, but warm. I had always regarded my friends as people to whom I could pour my heart out and might have been a little overheated in both language and action, fiercely loyal, but also demanding. Annette's manner cooled me down and I grew to appreciate her more and more as time passed.

Now, with our schooldays ending, we decided to apply for a nursery nurses' training course and chose to go together, I because I was afraid to go anywhere alone, and she because it suited her to go with me. We were both accepted in a college in Reading, a place with which I had absolutely no connections whatsoever. There could, therefore, be no link with Camphill, and I was sure that I would learn how to live correctly in the normal world. I felt that I could never do this unless I was forced, but I did not want to lay myself open to failure either. I hoped that Annette would help me, but I nevertheless quailed at the realisation of how much adjusting I was going to have to face.

The family decided that as I, the youngest, was now going to leave home, we should have one last family holiday together. So we hired a car, and obtained the use of a house from the parents of a young villager who lived with us, who had a holiday home in Donegal. Agi and Huib came over from Holland, because Huib was the only driver we had amongst us. Being part of Camphill meant that there were no private vehicles, only community cars driven by appointed drivers, and neither of my parents had ever learnt to drive. I travelled up to Derry by train because I would have to leave before the holiday was over and there was no space for me in the car. I had decided to fill the interim months before my course would start by going as an au pair to France.

My sister, Liz, had stayed for eight months with a family whom Susanne knew in France. She had gone there to improve her French before her A level exam and it had helped enormously. She enjoyed it so much that she invited me to come for a week, and I had loved it too, finding the Loire valley beautiful and being in France an exciting experience. Perhaps it was all the more interesting because the Monzies family lived in a chateau between Vierzon and Bourges, a beautiful, though rather run-down castle with turrets and bats and silk-covered walls. The grand room downstairs even had moth-eaten tapestries hanging on the walls. Madame rang a little brass bell to call in the maid for service between each of the four courses that were placed before us at dinner. I first tasted wine at the chateau. Liz went to stay with them to help them in their market garden. Now I had a job with a family down in the village near the chateau.

However, before this great adventure could begin, my family got together that summer as arranged, and we motored up north in an unusual heatwave. It was all a bit like a dream. We located the house up on the hillside near Buncrana in Donegal. It was big enough for us all, even allowing us to choose our own rooms. Not having to share was a holiday in itself. My bedroom had little rose patterns on the wallpaper and I woke each morning to the sound of the rooks cawing, just as they did in Glencraig, with the sun shining gloriously. It was one of those freak hot summers that happen once in a while. Ireland becomes a paradise in the heat. We swam and ate and read books and went for walks and talked and talked and talked. We did not fight once, which was the nicest part of that holiday.

My mother and father relaxed on deckchairs in the garden and read their Rudolf Steiner lectures, as they always did on holiday. We explored ancient sights in the area, the most notable being a huge fort that had been excavated and was set on the top of a hill over looking the bay. Huib made up the most extravagant tales of what it might have been used for and we laughed till we were sick and aching. My sister Liz and I managed to arouse a nest of wasps, which is the other memorable event of that holiday. We climbed the hill behind the house to get a good view because we were getting so fat and lazy that we thought it might be good for us. As we left the grass and entered the rough bracken, one of us stepped on the nest. A horde of the little stingers flew up and attacked us for all they were worth. We screamed and began to run down the mountain, the buzz furiously following us, tearing off our clothes until we arrived in the garden, naked and yelling with pain and laughter.

But then it was time for me to go. I packed my bags and Huib drove me to Derry to catch the train, the first on the long journey to Vierzon in France and the beginning of a new and independent life. I prayed that the homesickness would not raise its misery, and settled myself down in the carriage with a book that I was far too nervous to read.

Chapter X
INTERLUDE

I have a great deal for which to thank my parents and Camphill. Never, throughout my delightful childhood, had my parents' convictions been thrust upon me. I lived in the marvellous world of community with all its enthralling traditions, without the need to think about its spiritual background, or believe what my parents and their fellow community members believed. I simply lived happily in the bosom of Camphill as a child nestles in its cradle. It was always understood that when I grew up, I would leave to discover the magic and mystery of the 'outside world'. I was aware of my freedom without ever thinking about it.

Going to France to work as an au pair was just the first tiny step towards independence. And a tiny step it really was. The family with whom I was to live and work for were followers of Rudolf Steiner. They were friends of the French family for whom Lizzy had worked. I was to sleep in the chateau belonging to the Monzies and walk down everyday to the little square house in the only street of the village, next door to the village school, where Monsieur deLattre was the only teacher. I could not quite picture it. But I wanted an adventure and I was sure that I was going to have one. And I wanted to learn French, my previous short visit to France not having achieved this end.

I arrived at midnight in the railway station at Vierzon. I was exhausted and nervous and forgot the French word for 'exit'. Because my suitcase was so heavy that it took me a while to wrestle it off the train, and the hour was so late that there were no other passengers descending, there was no one on the platform whom I could follow out. I stood, panicked, looking at the signs overhead and not comprehending any of them. There was, indeed, only one to see, and I did not recognise the word that it bore. I walked frantically up and down that platform for what seemed eternity, with no one to ask, and unable to read.

Eventually, my fears subsided for want of any other outlet, and I followed a yellow line that led me outside. There stood a slight man, smoking a cigarette. He greeted me and I mumbled something, terrified because the last word of French had deserted me altogether. He led me to his car, in the back of which were the huddled sleeping bodies of three little girls wrapped in blankets. Madame deLattre had been delivered of a fourth girl the day before and was very ill in hospital. In order to collect me the poor man had had to bring his other children with him!

My comprehension of foreign languages has always been infinitely better than my ability to speak them, so I understood what Monsieur said, but could not answer him. We drove for an hour through the black night and he brought me to the chateau. I knew which room I was to use because it had been my sister's bedroom. I walked up the three flights of stairs as quietly as I could so that no one would be disturbed by my late arrival, and went to bed, to sleep soundly.

In the morning, I got up and went downstairs to see if there might be breakfast and to greet Monsieur and Madame before Monsieur deLattre would arrive to collect me as arranged. No one was there. The huge, forty-bedroomed chateau was quite, quite empty of human beings. I wandered around, once more filled with panic. Where was everybody? My imagination took wings. Were they dead? What had happened? Later, when my French was better, I learned that Monsieur deLattre had tried to tell me that they were away for the night and that they would be back the next afternoon, but of course I had understood not a word. Though I had been quite happy sleeping the sleep of the travel weary, I was now so scared that I could have screamed. I pulled myself together, reminding myself that I had wanted adventure and independence and to be my own boss, and now I was getting all that I had sought.

Monsieur eventually arrived to collect me. I was so glad to see him that I burst into tears. When we got down to his house, which in future I would find on foot, it was filled with boxes, the furniture stacked haphazardly in the kitchen, leaving a small space around the cooker and the sink, which had one water tap only, a cold one. He gestured to me that I was to take over, and off he went to open the school for the children's arrival.

I stood there, hearing his little daughters crying, away in the far distance of their bedroom, and tried to pull myself together. Clearly, not only had they had a new baby, but they had also just moved house and nothing had been unpacked except the beds, so that the children could sleep somewhere. Well, I once again reminded myself, I wanted adventure, and here it was!

Those first two weeks were conducted by way of experimentation. I knew how to clean, I knew how to wash dishes, but I could not speak the language and I had never cooked a proper meal in my eighteen years. I had prepared simple bread meals for supper and breakfast, but never a full-fledged dinner. My sisters had done that. On weekends at home, whenever there was a job to be done, I was not there! Now I was going to pay for being the youngest and the most spoilt. Monsieur deLattre was one of that breed of men who leave the housework to the women and go out to be the breadwinner. He could do nothing, and I also think *would* do nothing in the home. He was a lovely man, kind, quiet, gentle and humorous, but he never lifted a finger outside of his classroom, except to do the garden. He grew delicious vegetables, which made the cooking, once I had mastered it, a lovely thing to do.

I began by getting the girls up, a difficult affair because we did not know each other. Anique, Monique and Veronique became excellent allies, real friends and companions for all they were only four, three, and two years old. But it took time to build the relationship, and on that first day they cried and I cried quite a lot. However, I had seen how people looked after other people, and I had played with so many non-speaking children who had become my friends, that we overcame the language barrier by tone of voice and gestures.

Cooking was much more of a problem. How did one cook spaghetti? With lots of water, or with little? I knew that rice and spaghetti needed the opposites of water content, but which was which? I burnt both dishes only once and then realised that spaghetti needed a potful, and rice only double the amount. I felt as if I had conquered Everest by day three! I could do potatoes, that was really very simple, and I learned how to fry eggs. Then Monsieur produced minced meat. Now came my biggest challenge and with it my greatest discovery. I stood in that stone-floored kitchen, still filled with half-unpacked boxes, and stared at the bloody red meat. Suddenly I saw my mother's hands mixing mince for meatballs. I saw the flour, the eggs with their yellow yolks, I tasted the thyme and pepper on my tongue, and saw them, round and brown in the frying pan. I had found a deep well of visual and sensual memory just when I needed it. All those years of being allowed to watch people doing things – cooking, cleaning, repairing furniture, gardening, caring for children, creating plays for festivals, singing, decorating, knitting and sewing – all could be summoned up in my mind's eye and put to use by my hands. Camphill life had given me a resource of life-skills not to be beaten.

From that day on, I stopped crying and panicking and began to work. I organised the furniture, cooked lovely meals, scrubbed and polished, unpacked the clothes and made the house a home. But I made it into the home that I liked, forgetting Madame deLattre altogether. Monsieur visited her with the children every day and after some time she came home with the baby, Natalie.

Now the really hard part began. Madame took one look at the house, which I proudly presented to her, speaking a very broken French that the children had taught me, and she wanted everything changed. To my dismay, nothing could be left as I had arranged it. From her bed, she directed her husband and me, and we moved furniture all over again. I wanted to cry with fury and disappointment. It was as if all that I had done so willingly was undone in a stroke. I was forced to realise that it was not my home, and through this I learned another vitally important thing. I learned that people want things their own way and that I could not be the director of things all the time. Being the youngest in the family, and being the daughter of Barbara Lipsker, a much respected human being, meant nothing to people outside Camphill. In future, I realised that I would have to work for privileges, and that they would no longer be given naturally.

My French improved, my cooking became good, and I learned how to look after a newborn baby. I loved this part of the work most. Madame was ill for two months and so I was able to do much for little Natalie. I bathed her, changed her, and did most of the physical care during the day, Madame happily receiving the sweet smelling bundle to feed in her bed, propped up on cushions. The night care Monsieur provided, often looking drawn and pale in the mornings when I arrived to get the older girls up.

I worked hard. And Madame was a strict taskmaster. I had to polish the tiled floors on my hands and knees with red polish, and then shine them with a brush that had a strap over the wooden part in which to put my foot. I rubbed the brush over the floor with one foot. This was extremely gruelling, and on one famous day I fainted and found myself on the half-shined stone floor. Monsieur deLattre had to be fetched from his lessons next door by a distressed Anique, and he drove me up to the chateau to rest. I could not stop crying. I had worked from seven in the morning to ten at night for weeks, without a day off or even a lie in.

Madame Monzies, the lady of the chateau, became involved in my life at this point. She talked to the deLattres and from then on I had a lie in on Sundays, and a half day off on Tuesdays. Now life became more reasonable. I had time to read, which I did in French, and so my language improved. I was less irritable with the children and enjoyed the lovely autumn walks that could be taken through the woods that fringed the chateau. I was learning another valuable lesson for life: that rests are essential if one is to perform at one's best.

Nevertheless, in spite of the hard work, I liked the family very much. Once a month, Monsieur deLattre took me out to the cinema in Vierzon. Madame, when she could work again, helped with the cooking and cleaning and taught me how to make yoghurt and butter. I fetched the milk from the farm across the road every day, so it was as fresh as could be, but the first thing one had to do was to strain it. Never in my life had I seen such a farm. All the farms in Camphill had been kept scrupulously clean, and no one dared to bring muck into the dairy. On this farm, to get the milk you had to step over heaps of manure lying haphazardly in the yard and climb over a wooden step up into the dairy. The cows stood knee-deep in muck, and the farmers, two old bachelors, sat on three-legged stools and squeezed the frothy warm liquid straight and true into a dirty white enamelled bucket. Then it was poured into my can, bits of straw and manure floating on top! We survived this poisonous stuff by straining it through a cloth and pasteurising it in a clean stainless steel pot on the cooker.

The farmers were a delightful entertainment for me. At first nobody in the village spoke to me. They watched me, the foreigner, and took their time to accept me. One day, as I was scrubbing the front steps outside our house, one of the farmers came across the road and congratulated me on the pretty state of the front yard and the shiny clean steps. For a man who lived in squalor, he certainly appreciated cleanliness! From that day on, everyone spoke to me and asked after my health. I liked the visits to the farm as the winter drew in because I had to fetch the milk whilst the two men ate their supper. They sat at the dirty wooden table, a paraffin lamp giving a flickering light, and dipped their spoons into the eternal soup. They never seemed to eat anything else. They slurped and mouthed the vegetables and chunks of meat that floated on top of the garlic-flavoured dish, and dunked chunks of white French bread into the mess, using the last mouthful to clean their lips and cheeks, consuming it with glee and pleasure! And all the while, they quizzed me about the royal family, asking after each one's health as though I knew them personally. To please them, I made up stories (God forgive me!) that made them splutter into their soup with delight. They would tell me the latest village gossip in return, probably no less truthfully than the invented gossip they got from me.

They washed their clothes on Saturday afternoons, hanging the dark blue overalls out on the line stretched over the muck-strewn yard. On Sundays they went to mass in black suits with baggy trousers and light blue shirts, clean-shaven and bathed. For the rest of the week they used a bucket of water a day, drawn from the village pump. We, as the teacher's family, were privileged to have running water in the house. The rest of the village fetched theirs from the pump outside our house. It was a primitive way of life and I learned a great deal from observing their patience and acceptance of the hardships it offered. I learned most of all to appreciate all the good things that I had had, and to value the cleanliness and order that Camphill promoted by its way of life.

When I returned home at Christmas, I was a changed person. I met the warmth and familiarity of Glencraig with new eyes and an open heart. I saw how much growing up in a community can offer as skills for survival, as well as the power of adaptability that it had given to me. The warmth of my bed, the generosity of the space given to me for a holiday and the eagerness with which everyone met my accounts of life as an au pair, were very satisfying. And I was, at last, willing to participate in all the aspects of daily life.

I felt I had grown up, could manage my life, but that I did not want to live in this sheltered warmth any more. I wanted to go out, to see how normal people live, and to learn something about the ways of the world. I was sure that I would get this by going to college, having carefully chosen a town where I knew that anthroposophy and the work of Rudolf Steiner and Camphill were all quite unknown. I wanted to learn about child education and childcare as everyone else was doing it, and thus break away from the Camphill traditions and become a normal person. I was quite, quite sure that Camphill would never be my future, but I did not need to reject it, because my time in France had shown me of what value my previous life experience could be.

College was boarding school all over again. To my surprise we were expected to share a room. I slept with two other girls in a pretty room under the eves of the old house. It had a sloping beamed ceiling and each of us had a bed, locker, chair and cupboard. There was, however, absolutely no privacy. I was used to sharing, but this was something different. The girls gossiped and chatted till late hours of the night, each had their own radio and listened to the pop stations. Downstairs in the common room, the television was always on, and there was no corner that I could call my own, nor a moment without some background mechanical music. Sometimes I tried to escape by lying on my bed during the day and trying to read, but the cleaners objected to this. I found myself in another kind of community, one that was not set up to find each person's potential, but one that was merely a means to an end. We were there to be trained in the care and education of small children, but our own personal development held not the slightest bit of interest to the staff.

On arrival, I was issued with my uniform, a navy blue cotton dress, a black belt and white nylon apron, and a starched white cap. I had to wear black stockings or tights and black laced up shoes. Once dressed in this gear I felt quite proud to look like a nurse. We were also given woollen nurses' capes, which I loved wearing, especially when hitch-hiking, a form of travel to which I took like a duck to water.

The fees for my training had to be paid privately, as this was not a state-maintained college but under private management. It was registered as a children's home and students learned on the job. Trained staff managed the college and taught us. Miss Gardiner, the principal, stood over it all, wearing a tweed suit and speaking in a plummy voice that I learned to dread. My first interview with her was not a success.

She greeted me and promptly announced that I should forget anything I might have picked up of Camphill ways because this was a proper college of trained nursery nurses and Camphill was both unprofessional and sectarian. I was shocked. I had found out over the years that we were not the most popular amongst other caring bodies, but I did not know that we were considered unprofessional and untrained. I had realised that our community was not necessarily respected because it was often confused with 'commune', a kind of free-for-all attitude being expected by the prejudiced. But I had not anticipated that this negative judgement reached so far into the world of care.

I made the monumental error of asking her how she knew that Camphill was such a bad place. She looked at me with dislike and said that she had spent two weeks in Camphill in Aberdeen and had been appalled at the sentimental spiritual approach that she found there. Then she instructed me on the basic attitude that she expected of all her students: keep your mouth shut, don't think or ask questions, learn from the staff and be obedient. I left her sitting room, shaken and angry. How was I going to learn anything if I couldn't ask questions? My whole upbringing had taught me to consider free thinking as essential for growth and change. However, this was what I had chosen and now I was a part of the real world at last.

College consisted of two houses, one for the babies up to two years old and one large manor house in lovely grounds for those of two and upwards. All the children had been orphaned, or rejected by their family, or taken into care by the authorities. I was to start with the babies. They lived in nurseries with six babies in each, and were cared for by four students who did shift work. In the second year of the two-year training we all got a stint of night duty. We were overseen by a large, deep-bosomed lady with thin legs and very white hair called Nurse Ivy. She was a wonderful woman, caring and gentle and very good with these tiny infants. She was also kind to her students, but stood no nonsense. One did what Nurse Ivy said.

The work itself was lovely. It was a joy to handle the babies, play with them and be with them. But unfortunately this was not all. The lessons had to be got through and here I frequently came unglued. I found that so much of what I was now learning went counter to the Camphill approach to care and education. Where we, in Camphill, placed the child's inner nature, personality and soul needs first, knowing that the physical needs would reveal themselves if we took proper care of the inner development, here at college the physical needs came first and were the only ones worth bothering about. So if a baby spat out the bottle after six ounces of feed, we had to force the other two into the hapless infant, because at its given weight, eight ounces was recommended. If the baby, as it invariably did, vomited up the rest, then we were at fault. Half an hour later, we had to try again! Some of the little creatures hardly seemed to get any rest unless they had consumed the prescribed amount. I found this intolerable, thinking that maybe each had its own appetite. This was marked down on my report card at the end of the week.

The nurseries were very hot, and if we took a child out he or she had to be dressed in smart clothes, which were often not warm enough. This was another bone of contention. I felt that each child might have its own experience of warmth and might need individual dressing. What a sin that was, to dare to criticise the college methods! I was quite often brought before Miss Gardiner for, yet again making my own suggestions. I was told to be quiet and do as I was told. With hindsight, I can see that I was not the best student and wanted to do everything my own way. Should we all have done this, there would no doubt have been chaos. But I was so used to being encouraged to think and act for myself that the adjustment was enormous and it took me most of the first year to make it.

I had always been taught, and had learned my lesson well, that if you learn to love the children in your care, they will grow well and healthy. If they learn to love you, they will blossom and develop. Here at college, we were not allowed to form personal connections to the children. We were there to care for them only, and keep them safe. It was considered unprofessional to become attached to them. I could not obey this rule. I grew very attached to those in my care, feeling their loneliness and homelessness as a bitter pain in my soul.

Towards the end of the first year, a little girl, Antonia, arrived. She was placed in the isolation room, a glass-fronted cubical off the main corridor of nurseries. She was ten days old and suffered from hydrocephalus. Her head was huge and her face as beautiful as a pale white rose. She cried constantly in a high whimpering wail that tore at my heart. I stood outside her little room and looked at her, wanting to cry. Nurse Ivy passed by and told me to go and see Miss Gardiner. I thought I was probably in trouble again and went down, quite resigned to the usual telling off. But this time was different. With a slight air of discomfort, Miss Gardiner gruffly asked me if I would like to 'special' Antonia, as I had cared for disabled children before. I couldn't believe my luck! My luck continued, because Antonia took a liking to me and would feed with no one other than me. So I was encouraged to care for her day and night, only being absent for my statutory days off. This was the best time of all during those barren college years. And Antonia grew, stopped crying all the time and put on weight. She loved being outside in her pram and began to babble a bit.

In the beginning of my second year I was given a two-week holiday. I worried about who would take care of her in my absence. Miss Gardiner told me that Antonia was not my child and I had no right to be concerned. I had to take my holiday.

When I returned, Antonia had died. She took a convulsion and passed away in hospital. And I had not been there to help her, to hold her, or to comfort her. For the first time, I experienced Miss Gardiner as compassionate. She organised a single room for me. She said it was because I was antisocial and that the other students did not like sharing with me because I asked them to turn off their endless pop music, and because I did not go out with them but preferred to read. However, she also let me know that she understood my grief over the death of Antonia.

So I moved down to another road, parallel to the road in which the college stood, to a rented room. I spent the next year in a lovely attic, freezing cold in winter and boiling hot in the summer, but well and truly my own space at last. I hardly ever saw the landlady. She came and went mysteriously but the landlord I saw all too often. He used to come out of his bedroom just as I was mounting or dismounting the ladder, and feel my legs. I would try to escape without actually being rude to him. I took to creeping in and out of the house in order to avoid him.

This was only one of the surprises. The other, and much greater, was at Christmas. On coming home from my shift I passed by the open sitting-room door. There, in all its splendour stood the Christmas tree, candles, roses and copper signs hanging beautifully amid the fragrant branches! It seemed that the landlady was an anthroposophist. I had not escaped this world after all! But she knew little or nothing of Camphill and so I still felt reasonably free.

Working in the big house with the older children was not an easy time. Many of them had been abused and were exceedingly challenging. As a student one had little or no authority and they used this against us. I did not adapt well, never feeling quite free to be myself, having at last learnt to keep my mouth shut. But this was no help because it inhibited me and made me unable to act freely and with warmth. I was very glad that I only needed to do four months with them before going to the hospital to do my six weeks' sick nursing.

This was a lovely time, the hospital nurses being much less snobbish and silly than the students with whom I was training. The college girls all came from upper middle-class backgrounds and were, quite frankly, doing a training in order to be able to say that they had studied. But most of them had only one real aim in life: To get a job in a rich family and to marry well. I could not relate to such ambitions and so had little in common with them. However, the nurses in the hospital were committed and friendly, though the nurses' home in which I lodged was a dreadful place. It was Victorian and cold and lonely. I got lost quite frequently when walking from one ward to another, and often could not even find my bedroom. I was always late as a result. So I took to running, though we were forbidden to do so. A nurse never runs, we were told. But I did run, quite often, and on one occasion I bumped into a fire extinguisher which fell off the wall onto its nose and went off. The foam ran all the way down the miles of corridor and seemed to take eternity to stop erupting. I did not know where to begin to clear it up. However, I was lucky enough to meet two off-duty nurses who helped me with buckets and cloths. Thankfully I was also going off duty when the incident occurred and so could spare the hours it took to clean-up.

During my two years in Reading, the highlight was visiting Ans in Thornbury. Every free weekend, or when I had two days off, I hitch-hiked, in my nurse's cloak, to Thornbury for a sustaining taste of Camphill life. It was so refreshing to be once again in an environment of warmth and encouragement and interest. I could sleep well, eat healthy food and talk, talk, talk. I only realised how lonely I was when I entered The Hatch and felt a breath of relief and familiarity. I could talk about life at college and get things into some perspective so that when I returned I had renewed strength and determination to see it through. I tried to get to Thornbury for the festivals. I missed them terribly because now I was experiencing them as most people do. Easter was only chocolate eggs and paper bunnies on the walls. I decided to blow and paint eggs and make a kind of Easter altar, with a picture of the Risen Christ and primroses in mossy nests. But the other students laughed and said it was sentimental claptrap, and the children, following the example, broke the brittle eggshells.

I was at home for Christmas but I missed the Michaelmas festival altogether, not having time off, and having given up trying to bring the concept across at college. I began to try to love this new way of life and started to go out with the other girls to pubs and dances. But I could not bring myself to jiggle my hips about, and did not like alcohol, so I gave that up after a while. I also tried to move from boyfriend to boyfriend, but found that I was too choosy and still half in love with Peter and could not bear the physical touch of just any boy. So I gave that up too. Then I tried watching television so that at least I could talk to the other girls about the programmes they watched, and this was more successful. As a result, I watched a great deal of rubbish and began to read silly books as well. I felt that my standards were slipping and did not really try to retrieve them.

Though I had the company of Annette, maybe due to Miss Gardiner's dislike of me, she was often detailed to a different part of the course, or working in the other house. Miss Gardiner saw to it that we were well and truly separated for most of our college career. We did try to spend off-duty time together, but she got on much better with the other girls than I did and did not always want to spend all of her time with me. So the visits to Thornbury were like a breath of reviving fresh air and I treasured them very much.

Hitch-hiking I found easy. When I was wearing my nurse's cloak, people were always willing to stop for me. I got lifts with all kinds of people and had both good and bad experiences. On one occasion a man picked me up and suddenly turned off the main road down a narrow lane. I knew the route so well that I soon realised that he had something else in mind. He stopped in a deserted place and reached for me. I began to talk to him, asking him all kinds of things about his life. For once, my never silent tongue was a boon. I simply talked him dry and he took me back to the main road and dropped me off, thoroughly bored with the experience.

On another occasion some months later, when hitch-hiking again, I was picked up by two men in a lorry. They suddenly drew into a lay-by, and as the engine noises died one of them reached under the seat and pulled out a rifle. I thought that this was the end of me, but he smiled and said they always stopped there to shoot rabbits. They left the cab and were gone for fifteen minutes during which time I was able to calm my nerves. They returned with two dead animals, grinning cheerfully. They dropped me off at a motorway café, passing me on to another driver who delivered me safely to my destination. Mostly, however, my lifts were boringly uneventful. People were nice, friendly and helpful, and I saved myself a great deal of money travelling in this way. I was never afraid and perhaps that helped. I think it was because I had been brought up with so many odd people that a human being has rarely frightened me.

Sometimes I took the train to London. My sister, Lizzy, was studying eurythmy at Steiner House and I loved visiting her. She lived in a bedsit and cooked for herself. I admired her enormously. I thought that I was living real life, but college was nothing to living in London in a real bedsit and having to take jobs to make ends meet. She worked as a cleaning lady, or did ironing for old ladies, and she also cleaned in Helen Sielmann's flat once a week. I enjoyed these visits and enjoyed chatting to Helen, who by now was old and raddled and no longer a beauty. She did not like me very much, finding me strange because I did not have a man in my life. Neither did Lizzy, but she liked *her* a lot. She used to make us do exercises to accentuate our breasts and pull in our waists and we found it hilarious, giggling all the way home.

But London scared me. Coming from the country, I could not feel at home and did not like travelling on the underground. Lizzy, who had always been the shy sister, in need of protection, had now become the elder, more worldly one. I liked her better and better. We went to concerts and the cinema, and I helped her whenever she had to move, making her dreary bedsits homely and inhabitable for her.

Towards the end of my training, I was sent to a maternity hospital in Melton Mowbray. We had to learn about the newborn and about delivering babies, though our training would not qualify us to become midwives. However, it did qualify us to work in maternity wards and with premature babies. I loved that little country hospital, loved the nurses' home with its bright painted walls, and fresh fruit placed in a wooden bowl in every nurse's bedroom once a week. The work was lovely. The mothers, northern and down-to-earth, were all sweet, and the newborn babies, all loved and wanted, were a delight. I became so relaxed and happy that I finally began to feel at home in this outside world to which I had committed myself. I went out to parties with the other nurses, and even taught myself to dance the Twist and other gyrating fancies of the Sixties!

At one such party I met some young men who were in the RAF. Loud though they were, and often drunk, they were lively and interesting. One boy came from Scotland and his voice drew me. Memories of the Scottish Highlands rose up into my throat. I was so drawn by his accent that I could not tear myself away. He started to take me out, to pubs and for drives. The more I got to know him, the less I liked him, but I could not keep away from his voice.

When I returned to college, after the three months' maternity practice was over, I discovered that I was pregnant. This was a huge shock to me. I had never told my parents that I had had relationships with boys. I felt that they would not be able to cope with this, nor understand it. Sex had never been something that I could discuss with them. Now I would have to tell them, that not only had I slept with someone but that I was also expecting a baby and they would become grandparents.

My eldest sister was expecting her first baby and now so was I. How could I tell *them*? What should I do? I did not feel at all well, and then an epidemic of German measles hit the college. I had no idea whether I had had this disease and did not know what to do. So, sensibly, I went to the doctor. He did a pregnancy test and then advised me to have an abortion. After all, he said soothingly, the baby was illegitimate, I had no means of keeping it, I had not told my parents and because of the risk that the baby would be handicapped, the NHS would pay for the abortion. I said I would think it over.

Throughout my whole life I had been taught that life is sacred and that handicapped people are as entitled to life as those not handicapped. Now I was being put thoroughly to the test. I did not think that I had contracted the German measles, but I had had a sore throat and the doctor said that it was probably a slight attack after all. Would the baby be damaged? Did I want the baby? The father was not in the least interested when I told him and announced that it was my responsibility entirely. So I had to make the decision alone. Finally, I went to Miss Gardiner and told her I was pregnant. She looked at me in stony horror and found the answer to her problem of my possibly contaminating the other girls by putting me on night duty. She said it was a good thing that at least I had my own room!

During those nights I learnt a great deal about how people can rise above themselves in a crisis. The girl who shared the duty with me was wonderful. She let me sleep and covered for me. When I had to prepare the breakfasts for the babies she helped because I had terrible morning sickness. Sometimes we had to boil sheep brains, skin them and mash them to put on fingers of toast for the toddlers' morning meal. It was supposed to be highly nutritional! The greyish-white substance made me puke. This kind girl did all the horrible stuff for me and told no one.

I had time to think, during night duty, and I remembered a visit that my sister Lizzy and I had made to Delrow, a Camphill community near Watford, where Peter Roth was visiting. I had learned to love him from the Botton days and was happy to find an occasion to see him. I told him about my training and about the children, abandoned and unloved, with whom I worked. He said that I should start a community for underprivileged and deprived children, and I laughed because I knew that Camphill was not going to be my future. I asked him if he thought that a staff child would ever have a handicapped child. He said this would never happen.

Now he was going to be proved wrong. Not that there was any confirmation of my child being handicapped, but the probability was very high indeed. I suddenly realised that such a child would be handicapped only in as much as it lacked understanding, love, and education. The love I already had; the understanding and education Camphill could help me with. So I told the doctor that abortion was not an option. Then I turned to my sister, Agi, for help. She was wonderful. She seemed so happy to have me accompany her through her own pregnancy with mine. She said that I should tell our parents and then come to stay with her for a while.

Now I had the courage to phone my parents. My father said

he was very happy to have a grandchild who would bear his name because otherwise Lipsker would die out with him! My mother only asked if I was happy and I lied and said that I was. She then said she was happy too, and when was I coming home? I felt as small as a worm because, although I knew that they would always stand by me, I also knew that I had hurt them atrociously. So I left college four weeks before graduation by special dispensation and a promise of still receiving my certificate, and went to Holland to stay for a month with my sister, Agi, and her husband, Huib.

It was like heaven to be in a warm and undemanding little flat out in the countryside with people who loved me and did not treat me like a dirty pig. I ate well, and slept well, and laughed and helped Agi preparing things for her baby. It snowed and we went for walks and knitted baby things and slowly I began to look forward to my baby being born. That it might or might not be disabled I put out of my mind. It seemed irrelevant and was anyway a speculation.

During that visit, Agi took me to see some friends of hers, a doctor and his wife, whose extended family were too complicated to take in, some being real sons and daughters, others stepsons and daughters. Sim, the eldest, was going to Glencraig to become the assistant farmer, and he and I decided to travel together. He was large and friendly like a great St Bernard dog, and we loved each other without much effort. We became very good friends as the years passed.

And so I came back to Camphill, to Glencraig. The reaction of my friends was outstanding. In the late Sixties, it was still not considered proper to be an unmarried mother and I feared what people would say. But without exception, they greeted me with joy and all seemed to look forward to my baby more than I did! People knitted me things. The Königs lent me their cradle, saying that I could practise motherhood on their two sons – not that I needed it. Wasn't it a good thing that I had trained to look after babies? They said I would be the best mother in the place.

No one turned against me. There was only one hurt dealt to me, when someone took me aside to ask if I realised what damage I had done to my parents by becoming pregnant without a husband. I could not answer her, because it seemed as if my parents were very happy and not the least hurt. It seemed to me that *I* was hurt, that I had taken away my own childhood. And it seemed to me that she had no right to put words into my parents' mouths that they had not uttered. I was coming up against the downside of community: where people feel that they should say what they imagine others want to say. So I avoided her for a while, and in the end I forgave her, because she was otherwise always kind and supportive.

We were still living in Brendan, but now I had a room of my own. It had a balcony and looked out over the garden. Beattie was still the housemother and ran us all with a very firm and loving hand. I had very little to do, because I was neither a child nor a co-worker. Moreover, I was pregnant and so not expected to work very hard. I was given space to be, and so to find my own future. As a contribution to my living I made suppers for overworked housemothers, babysat for the Königs and Susanne, and helped Beattie as much as she would let me. Saralies and Johannes were delighted that I was now living in Glencraig, and I had Sim to have fun with. But I was lonely. I used to lie in bed at night and talk to my unborn baby, telling it that all would be well and that as soon as it was born and we were ready, we would find a home where I could work and bring it up. It was neither boy nor girl in my mind, just baby. Secretly, I already knew that things would not be so easy. If the child were handicapped, would I be able to get a job? Did I want my baby in a nursery all day whilst I worked? I could not answer these questions.

Sometimes, mother would look as if she wanted to ask after the baby's father, but I always forestalled her. I did not want to talk about him. I had been given a lifetime's example of freedom, and I felt that he had a perfect right not to want the baby. I had not loved him, so I did not deserve his concern, and clearly he had not loved me, so we were better apart. But I felt the loneliness and so much wanted a real home for my baby and me.

Susan and Johnnie were a great comfort. Susan knitted baggy baby clothes and sat chatting with me in the lonely evenings. She was always bright and cheerful and kind. Johnnie was funny and big-hearted and laughed at me when I felt sorry for myself. Secretly I longed to become a housemother and have the chance to live with these lovely people, but I did not think I was really capable, neither did I think that I would be considered responsible enough to do this job.

In those long days of pregnancy, Frédérique, whom I had got to know in the Ceridwen days, when we still lived with children, became a good friend. She had known Sim from Holland. Before coming to Glencraig, she had lived with his extended family and they were like brother and sister. Through him I got to know her much better, and grew more and more fond of this quiet, unassuming, humorous person. I still felt that I was on the fringe of life in Glencraig but I could see how I might become more involved.

In May, two months before my baby was to be born, Agi gave birth to stillborn twins. This was shocking and hugely painful. My sister, married and with everything in place, had not held on to her babies. I, who was unmarried and ashamed of myself, was going to give my parents their first grandchild, out of wedlock. It seemed terribly unfair and awful. But my sister said that life sometimes dealt odd blows and that she would come to be with me when my baby came. Had she not lost her twins, she wouldn't have been able to do so, and maybe that was what was meant through all this. I could not have felt more loved and cared for, both by my family and in Glencraig.

The contrast when I went to the hospital for antenatal check-ups was enormous. Here I was treated like a prostitute because I would not give them the baby's father's name. I had decided that if he did not want contact with us, then he should also have no rights over us. They asked me every time I attended the clinics whether I had arranged for adoption, and each time I told them that I was keeping the baby. They sent a social worker out to talk to me. They prodded me around and took endless blood samples. It was horrid and degrading. I had to sit on a chair with my knickers off waiting to be humiliated by student doctors, whom they seemed to line up just to poke at me. The married mothers were treated much more deferentially. Then, on 12 July, my daughter Helen Barbara was born. Agi, true to her word, came to be with me, but in those days even the father had to force his way in to be present, and mere sisters did not stand a chance. Nevertheless, after much trouble and a long labour, my daughter came into the world.

And she was beautiful. She looked like a perfect princess with black hair and blue eyes and shell-pink skin and nails. But she would not cry. She whimpered and wailed and lay very still in my arms. They put me into a separate room (probably so as not to contaminate the married mothers) and I loved the peace. Whilst in labour, I had heard the gunshots and riots out in the Falls Road and the nurses all expected me to call her Mary. But I was happy and at peace and glad to have my family around me, and to know I would be returning to Glencraig with this little mite who seemed so unwilling to be in the world. She did not take easily to the breast and we were to face a great struggle over this, until I decided that a happy baby and mother were more important than the rules, and put her on the bottle. After that she began to thrive and grow and take more kindly to life.

We moved to Pestalozzi when she was three months old. My mother had asked to live in a small house and to retire from houseparenting as she felt older and thought that I could take on the house for her. The Königs moved to a bigger house, and we took up residence in the old and charming farmer's cottage. But working with my mother was not easy. I did not feel free; I did not feel that I could really make a home for myself and my child in my mother's house, much as we cared for each other. She wanted me to do things her way and I wanted to do them my way. Besides, we had four young men to care for and one of them had a fixation on young mothers. He could not refrain from trying to strangle me whenever he got the chance. And though I liked him because he was a nice young man and could not help his fixation, it was sometimes rather scary to be left alone in the house with him.

Moreover, I had to unlearn many habits that I had picked up in college. I did not dress my daughter warmly enough and so she cried a lot, and it took me a while, with great forbearance and hints on my mother's part, to realise what was wrong with her. I had to learn that she needed lots of sleep, that she needed not to have to finish every feed, as I had been taught, and that she could not cope with too much stimulation. I was slowly realising that, as I had feared, I could not contemplate leaving Camphill. I would have to stay in order to give Helen Barbara a home in which she could flourish. Though she did not seem to be handicapped and was most certainly not blind, as I had secretly feared for a rubella baby, she did seem to need extra special care. Now I was going to have to make a choice. If I left, I needed a job, and I could not seem to manage to get this organised. If I stayed, I could not do so in my mother's house as an eternal staff child. I would have to become a co-worker.

My mother and father were a tremendous support. Not once did they put any pressure on me. Agi had to return to Holland, but Lizzy came to visit as often as her training allowed, and was such a good aunt to Helen Barbara, as well as a great source of encouragement to me. The community too stood by me, making me feel welcome and useful, but never once asking more of me than I wanted to give. I was entirely free to make up my own mind. I could have stayed as a live-in working guest forever. And then, one day, Annemarie came to see me. She said that they were short of houseparents and that Dell o'Grace was available to me, with four villagers and an older lady to help me, if I wanted to take it on. I was aghast. Did they really think that I could be a housemother? Could I do such a task and be reliable and responsible? I had been taught to care for little children. Could I look after adults properly?

I thought I would have to discuss this proposition with my friends. Through Sim and Frédérique, I had become acquainted with Rob, her brother and Sim's friend. He had come to Glencraig at the same time as Sim and I, to do the three-year training course in curative education run by the Glencraig community. He was tubby, warm and undemanding. And he loved Helen Barbara unstintingly. She loved him too and would smile at him sooner than at me. Rob thought my being housemother would be great. He said that at last there would be a house in the community where young co-workers could gather and have fun in the evenings. Besides, he said, it was filthy and I could clean it up! The others also, thought the idea appealing, and encouraged me to try. Feeling that there must have been some mistake, and that the whole community had taken the child that I was for a real grown-up, I timidly accepted the offer of becoming the housemother in Dell o'Grace. Helen Barbara was now four months old.

Chapter XI
COMING HOME

Dell o'Grace was indeed filthy. My sister, Lizzy, who was home on a holiday, helped me to clean it. We scrubbed and scrubbed and scrubbed. I very much wanted to paint as well, but time and money did not allow. Glencraig at this time had divided itself into a school community and village community. The school, because it received fees for the children, had money. The village, which received only a small amount from the Department of Employment and was supposed to earn the rest from its work output, had very little money. Dell o'Grace was a village house so I had to get used to a tight budget and making do. The living unit was built around the pottery, a large workshop which had a good output financially speaking, but which also had a good output of dust and clay that walked itself upstairs on the villagers' and co-workers' feet alike. Dirt has no enemies when it creeps. So for the time that I lived in the lovely cottage right by the sea, up on the rocks with the waves thundering when there was a storm and the seabirds crying lonesomely, I did an awful lot of cleaning.

However, as start to the career of houseparenting, there could be no better household. It was small, with only four villagers, and an elderly lady, Elizabeth, fondly know as Patchie, coined from her unpronounceable Polish surname, and myself and Helen Barbara. At last I had my own home. I felt enormously privileged at the trust that was extended to me by the community, and swore to do my very best. Annemarie König had offered her support as godmother to us all and so I embarked on a new way of life, knowing that other people thought I was a grown-up, even though I did not believe this at all. They only thought I was fully adult because I had a child! I would have to prove that their mistake had some foundation. I reminded myself that when I had realised that I was pregnant, my greatest fear was that I was too much of a child to bring up another child, and I had wondered anxiously how we were going to manage. But I also remembered that when I thought of my child and me as 'us', then I knew that we were in it together, and together we would grow up, learning from each other. There was no reason why I should not apply the same attitude towards my new career.

Someone I did not count on, but who emerged as a wonder and endless resource of strength and help, was my mother. Through thick and thin, she stood by us, never forcing her ideas but always ready to guide, assist, instruct and comfort. This last was what I needed most. It is a lonely business to bring up a child single-handedly, as many one-parent families know. Now I was to become a single houseparent, responsible for five other people apart from myself and my daughter. What faith Glencraig had! There was no question about letting them down. I would prove their good faith by my goodwill.

At first, cleaning and cooking and beautifying took all my energy and time. Dell o'Grace was going to become the best house of them all. I pushed myself madly to keep up with my own standard, and Helen Barbara patiently cooperated, being an extremely good baby. She only ever cried when there was something wrong, and slept all through the night. What a boon that was!

I was beginning to wonder whether all was well with her. She was so beautiful, and so thin. Although I fed her properly, she did not gain enough weight. Moreover, she did not like being cuddled when facing me. She always wriggled around to keep her back pressed up against my breasts. Then she would laugh and gurgle like any other baby. And she seldom cried. But when I voiced these slight anxieties, everyone said that this would change as she grew older. It was all quite normal. Secretly, I knew it was not normal, and took every opportunity, verbally and through my actions, to tell my darling daughter that life was going to be all right. I assured her loudly and with cuddles that we were together and so it would work out fine.

But life as a single houseparent was very hard. I wanted a social life too, and invited my friends to Dell o'Grace in the evenings for get-togethers that lasted late into the night. We read

Winnie-the-Pooh, Shakespeare, poetry and drama. We listened to music, I played my guitar and we learned endless folk songs, drinking cups of tea and home-made elderberry juice, the berries for which I picked and processed. It was delicious when warmed, with a dash of lemon in it.

The sitting room of the house was meant to be a display for the pots from the workshop below. It was a big room overlooking the sea, in which the seals bobbed about in calm weather. I could stand for hours, watching their antics. The kitchen too looked out over the lough and when one sat down to a meal, because of the height of the window sill, one imagined oneself on a boat. In stormy weather, I sometimes even felt seasick!

To help me manage the house, I begged for a housefather, and so Sim came to live with us, having to sleep in the sitting room because there were no more bedrooms. So I begged again, and a very tiny room was built up over the stairs with drawers for clothes set under the bed, so that at least a locker could fit in for a bedside light. Sim moved in to this minute room and now we were a house community. But Sim was courting and eventually he got married and moved out, so I had a succession of housefathers for the next two years.

In the school community, it was possible to follow a training course as part of the education for new volunteers. Co-workers following the course were expected to gain some experience of living with adults. The male students came to Dell o'Grace to help me and gain the added dimension of working as a housefather and thus I made many and good friends. There is nothing like having to work together for people to get to know each other. These friendships always remained just that, a working partnership. And I loved it. How safe it was to have so many dear companions with no emotional strings to pull! It was a good time for healing.

Patchie was an invaluable source of warmth and maturity. She suffered from a bad back and could do little physical work, but she upheld me in all my efforts and experiments, assisting with the care of the men, an aspect of houseparenting that I found I could not do. I was still too much of a child to wash and dress a grown man, especially one who sometimes soiled himself. But I loved to help the girls with their hair and nails, and loved to see them looking pretty and well dressed.

Hilary was my mainstay. She became my assistant housemother, because she knew better what was needed than I did. She taught me everything, reminding me of details and stepping in when Patchie was ill, which was quite often. Many a morning, by the time I got up, anxious and troubled with my responsibilities, I would find Michael and Jeffrey already up, teeth brushed and hair combed. Airing the bedrooms and making the beds was a piece of cake, as long as I did not need to dress and wash the boys! Hilary had been up extra early to do them for me, knowing that Patchie was once again incapacitated with her back. On one occasion, after a migraine and a broken night's sleep, I only woke at nine o'clock, leaping out of bed in a panic and wondering why it was so quiet. On the kitchen table was a note, written by Caroline who could write, though Hilary could not – stating that everything was in order and that I should sleep on peacefully till I was better. It was signed in big crooked capitals by Hilary.

Caroline was quiet, ladylike and kept her hands folded most of the time. At first she did nothing, remaining silent and incapable. The housemothers' group, which made the arrangements about who should live where, had decided she would be happy in Dell o'Grace because of the vibrant Hilary. But this status quo did not last. On one occasion I suffered such a mammoth migraine that I could hardly feed Helen Barbara, let alone cope with the household. I took painkillers and got through the day by neglecting all but the most essential. So the nappies did not get washed. The next day, to my horror, I could not find the dirty-nappy bucket. I searched and searched and eventually found it, clean and empty, beside the airing cupboard. I looked inside and there hung the nappies, white and sweet smelling. I burst into tears. Who had been the good fairy? At lunch I asked the question and Caroline whispered, hands folded as usual, 'I did it.'

From that time on, she became my household helper, friend, and a nursery maid to Helen Barbara. No more responsible a person could anyone find in this capacity. I knew that my daughter would not only be safe, but would also be encouraged to develop and would have a companion who never tired of playing with her, outside in the sun, or inside in the rain. Caroline began to talk much more, and became a rock of stability.

As for the men, Jeffrey was the house clown, funny and dear and very, very lazy. But we were amply repaid for his dependence by his excellent talent for mimicry. He played us all, hook, line and sinker and never missed a gesture or facial expression. Sometimes this could be irritating, because gazing in one's own mirror showed weaknesses as well as strengths, but we loved him very much and so forgave him and learned a lot in the bargain.

Michael was the most disabled, not able to speak, being deaf and paraplegic. But he was a truly humble soul, undemanding and patient. Sometimes this drove me to distraction and I pushed him to be less of a sheep because my choleric nature wanted more input from him. Then tears would well up in his eyes and he would pat me on the back as if to say, 'Don't try so hard. It will be all right. I forgive you.' And this would either make me rage more out of guilt, or make me cry in penitence for my disgracefully impatient nature.

And they all loved Helen Barbara. I think I was probably forgiven for all my errors and for the rages that I sometimes suffered, though I generally went outside or to my room to indulge in the tears that they brought, because of the love they bore for her. They would play with her and mind her faithfully, each in their own fashion. Hilary, bustling and talkative, her hair hanging greasily around her pockmarked face, but with a beaming smile and cheerful manner, would sit clumsily on the floor and pick up the toys that Helen Barbara liked to throw down. They never seemed to tire of this game. Caroline's speciality was the peek-a-boo game. She could play it for hours. She also took Helen Barbara for a walk, patiently assisted her efforts to get up onto her feet and she watched her for me when she wanted to explore the passage that led to the stairs. She was a warm and steady minder, and I knew that as long as Caroline was there, Helen Barbara would be in very safe hands.

Jeffrey sat in his favourite armchair, an imaginary book in his one hand and an invisible cigarette in the other, mumbling soothing phrases at the baby in an absent-minded fashion, which kept her placidly entertained whilst in her playpen for safety. He could be relied on to tell me if she might be getting up to mischief, but often only after she had spilled the flower vase, or pulled down something on her head. He enjoyed dramas, and so when he was minding her, I usually put her safely in the playpen out of harm's way; but his company, undemanding as it was, kept her happy. Only Michael could not actually do anything for her, but during the meals he smiled at her encouragingly whilst I fed her, and this distracted her well enough for the spoon to be pushed into her mouth. She was not a good feeder, and had no real interest in eating.

I also had my father to help me. He came every morning and took his little granddaughter for a walk, first in the pram, then in the pushchair as she got bigger, so that I could have an hour to myself. He would deliver the post and then take her out, chatting and singing all the songs that I had heard as a child, his pipe puffing away merrily. They loved each other very much, grandfather and granddaughter. She seemed much less withdrawn when with him.

With all this generous help, I was learning to be a mother. But with regard to my new career, there was one important aspect of housemothering that I refused to take upon myself. This was to hold the Bible Evening every Saturday, and to go to the service on a Sunday. I was not a real *committed* co-worker, I declared. I was a housemother only to help out and only until Helen Barbara would be strong enough to come out into the real world with me. I did not believe in all the religious trappings of Camphill, I would find my own way in these matters. I was quite outspoken when I reported to the housemothers' group, as this was the body responsible for my work. They smiled, the other housemothers, and answered that Patchie would carry this part of my duties. So I prepared the table and the food every Saturday and left the rest to her. On Sundays I cooked enormous delicious lunches as a compensation for the niggling guilt that I felt at refusing to take up the inner tasks of houseparenting. But I had not completed my exploration into independence. It was life circumstances and the neediness of my daughter that had interfered in its natural process. I still needed to rebel, and the great heart of Camphill understood this and let me be.

My first Christmas as a housemother was a thing to remember

with humility and shame. I wanted it to be the best, the most real and the most successful. I needed to prove myself to myself and to the community, probably because I had still not clarified my involvement and lived in uncomfortable ambivalence. I worked myself and everybody else into a frenzy of baking, cooking, cleaning and decorating. No house had ever looked so fair, and no people had ever cared less than my house community. They just wanted a bit of peace and quiet! But they bore up stoically until Christmas Eve, when disaster struck.

Needless to say, I had developed a terrific migraine once again and was tottering around trying to dress the tree, all by myself, so that it would be a surprise, as all good Christmas trees should be. I had cooked the meal, bathed the girls and done their hair perfectly, had set the table delightfully and tidied everybody's rooms. They were all sitting stiffly in the kitchen, not daring to move for fear of upsetting me, and I was now getting Helen Barbara ready so that we could all go to the Christmas community play and then come home to the perfect Christmas meal. Somewhere in my heart I did not feel right. It was all outside of me; I had no peace inside, my head pounded and I wanted to die. I felt so completely and utterly alone.

Just before we were to go to the hall, I peeped in through the door of the sitting room to give a last look at the tree, and burst into horrified sobs. There it lay, candles broken, copper signs a tangle and the paper roses squashed. It had fallen down! Hilary peered over my shoulder and announced firmly, 'Never mind. It won't run away. We'll put it back up after the play. We'll all help you. Stop fussing, God won't mind.'

What a lesson I learned! We did indeed put it back up – all of us together, with a lot of laughter and fun. We had our supper late, eating with joy and companionship. We had, after all, made Christmas together in spite of my misguided efforts, which might have utterly spoiled it all. How I loved them!

The next day I woke up wondering what was different. I realised that I had no pain in my head! I felt like someone newborn. Only then did I realise that I had had a migraine for the last six months. At last I was free of it. I had grown so used to it that it was only when it got to a pitch of unbearable pain that I felt it at all. Now I was pain-free. The relief was tremendous, not only physically, but also mentally. I could begin to really live with my friends in the house and lean on them as they leaned on me. I had begun my road to community, though I did not yet fully realise it.

The social life in Dell o'Grace continued. Sometimes, on Sunday mornings, Rob would call by with his dormitory and I would join them for a walk, taking Helen Barbara along. Because of my newfound ability to share the tasks, Patchie cooked the lunch. I was learning to delegate. Helen Barbara loved these walks, enjoying the fun and lightness that was Rob's natural way of being. He often came to supper on his afternoon off, and helped to put her to bed. Sometimes I wondered which one of us he was really visiting, Helen Barbara or me? But mostly I just enjoyed the teasing and light-heartedness of his visits. Johannes too continued to come, more so than ever because now I was mistress in my own home and could have him to meals at any time. He practically lived with me during his school holidays. I was very happy in the Dell o'Grace years, the loneliness becoming a faint discomfort far in the background of my consciousness.

Then a redheaded young man from New Zealand arrived in the community. He joined the school to follow the training course, and after falling in love with a variety of young beauties, he began madly to court Frédérique. Being a cautious person, she watched his efforts with a wry smile, and took some time to become hooked. Because we were a group of friends, he joined our social life. He too was called Johannes. Perhaps a certain cheek goes with that name because, like my small friend, he was also capable of turning the world upside down. He had a vivid imagination but he transformed it into artistic things, unlike the younger Johannes, who could still be very naughty. Our indulgence in singing, theatre and poetry intensified. He was mad and artistic and brightly alive and captivated us all, all but Frédérique, who remained very cautious and kept her distance. This only enticed him the more. What he could not have, he wanted very badly. He was a charming but rather spoilt young man. Through him, Michael, another New Zealander, arrived and he came to be my housefather. The group of friends around Dell o'Grace was growing.

Michael had a serious side to him. He and Johannes could argue all night about whether there was, or was not, a particular angelic being! They could also sit, drink herb tea, and giggle for no accountable reason that anyone other than the two of them could fathom. Sometimes, I felt that I was only there to provide a warm and cosy place for their discussions. But gradually, as our friendship grew, I joined their crazy imaginary world. We talked philosophy for hours and giggled like geese. After all, it was the end of the Sixties, and most of the younger generation were madder than we were. I had entered a lovely and unique time. Through these intensive late nights, I began to *think*, not only feel something about Camphill and community living.

Michael was a good housefather and did not mind any of the work that came his way in the house. We argued about the way of life in Camphill, he wanting more of the Sixties type of commune and I finding myself, to my horror, arguing for the Camphill approach to community. Somewhere in these discussions it was being borne on me that I loved Camphill, not just as my home and as a refuge in times of need, but as an impulse in its own right. I began to question my commitment. I started to hold the occasional Bible Evening, and once or twice I went to the service, 'just to try it out'. I could not yet admit outright that I was here, not just to feel safe, but because I wanted to be in Camphill.

In my second year of Dell o'Grace, Rob began to visit very regularly and eventually we both realised that our relationship had moved from friendship to love. Now I had to tell my parents. We went to visit them after Bible Evening, one Saturday night. These were always relaxed evenings in the community and people used them for quiet talks and peaceful social gatherings. My father, however, usually went to bed immediately after the Bible Evening was over, and I had to ask him to wait up until we came because we had something important to tell him. When we got there he said that he could understand why *I* wanted to see him, but why Rob?

This made it very easy to announce our intentions. They were both unstintingly happy and supportive, though my mother did say cautiously that perhaps we should wait a year or two until we were a bit older. I was twenty-three and Rob twenty-two. We were not prepared to follow her advice. We stated that we had known each other as good friends for so long that we didn't need to wait. So that was that.

Rob naturally wanted to spend as much time as he could together with me. He lived in a children's house run by two unmarried women. They did not have a great deal of patience with this idea and so we saw each other only at night. With the very small room above the stairs for a housefather, the sitting room could be our meeting point, and I was glad that I had kept a bed in it, because Helen Barbara and I shared a room and I could not bring myself to disturb her. Rob must have been very tired, caring for six boys ranging from six to eighteen years old and having to find time for me and Helen Barbara as well. But he was a man whose patience never let him down, and he peacefully went from one duty to another, never seeming to get into a flap. And our friends were happy for us. Frédérique, who loved her 'little brother' very much, was happy to welcome me into the family. I hoped her parents would get used to the idea too.

Apart from the late evenings and free afternoons, Rob and I found another delightful space in which to meet. I had joined the training course as a special student. Usually, people in the village were not allowed to join the course. One had to live in a schoolhouse and take care of children to qualify for a place. But I bent the rules. As a staff child, I knew how to do this! I went to see Hans Heinrich. He was the doctor and principal of Glencraig, and to pull any strings one must always start at the top. Because of Helen Barbara, I thought that I qualified as looking after a child. And besides, I disliked the barriers that were growing between school and village. I had friends in both parts of the community and would not abandon them because we had different outlooks. Hans Heinrich agreed that I might become a bridge and allowed me onto the course.

I loved it! At last I was actually learning the theory behind the practice of community building, curative education and village life. I was beginning to want to learn more about anthroposophy, the philosophy that had been the background to my whole lifestyle and upbringing. So much of what I had rejected was starting to make sense to me and I wanted to know more about it.

I particularly enjoyed the artistic and social side that the training course offered. I could work, learn and take care of my daughter, all without leaving home! This was a wonderful and privileged experience. Certainly, it was also rather insular and inbred, but it was so interesting and stimulating that I did not mind a bit. If, through my life circumstances and the needs of my daughter, I was prevented from going out into the world, by nature of the multinational and multicultural young co-workers who came to the course, the world was coming to me. What a gift!

Rob and I decided on the date of our wedding in the middle of a play rehearsal of Shakespeare's *Tempest*. Richard Poole, whose family had taken care of Liz during the changeover from Heathcot to Botton, was an expert on the great dramatist. Every year he came to lecture on the training course and unfolded the mysteries of Shakespeare's great wisdom regarding the human soul. It was an extremely lively way to learn human psychology. We studied his dramas, learning to analyse all the dark and light qualities that live in every human being. As a grand finale to this popular course, he directed us in a production of one or two of the plays. They were fun to do and usually delightful to watch. Where we were unprofessional, we made up for in enthusiasm.

He cast me as Ariel. What a sight! I was chubby, short and round. Never a more earthly Ariel could anyone have seen. And the only reason he insisted that I took the part was because I had done eurythmy in school and no one else had. What a silly reason, because graceful I was not. Nevertheless, it was great fun to flit about the stage like a baby elephant. It was altogether not one of the greatest productions.

Othello was the other drama that was being performed by another group, and Johannes, picked to be Prospero, was furious at not being chosen to do Othello. Sim had drawn that straw. As these two young men were not always good friends, animosity raged. As a punishment to Richard for having done such a dreadful thing, Johannes played the great magician in a wooden and gloomy manner, quite deliberately sabotaging what was already a bad production. A fat Ariel only served to make it worse. But at least I knew my lines, which he had not bothered to study at all. Poor Richard, what a time we gave him! However, to compensate, and much to Johannes' disgust, the *Othello* group was superb, Sim outshining everyone in his performance of raging grief.

Being bored offstage whilst Prospero limped through his long speeches, and sitting as quietly as we could as the play continued down its unfortunate path, Rob, dressed as the Bosun and trying to act drunk, and I in my eurythmy veils of silken cloth, smoked cigarettes together and planned our marriage. The only spoke in an otherwise smoothly rolling wheel was the fact that he was going to be called up for his military service in Holland; I did not want to go with him. I wanted us to stay safely in Dell o'Grace. I felt keenly and anxiously the responsibility of Helen Barbara's special needs. I was unsure of how we would live.

Besides, when we decided to get married, Rob had phoned his parents to tell them the good news and had forgotten to inform them that I already had a child. It was so natural for him that it had not entered his head that it might not be as natural for them! So he had to phone them a second time. And quite understandably, they were shocked. To cap it all, I found out that he had not told them that Helen Barbara was in need of special care! At this moment, in the midst of our Shakespeare production, we were quarrelling about his oversight.

A few months previously, Helen Barbara's condition of health had begun to be a real worry. She did not talk or walk, and was continuing to lose weight whilst being fed on healthy organic food. What could be the matter with her? She often vomited and no doctor seemed to know what was wrong. Eventually, she had to be admitted to hospital.

This was the only time that I can say that the community let me down. I was highly distressed because of having to leave her alone and they would not let me stay with her. I could only go for visiting times, an hour in the afternoons and an hour in the evenings. This was quite unacceptable to me, because I knew that she needed me for far more than just a visit. She was so tender and remote and did not make proper contact with people. And she was only thirteen months old. I wanted to be with her all the time.

My house community, however, were very supportive. I got up very early everyday, after a sleepless night of worrying about Helen Barbara, and cooked the lunch, leaving it in the warming oven of the Aga. Christof drove me into the hospital at ten o'clock, which was the earliest time they would let me in. Then I stayed with her all day, and Christof would collect me at seven in the evening, when she had gone to sleep. It was an agonising time, and I could hardly keep myself together. But no one visited me, except on one occasion, which was to tell me that it was quite impossible to expect Christof to drive me around and that I should take public transport. This was really very obstructive. To get from where we lived to the hospital involved taking three buses, and would have meant three hours' travel. I said nothing. I just got up earlier and walked over the hills. This took me only one and a half hours. Christof continued to collect me, but I sometimes had to wait from seven till ten o'clock, until he was free to drive.

I hated everybody with a vengeance. They said that I was emotional and that my daughter would be fine without me in the huge, impersonal hospital. And I knew that this was not true. By the time she had been in for three weeks, she had been diagnosed as having a coeliac condition, and with a gluten-free diet she would grow and gain weight. But they would not let her out until she had gained the weight that she had lost whilst being in hospital. And I knew that she would never regain this weight because she was pining for me and home. So I officially discharged her, much to the community's disgust. They said I was endangering her health. She looked like a concentration camp victim when I brought her home, and I could hardly bear the community criticism. It was a dreadful time in both our lives. I date her autism from this experience.

However, once home again and taking easily to her new diet, she started crawling and getting herself around, often on her bottom, like a rowing boat, using her hands as oars in the air for momentum. She was not going to be an ordinary child and I knew that I needed the support of a Camphill education and lifestyle for her to develop properly.

So Rob began a process of getting legal dispensation from the

Dutch military so that he could be exempt from service. And then we could stay in Glencraig and become houseparents together. All of a sudden, the support returned. People were incredibly helpful and wrote letters saying how necessary it was for Glencraig's continued development that Rob should work with us, and that he had special responsibility for particular children and was therefore a vital part of their future development! Eventually the dispensation was granted.

Somehow, during this dark time, something registered. I realised that Camphill was a dream in the making. It was not a community of perfection and fact. It was an attempt to create a new social order and that this new way of life was not yet fully born. It could only happen as a factor in this world if each of us, individually, conquered our petty greed, opportunism, irritations and darkness of soul. It was an ideal that could only be realised by people who, with all their faults and failings, in good faith and with goodwill, could make this effort worthwhile. Camphill would only become what it strove to be if there were people who made it real.

Finally, I had arrived. I had become the grown-up others saw I might become. Now, in the midst of misery and resentment, entangled by the great goodness and generosity that I had been embedded in all my life, I wanted to stay. I wanted to be one of the human beings who give their goodwill out of freedom to help this new social order to be born.

So we were married in Glencraig. It was now my turn to be the bride in a huge and festive community wedding. Though I had never qualified as the May Queen, now I could wear flowers in my hair. My sister, Agi, picked wide-open wild roses from the tangled bushes in the playground and artfully pinned them in a crown on my messy curls. Rob wore a dark blue suit, purchased by his father in a big posh man's shop in Holland. He had to use safety pins provided by his sister, Hetty, to tighten the waistband, because he had lost so much weight coming up to the great day. Everyone was there. We had set the date for the first week in July so that our friends in Glencraig could attend. Children and villagers and co-workers gathered to send us off down the road towards what *we* knew would be wedded bliss and what *they* predicted might become tribulation!

It was a strange day. The weather went from rain, to storm, to sun and to cloud. We were the first couple to be married in the newly built chapel, and someone had made an arch of flowers around the door. Helen Barbara wore a pretty dress that my mother had bought her and stood at the back with my sister Lizzy taking care of her. She had, two weeks before the great day, at last learned to walk! I was filled with a mixture of fear, warmth and laughter. Now that she was mobile, would her next milestones come more easily? Would she ever begin to talk? She skipped about, as confident as a little fairy. Rob loved her; we all loved each other.

We had a Norwegian wedding cake, ring upon ring of almond pastry, and everybody got a little piece of it except Rob and myself, who were so busy being congratulated that it got eaten before we could have any. The wedding meal was spread over a huge table, decorated with summer flowers, and so many people were there, family, old friends and new friends. My father gave a speech in which he congratulated Rob for having the courage to take me on and for taking me off his hands! Jens, my adopted, godfather was our witness, as was Miriam, who had once called herself Renate and had returned to Glencraig with her little daughter. Despite the long separation, she and I had remained very good friends, almost sisters. Only Pauly was missing. I had sadly lost track of him.

Frédérique, now my sister-in-law, Sim, Hilary, Caroline, Jeffrey, Michael, Patchie, my sisters, my parents, Auntie Jeanette, and even my mother's brother, Aba, (still a practising Orthodox Jew), had come to witness our wedding. Rob's parents, the tallest people I had ever met, and whom I hoped would grow to love me, and his other two sister's, Hetty and Jossie, had also come to take part in the momentous decision that their beloved only son had made. Christof and Annemarie, Johannes and Saralies, Turid, Hans Heinrich and even Peter Oram, all were there enjoying the fun of a community celebration. The lump in my throat that had been such a constant companion was now a thickening of love and gratitude for the way in which I had been brought up. I was happy and at peace with myself and with Camphill.

When I was a little girl, whining as little children sometimes do, my father always said, 'If you are bored, it's because you are boring. Look around you! Never say life is hard, say it's interesting.'

I knew that surrounded by my family, with Rob and my daughter, within the variety and richness of the Camphill community, life would always be interesting and I would never be bored.

Printed in the United Kingdom
by Lightning Source UK Ltd.
2027